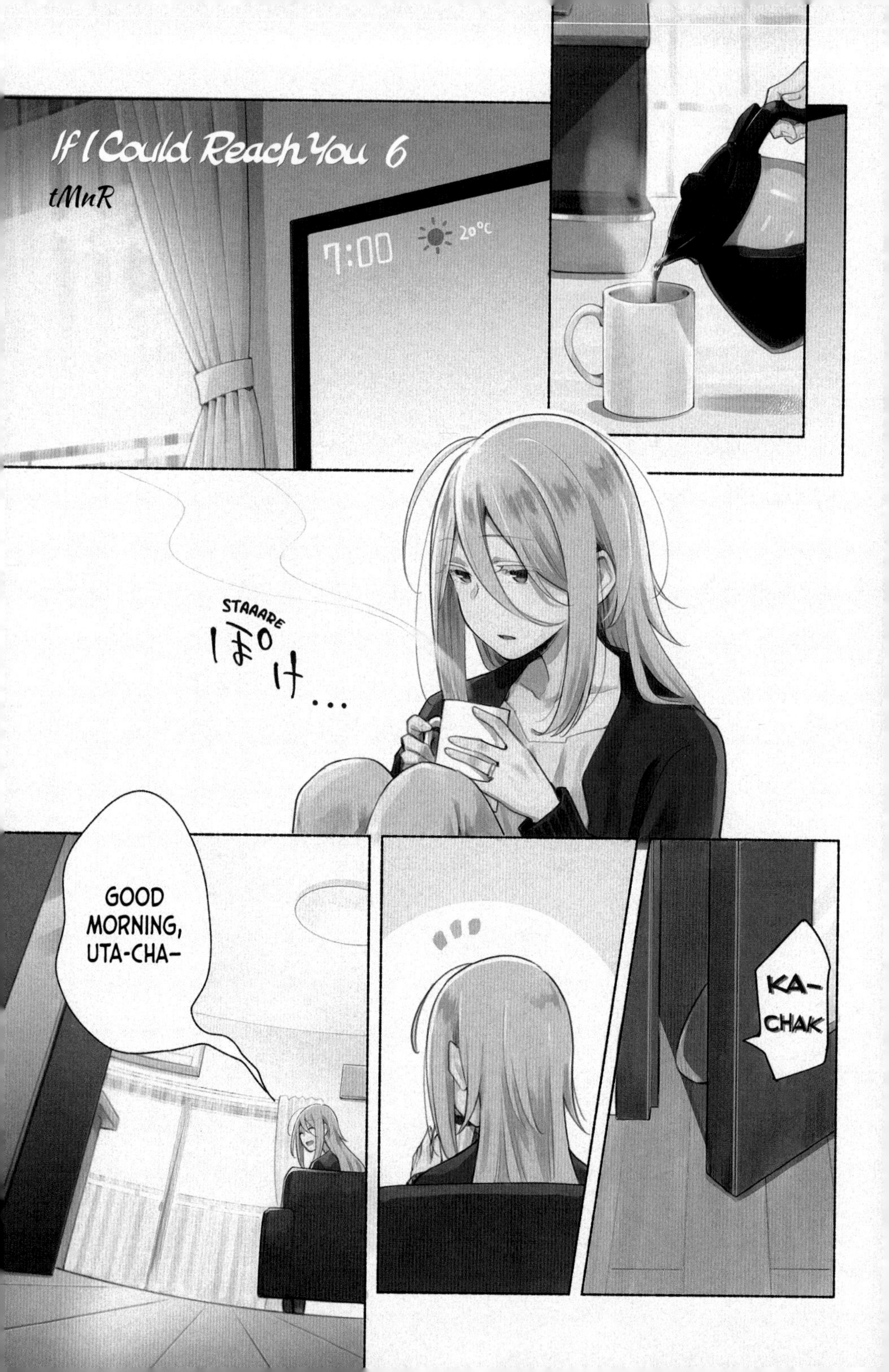
If I Could Reach You 6
tMnR
STAAARE
ぽけ…
KA-CHAK
GOOD MORNING, UTA-CHA-

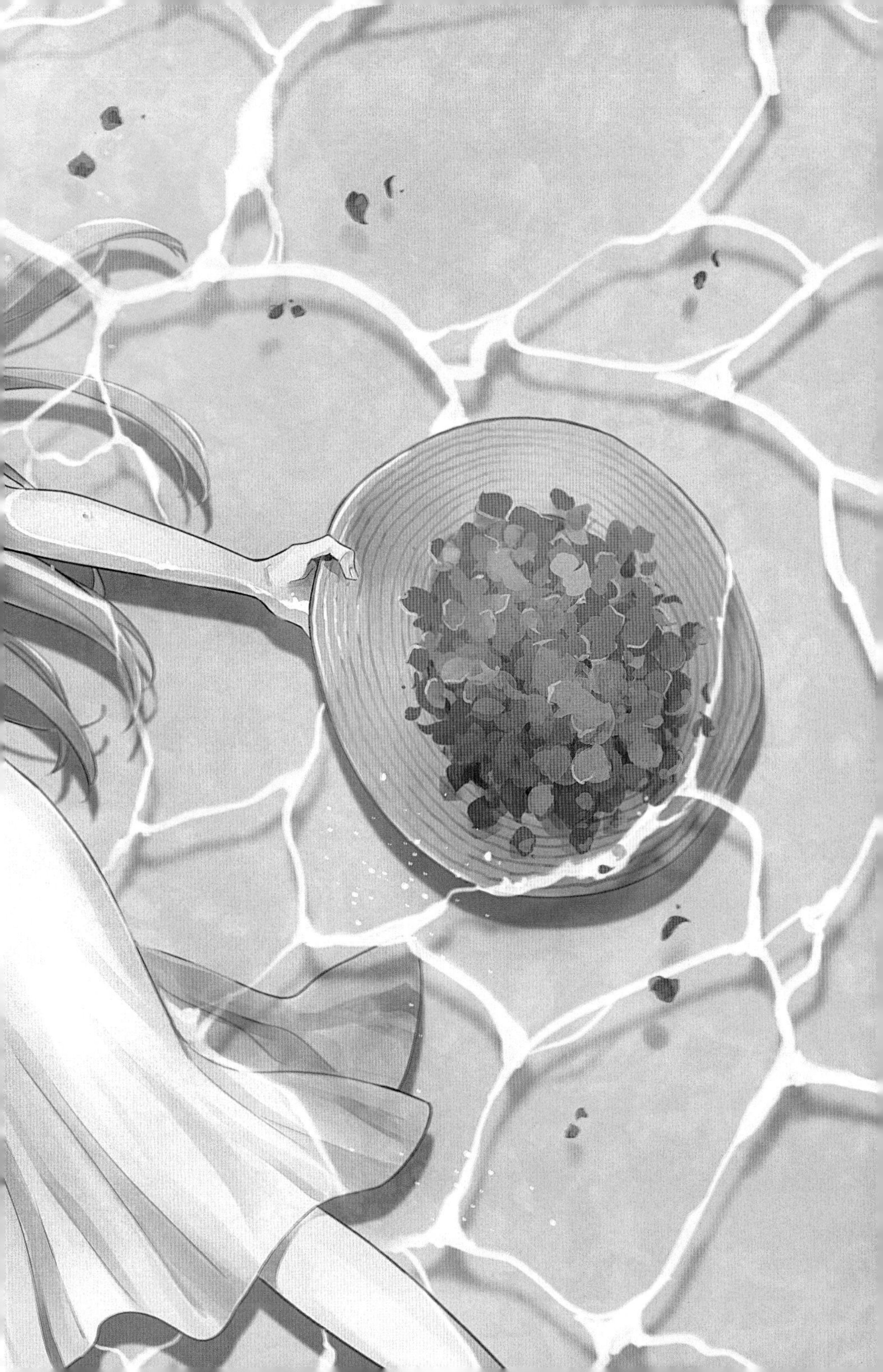

Chapter 26

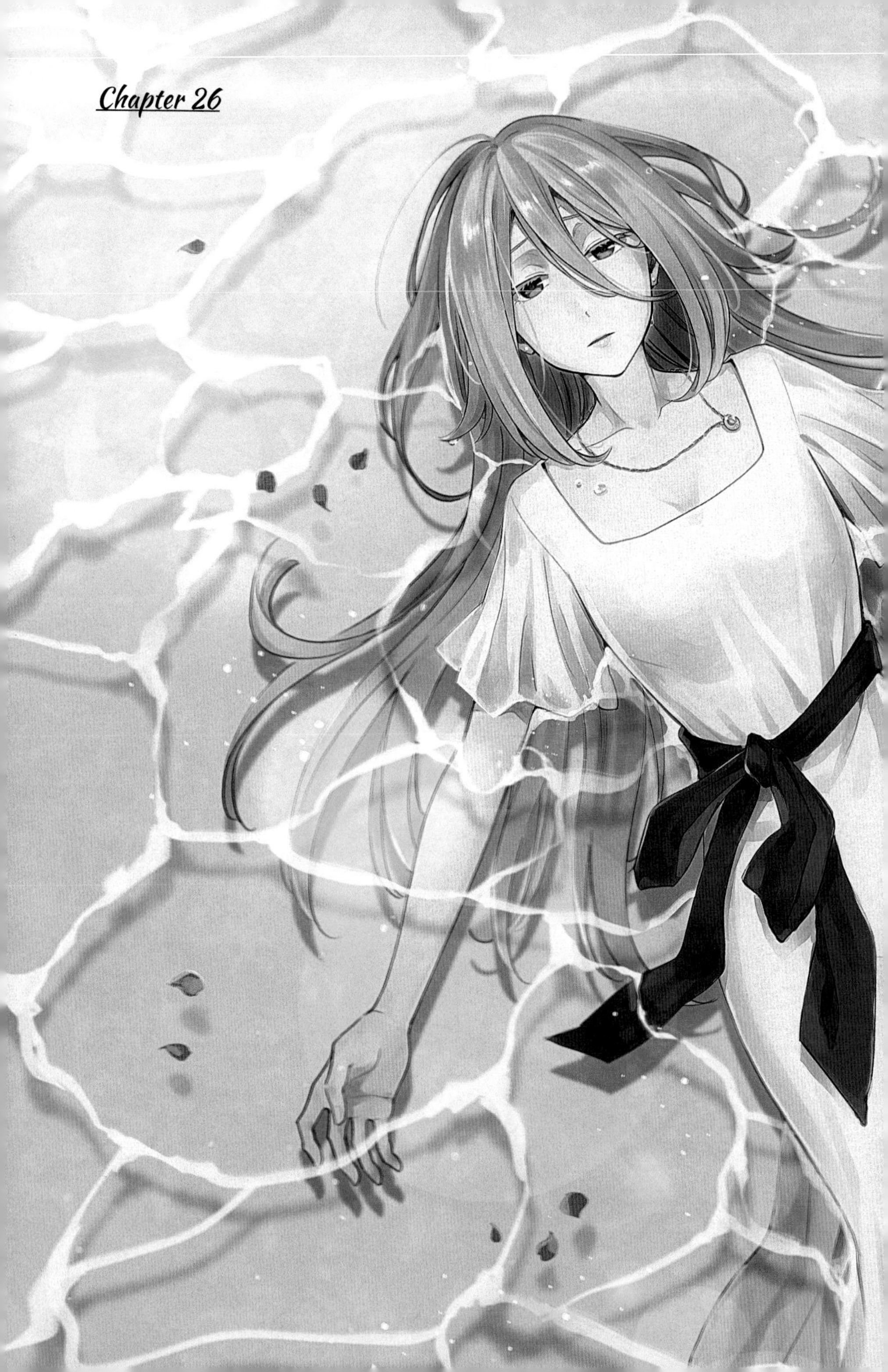

If I Could Reach You

6

C O N T E N T S

Chapter 26
003

Chapter 27
035

Chapter 28
063

Chapter 29
093

Chapter 30
124

Afterword
163

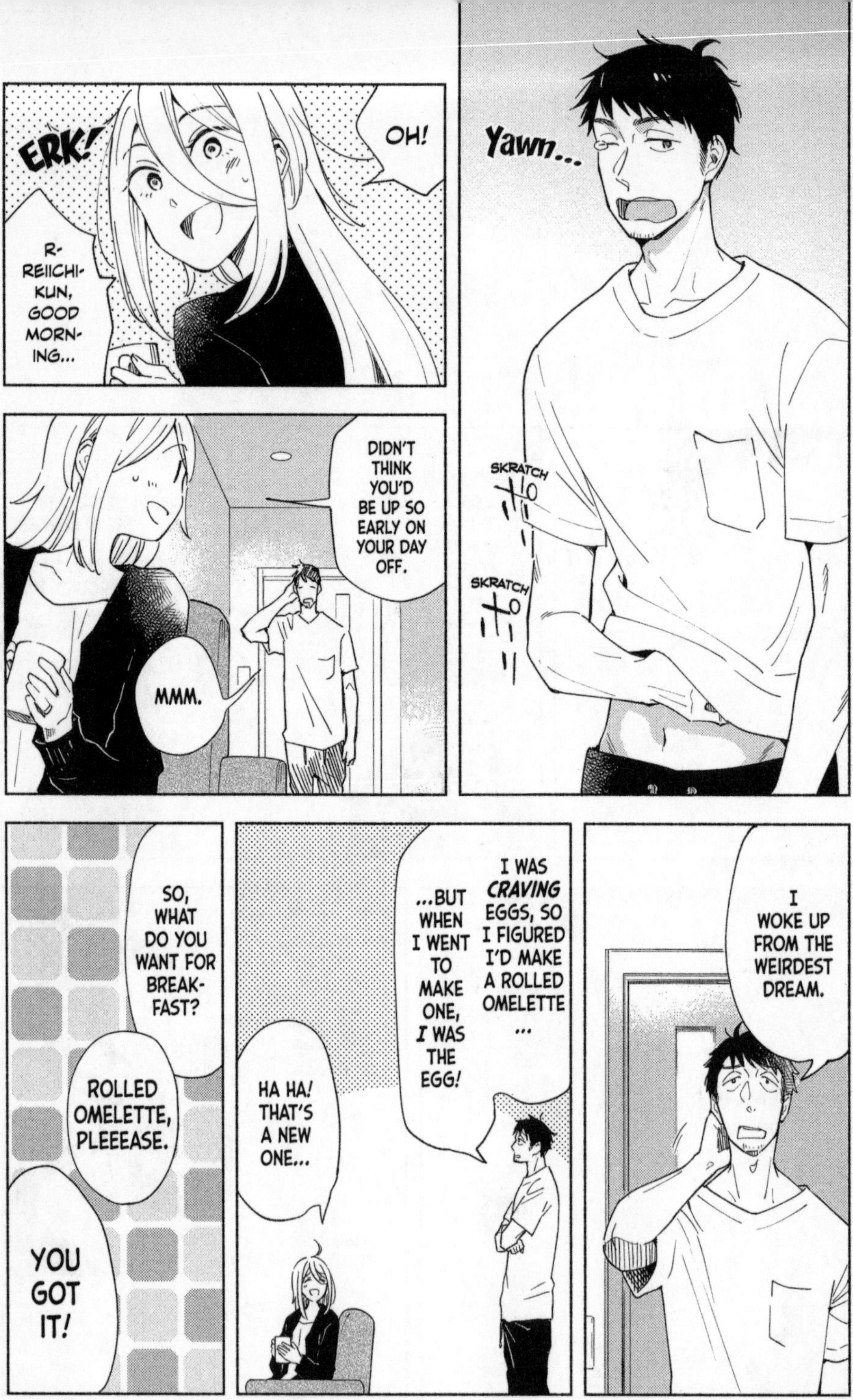
Yawn...
SKRATCH
SKRATCH
OH!
ERK!
R-REIICHI-KUN, GOOD MORNING...
DIDN'T THINK YOU'D BE UP SO EARLY ON YOUR DAY OFF.
MMM.
I WOKE UP FROM THE WEIRDEST DREAM.
I WAS *CRAVING* EGGS, SO I FIGURED I'D MAKE A ROLLED OMELETTE ...
...BUT WHEN I WENT TO MAKE ONE, *I* WAS THE EGG!
HA HA! THAT'S A NEW ONE...
SO, WHAT DO YOU WANT FOR BREAKFAST?
ROLLED OMELETTE, PLEEEASE.
YOU GOT IT!

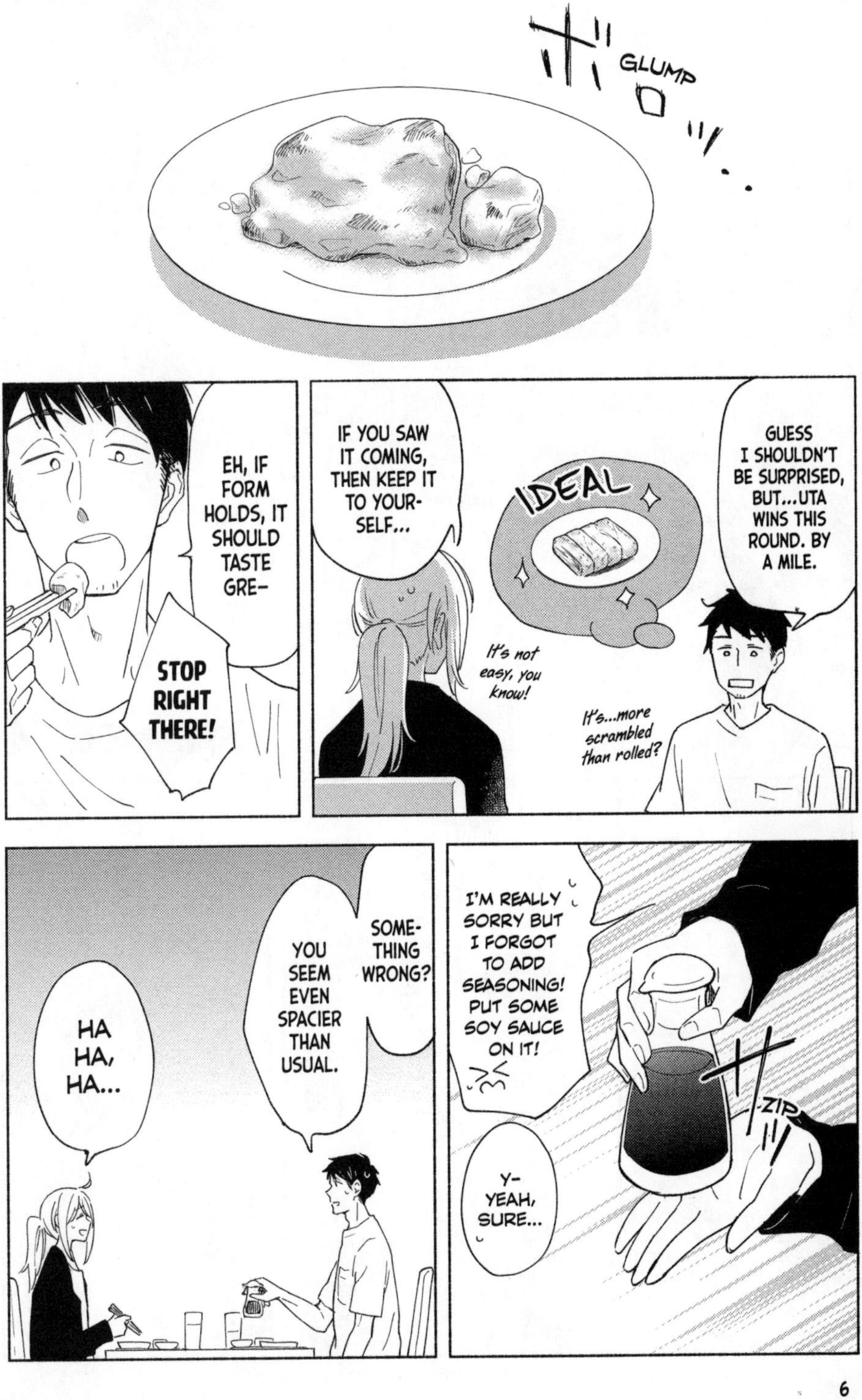
GLUMP
GUESS I SHOULDN'T BE SURPRISED, BUT...UTA WINS THIS ROUND. BY A MILE.
It's...more scrambled than rolled?
IDEAL
It's not easy, you know!
IF YOU SAW IT COMING, THEN KEEP IT TO YOURSELF...
EH, IF FORM HOLDS, IT SHOULD TASTE GRE–
STOP RIGHT THERE!
I'M REALLY SORRY BUT I FORGOT TO ADD SEASONING! PUT SOME SOY SAUCE ON IT!
ZIP
Y-YEAH, SURE...
SOMETHING WRONG?
YOU SEEM EVEN SPACIER THAN USUAL.
HA HA, HA...

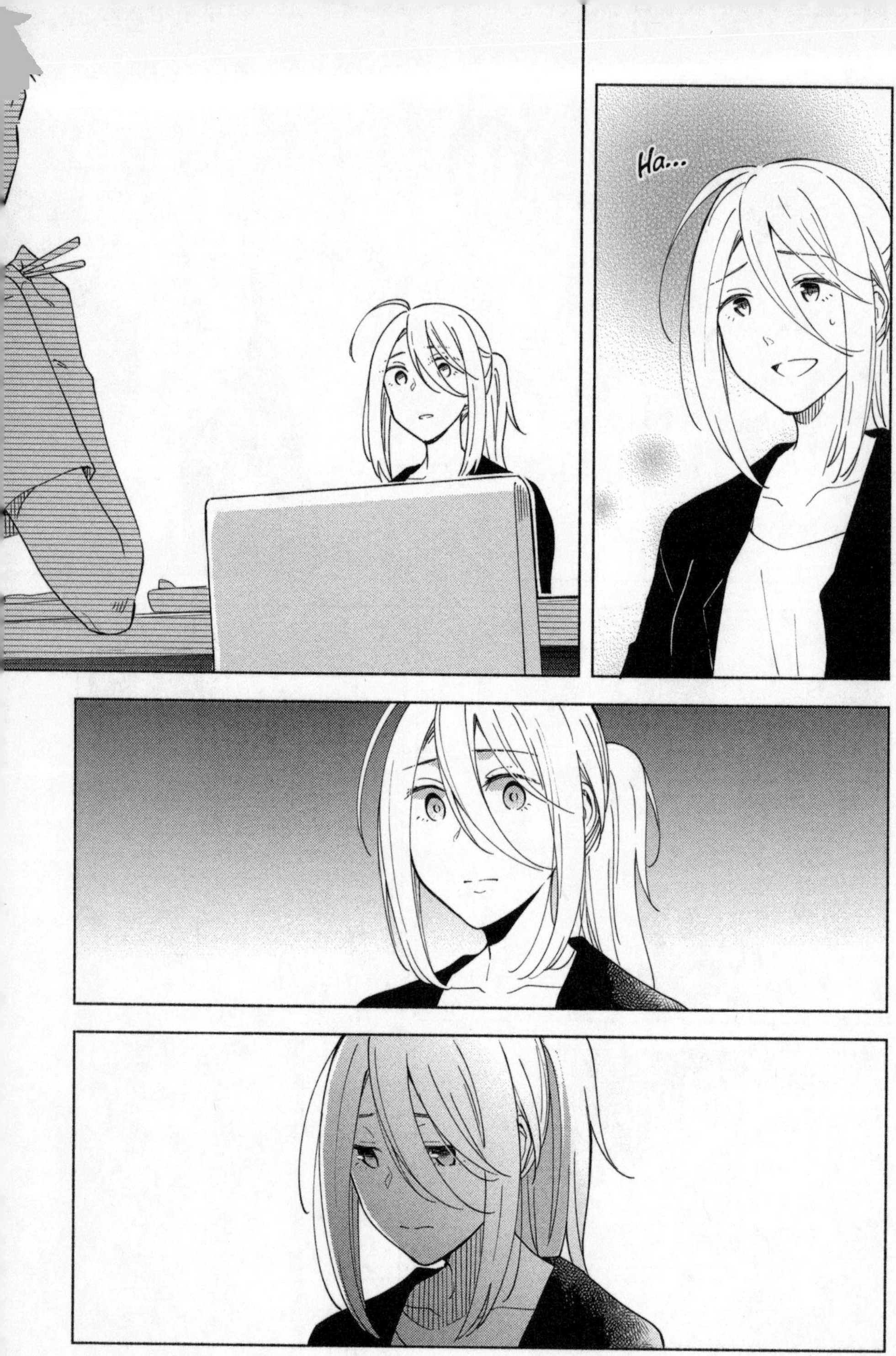
Ha...

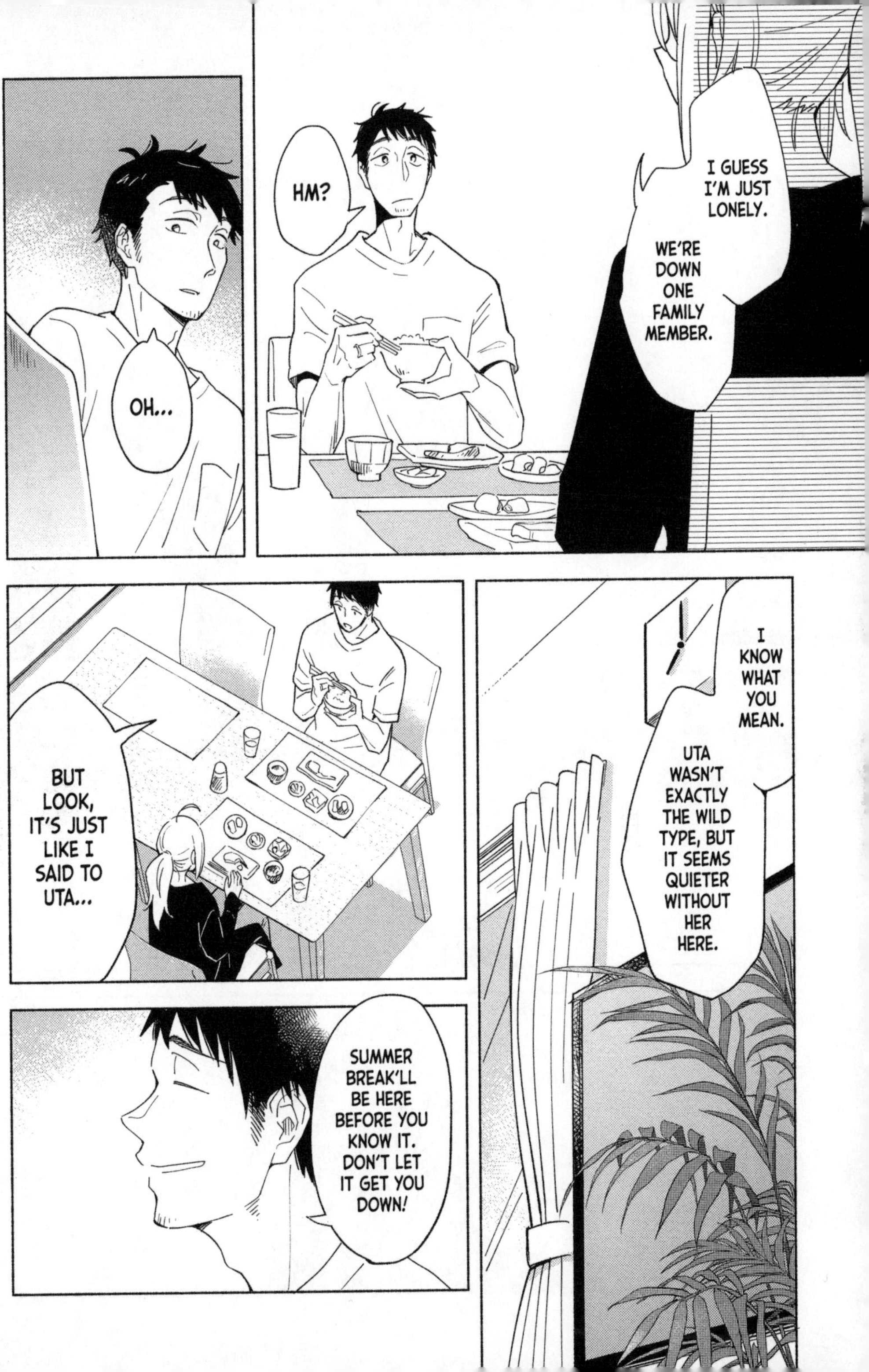
I GUESS I'M JUST LONELY.
WE'RE DOWN ONE FAMILY MEMBER.
HM?
OH...
I KNOW WHAT YOU MEAN.
UTA WASN'T EXACTLY THE WILD TYPE, BUT IT SEEMS QUIETER WITHOUT HER HERE.
BUT LOOK, IT'S JUST LIKE I SAID TO UTA...
SUMMER BREAK'LL BE HERE BEFORE YOU KNOW IT. DON'T LET IT GET YOU DOWN!

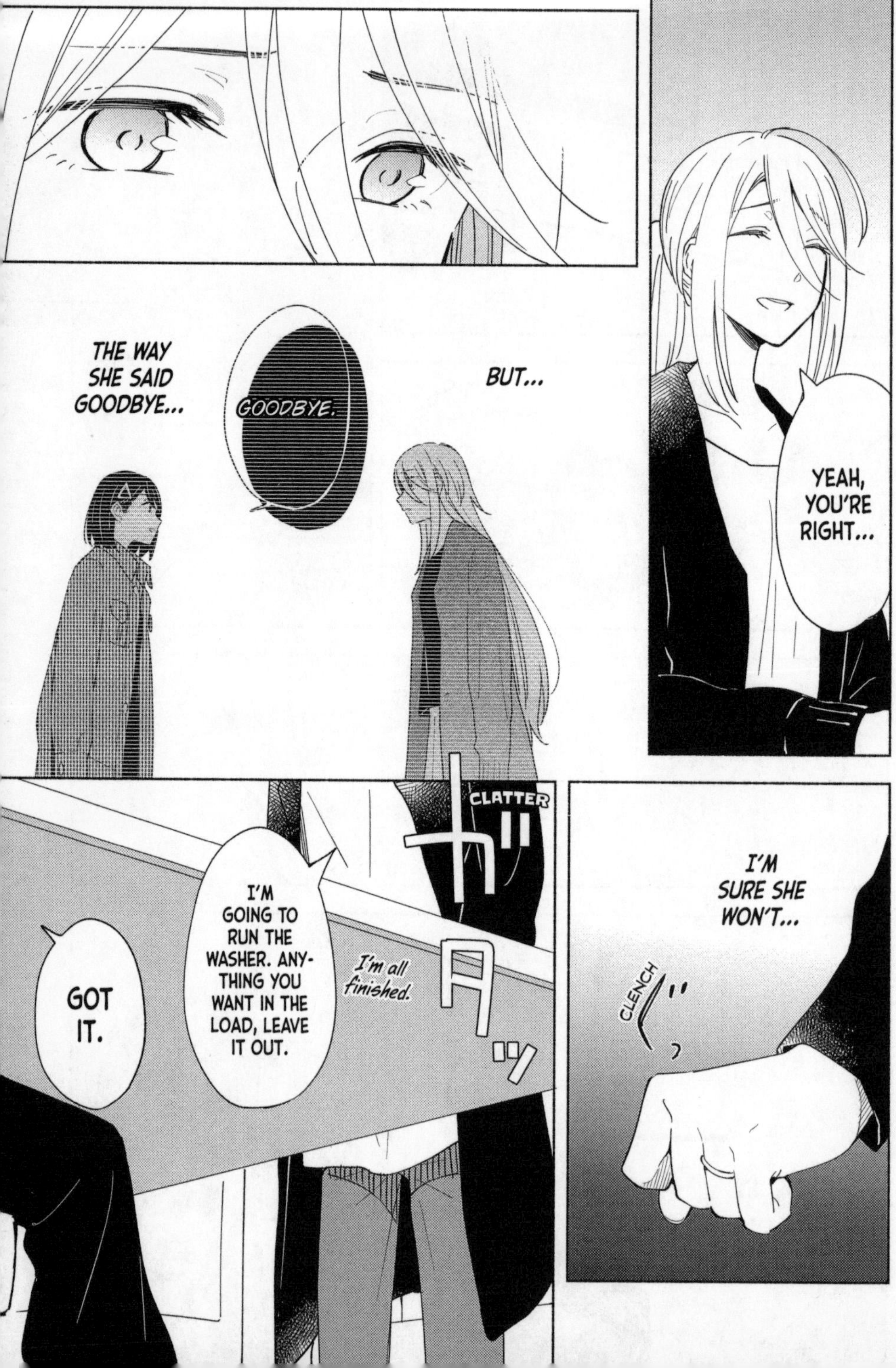
YEAH, YOU'RE RIGHT...
BUT...
GOODBYE.
THE WAY SHE SAID GOODBYE...
I'M SURE SHE WON'T...
CLENCH
CLATTER
I'm all finished.
I'M GOING TO RUN THE WASHER. ANY-THING YOU WANT IN THE LOAD, LEAVE IT OUT.
GOT IT.

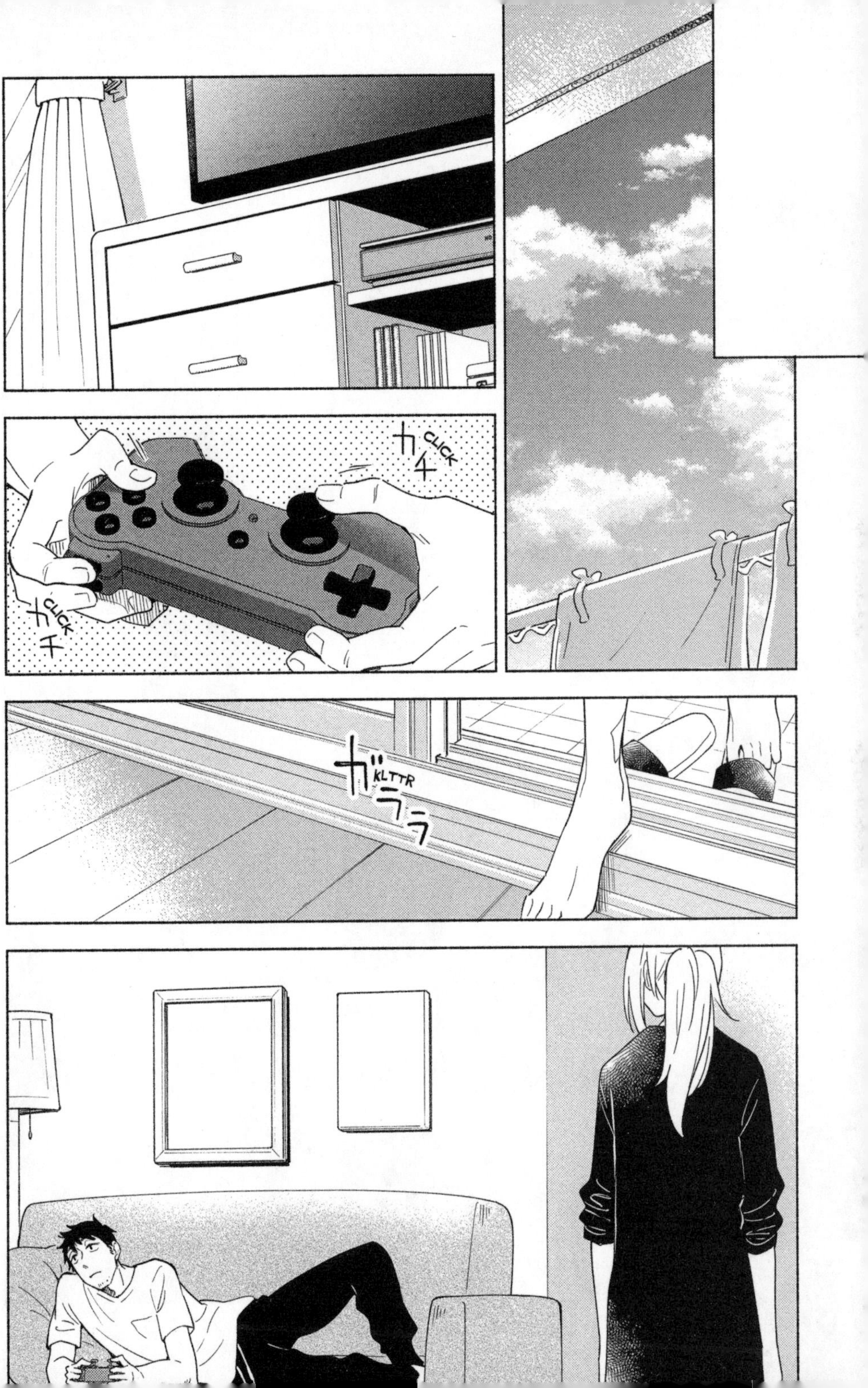
カチ
CLICK
カチ
CLICK
ガララ
KLTTR

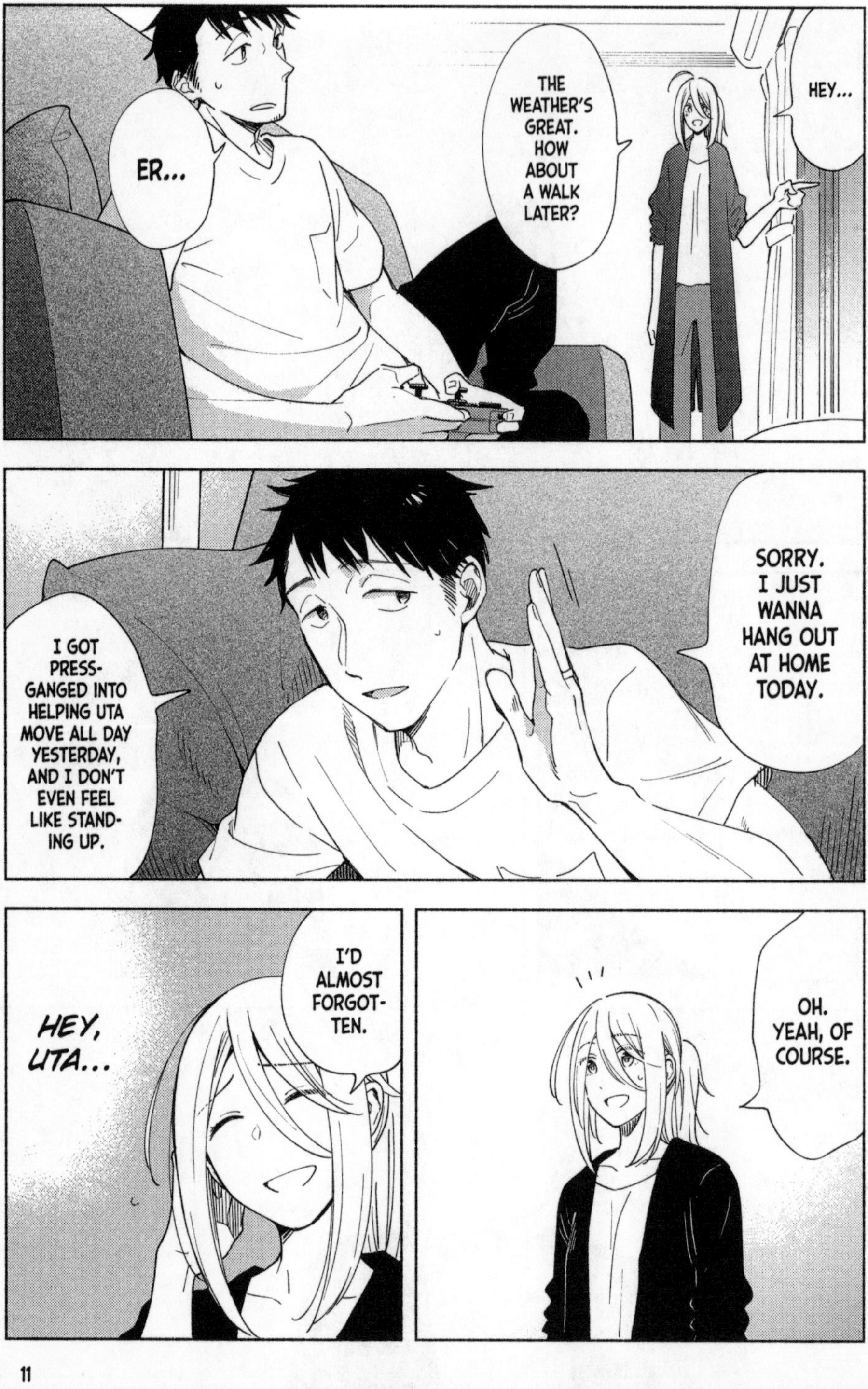
HEY...
THE WEATHER'S GREAT. HOW ABOUT A WALK LATER?
ER...
SORRY. I JUST WANNA HANG OUT AT HOME TODAY.
I GOT PRESS-GANGED INTO HELPING UTA MOVE ALL DAY YESTERDAY, AND I DON'T EVEN FEEL LIKE STANDING UP.
OH. YEAH, OF COURSE.
I'D ALMOST FORGOTTEN.
HEY, UTA...

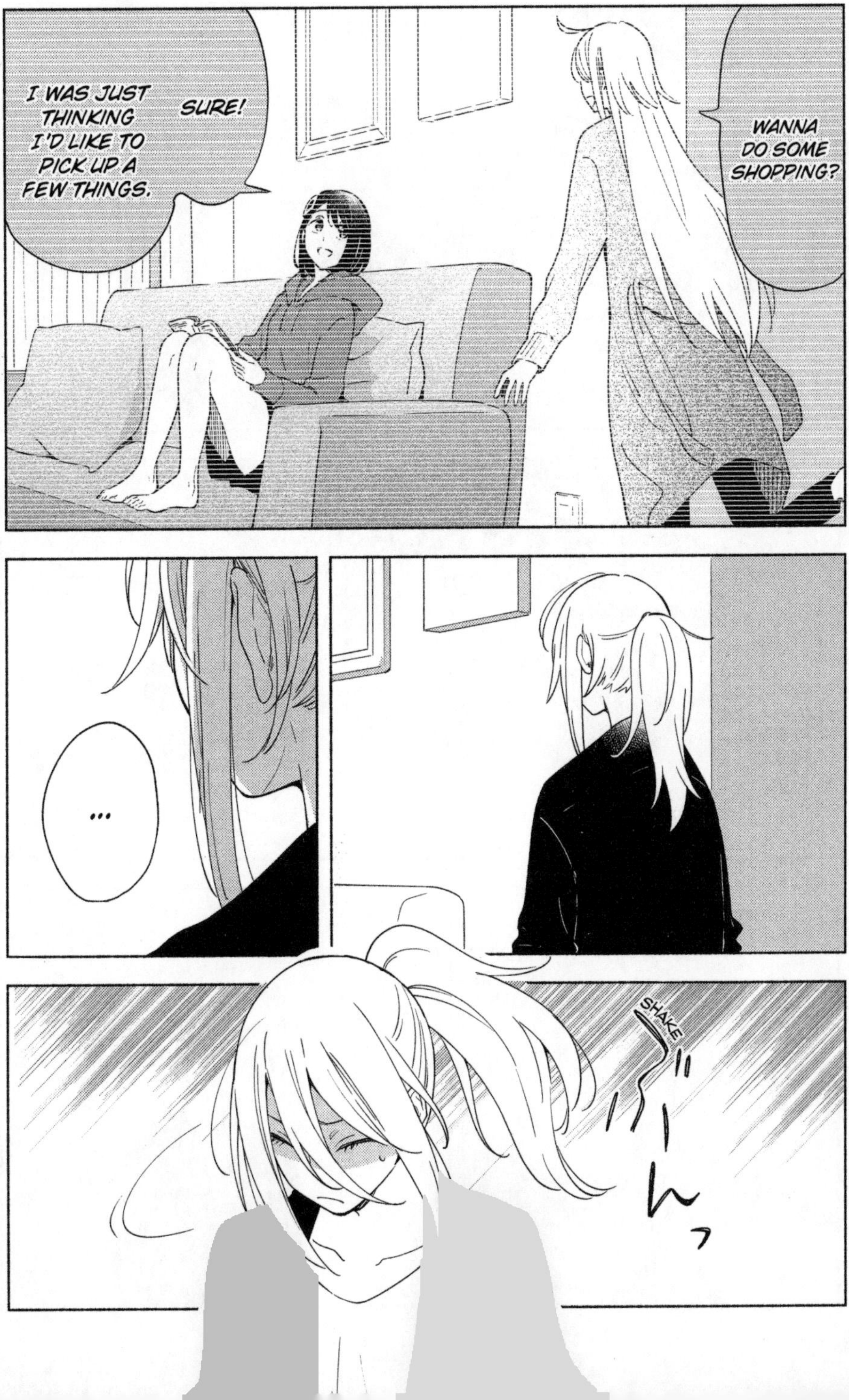
WANNA DO SOME SHOPPING?
SURE!
I WAS JUST THINKING I'D LIKE TO PICK UP A FEW THINGS.
...
SHAKE

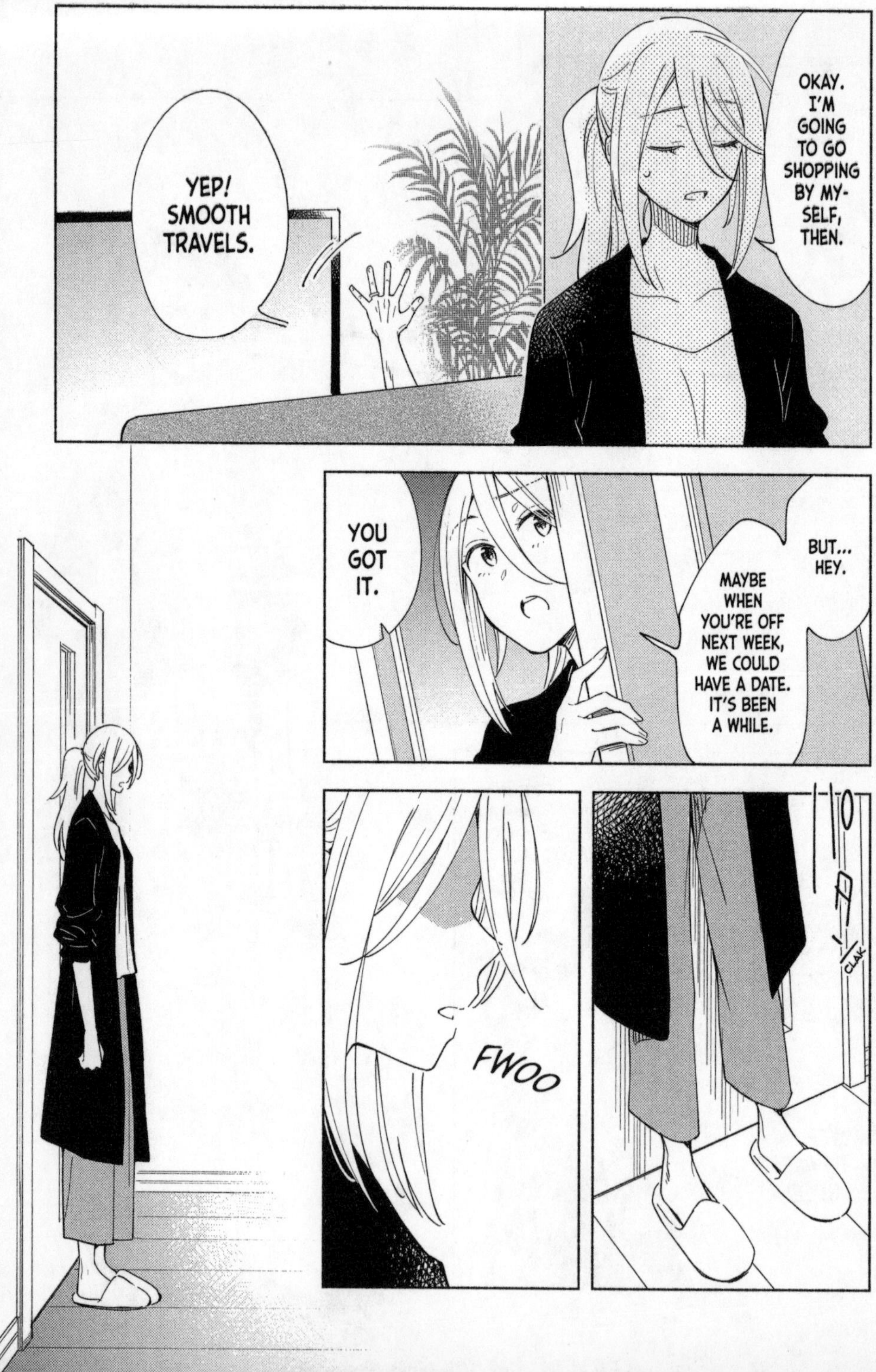
OKAY. I'M GOING TO GO SHOPPING BY MY-SELF, THEN.
YEP! SMOOTH TRAVELS.
BUT... HEY.
MAYBE WHEN YOU'RE OFF NEXT WEEK, WE COULD HAVE A DATE. IT'S BEEN A WHILE.
YOU GOT IT.
CLAK
FWOO

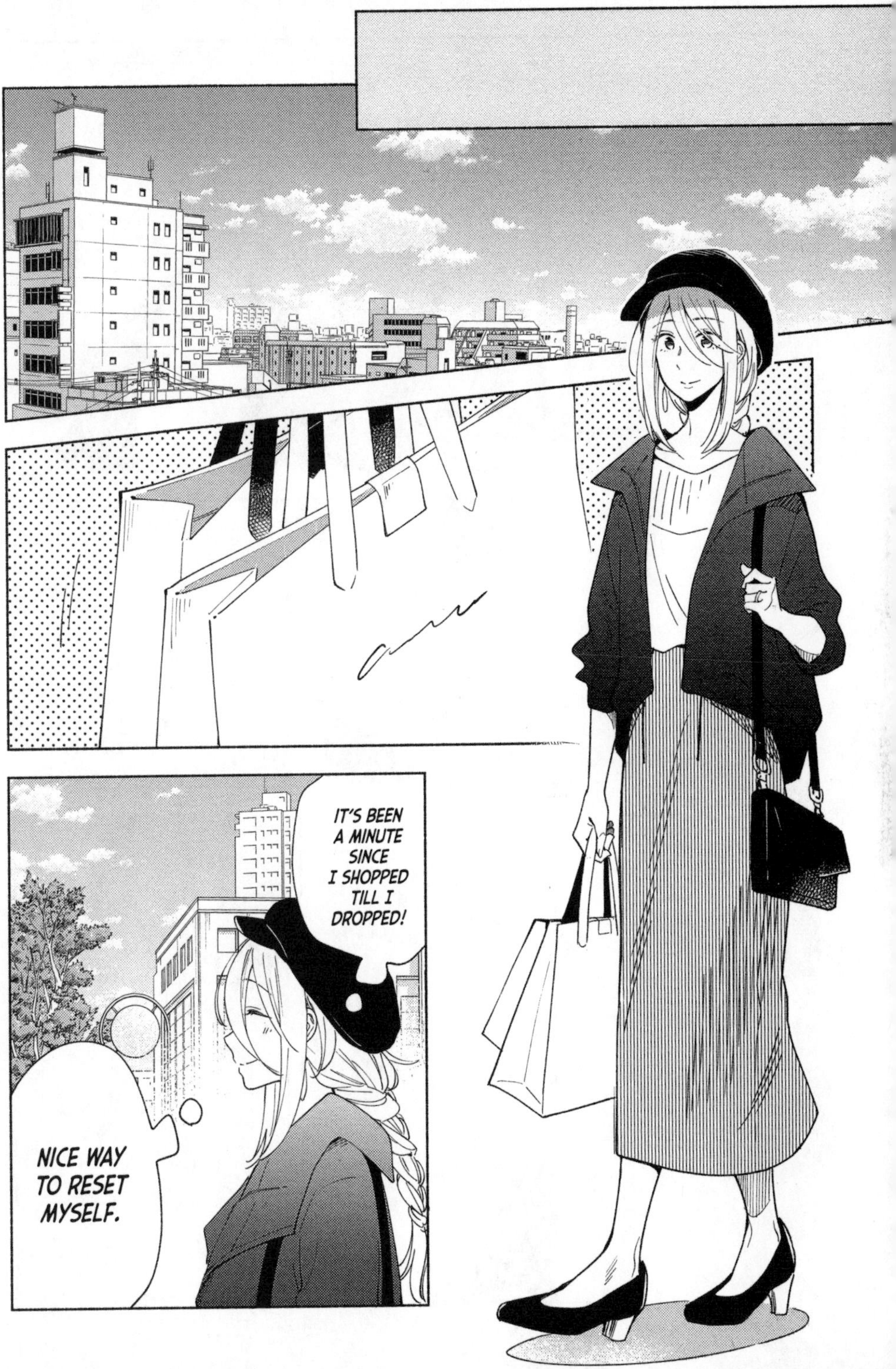
IT'S BEEN A MINUTE SINCE I SHOPPED TILL I DROPPED!
NICE WAY TO RESET MYSELF.

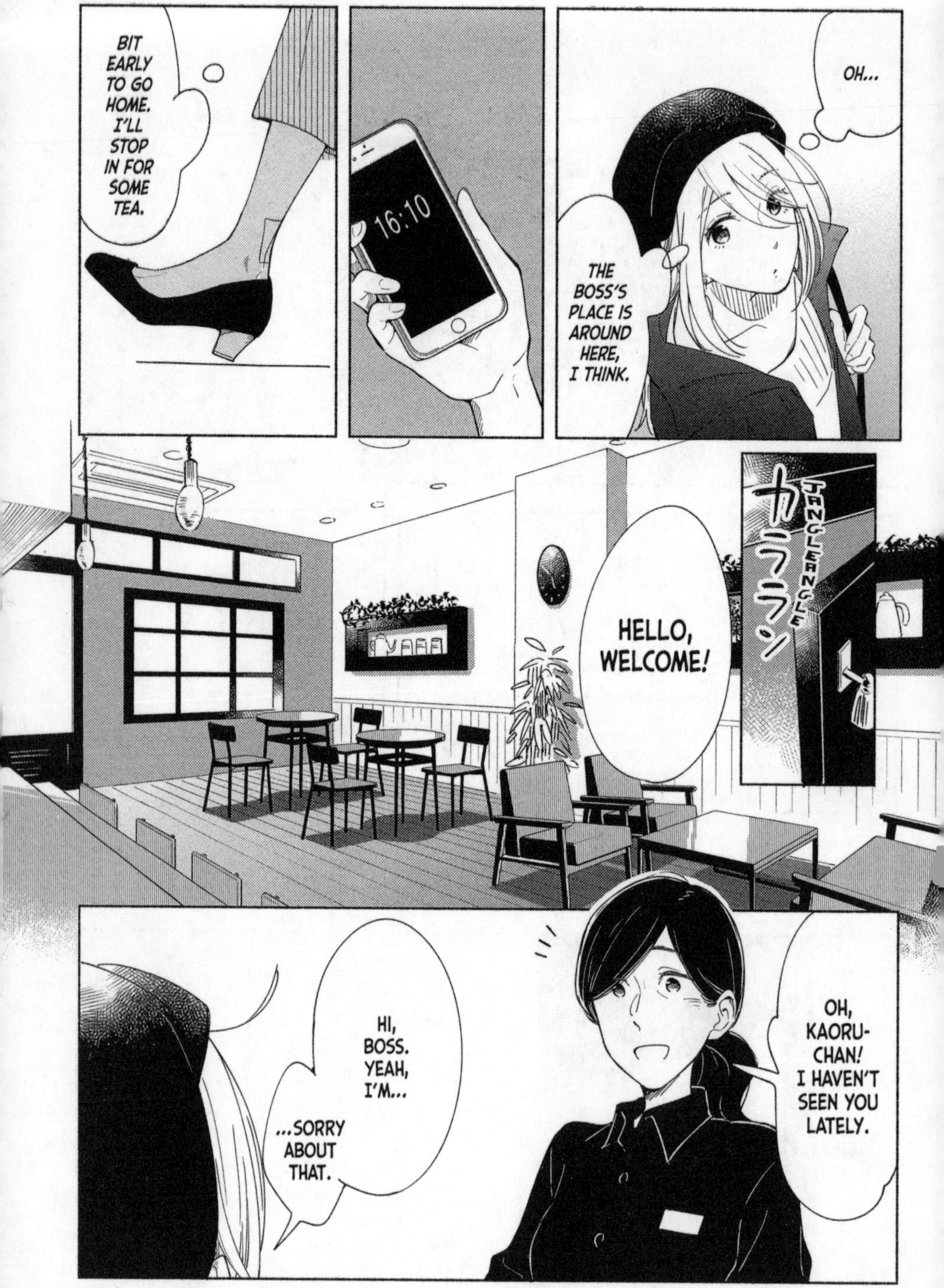
OH...
THE BOSS'S PLACE IS AROUND HERE, I THINK.
16:10
BIT EARLY TO GO HOME. I'LL STOP IN FOR SOME TEA.
カラン
JANGLEANGLE
HELLO, WELCOME!
OH, KAORU-CHAN! I HAVEN'T SEEN YOU LATELY.
HI, BOSS. YEAH, I'M...
...SORRY ABOUT THAT.

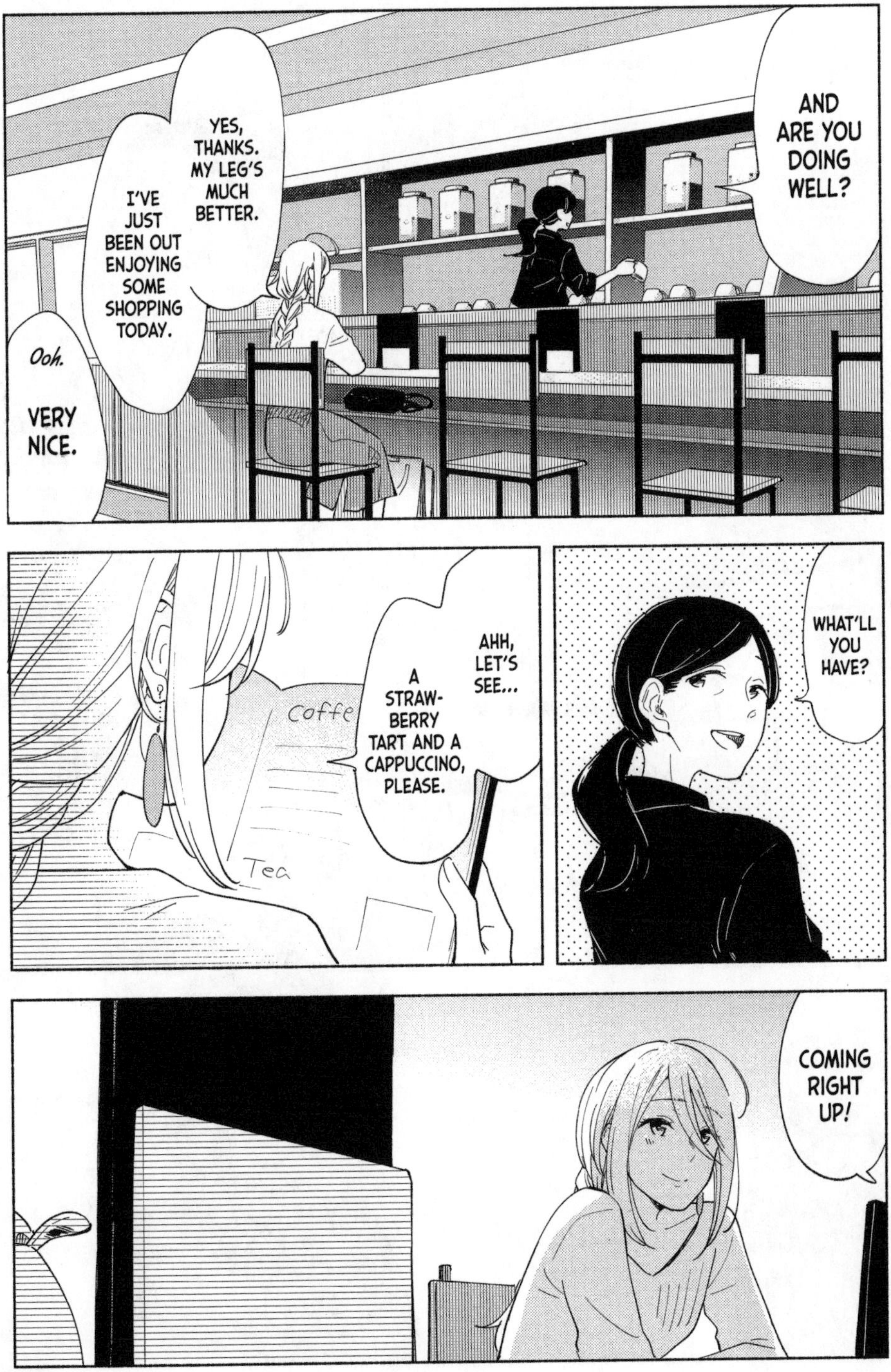
AND ARE YOU DOING WELL?
YES, THANKS. MY LEG'S MUCH BETTER.
I'VE JUST BEEN OUT ENJOYING SOME SHOPPING TODAY.
Ooh.
VERY NICE.
WHAT'LL YOU HAVE?
AHH, LET'S SEE...
A STRAW-BERRY TART AND A CAPPUCCINO, PLEASE.
Coffe
Tea
COMING RIGHT UP!

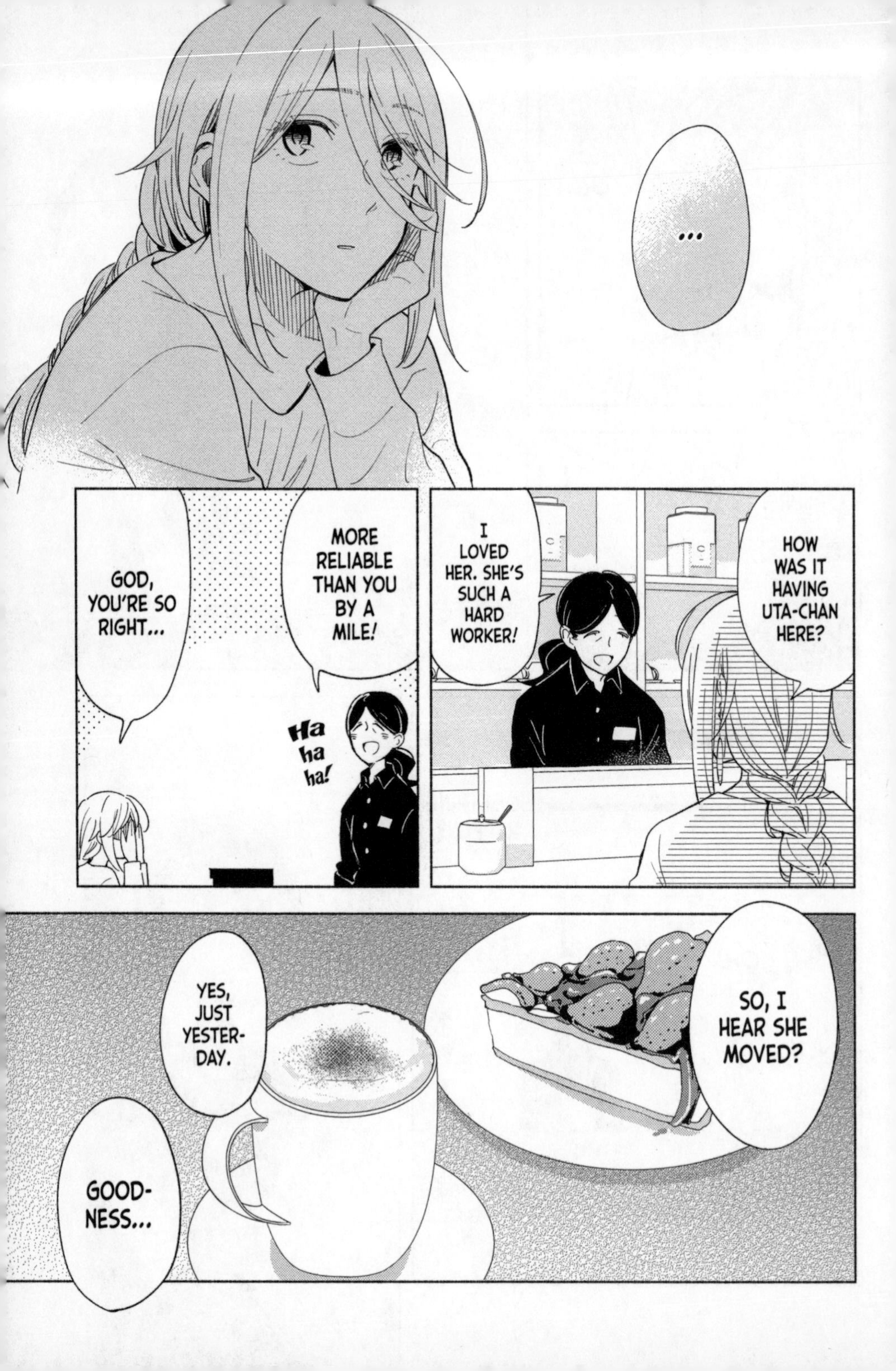
...
HOW WAS IT HAVING UTA-CHAN HERE?
I LOVED HER. SHE'S SUCH A HARD WORKER!
MORE RELIABLE THAN YOU BY A MILE!
Ha ha ha!
GOD, YOU'RE SO RIGHT...
SO, I HEAR SHE MOVED?
YES, JUST YESTER-DAY.
GOOD-NESS...

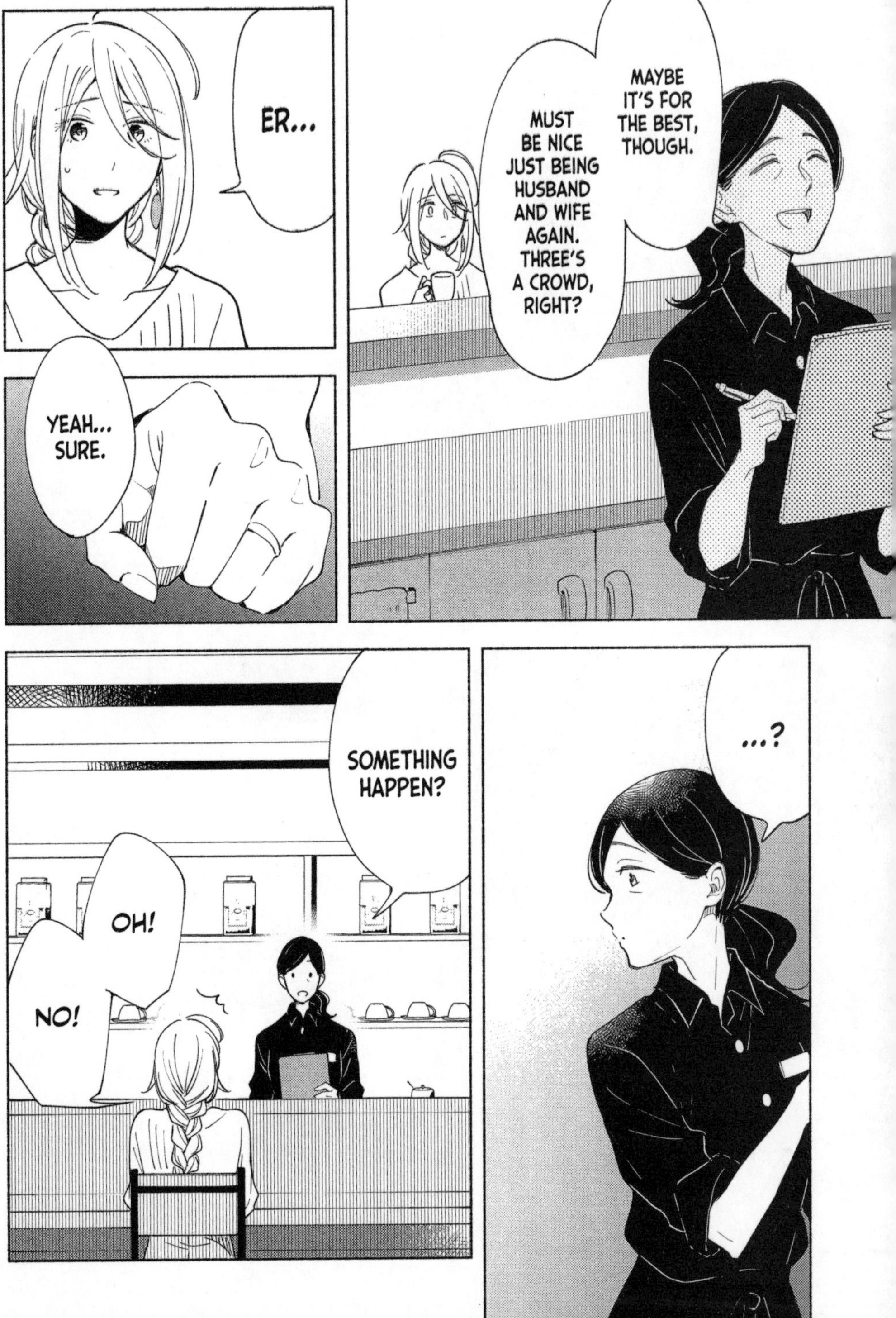
MAYBE IT'S FOR THE BEST, THOUGH.
MUST BE NICE JUST BEING HUSBAND AND WIFE AGAIN. THREE'S A CROWD, RIGHT?
ER...
YEAH... SURE.
...?
SOMETHING HAPPEN?
OH!
NO!

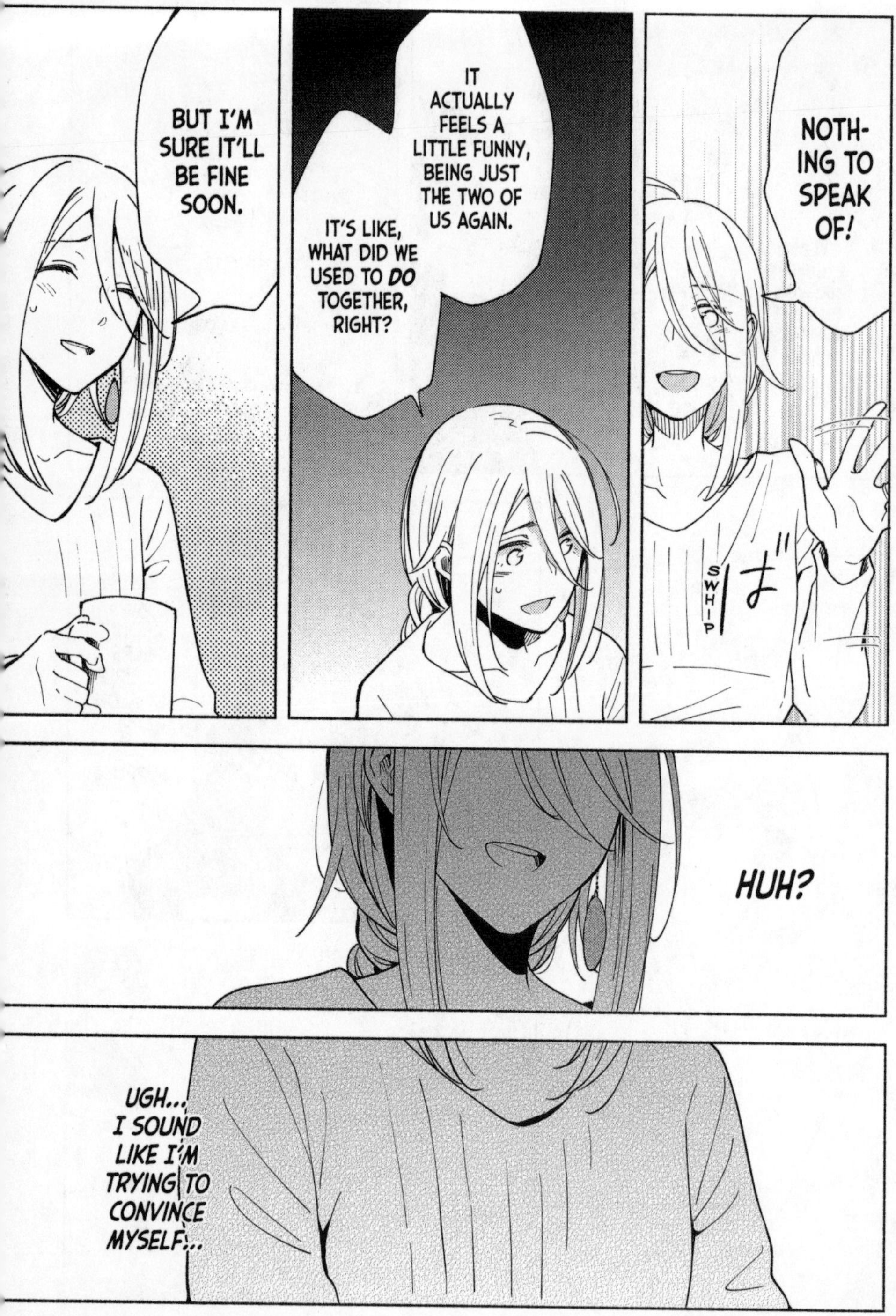
NOTH-ING TO SPEAK OF!
SWHIP
ば
IT ACTUALLY FEELS A LITTLE FUNNY, BEING JUST THE TWO OF US AGAIN.
IT'S LIKE, WHAT DID WE USED TO *DO* TOGETHER, RIGHT?
BUT I'M SURE IT'LL BE FINE SOON.
HUH?
UGH... I SOUND LIKE I'M TRYING TO CONVINCE MYSELF...

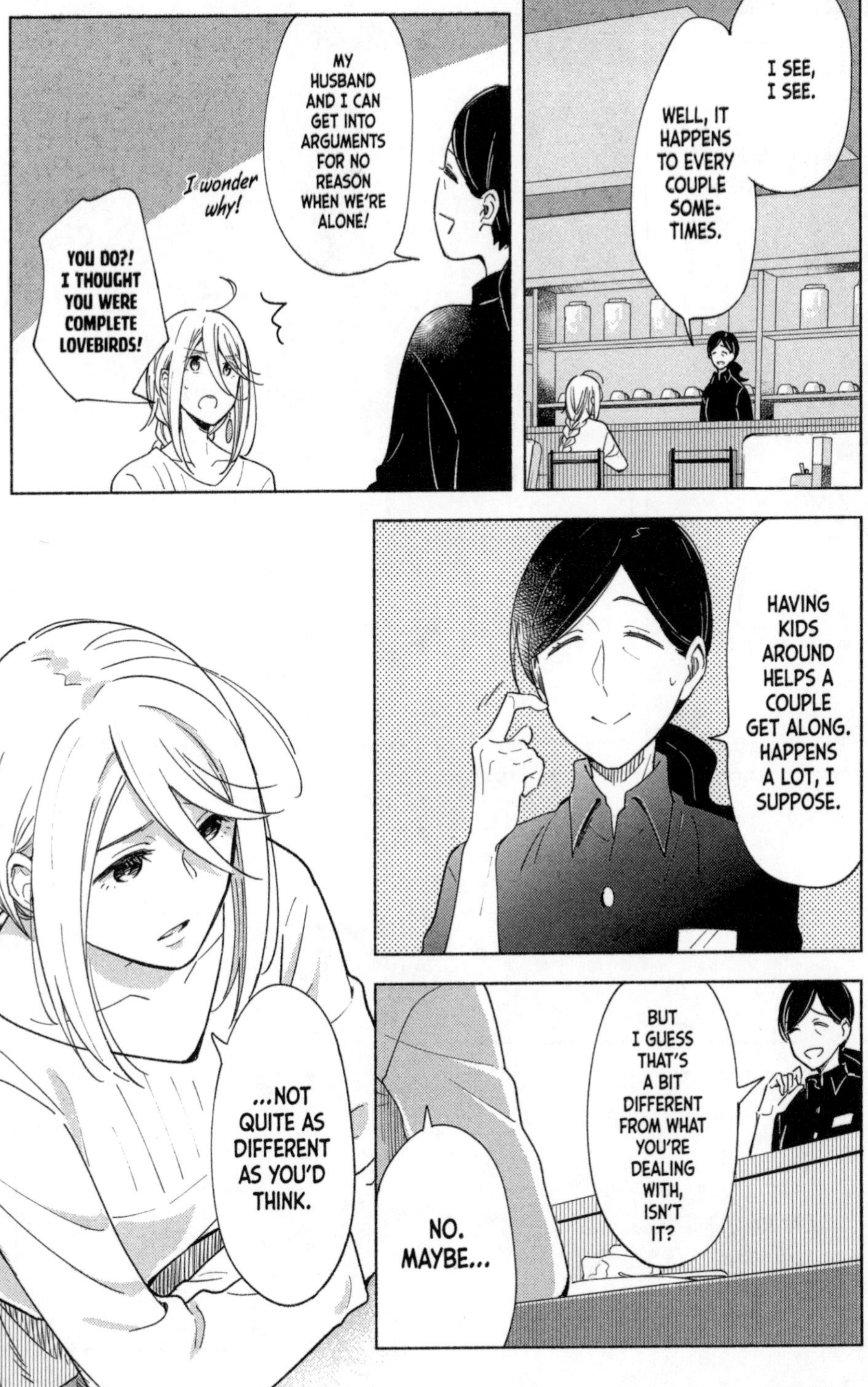
I SEE, I SEE.
WELL, IT HAPPENS TO EVERY COUPLE SOME-TIMES.
MY HUSBAND AND I CAN GET INTO ARGUMENTS FOR NO REASON WHEN WE'RE ALONE!
I wonder why!
YOU DO?! I THOUGHT YOU WERE COMPLETE LOVEBIRDS!
HAVING KIDS AROUND HELPS A COUPLE GET ALONG. HAPPENS A LOT, I SUPPOSE.
BUT I GUESS THAT'S A BIT DIFFERENT FROM WHAT YOU'RE DEALING WITH, ISN'T IT?
NO. MAYBE...
...NOT QUITE AS DIFFERENT AS YOU'D THINK.

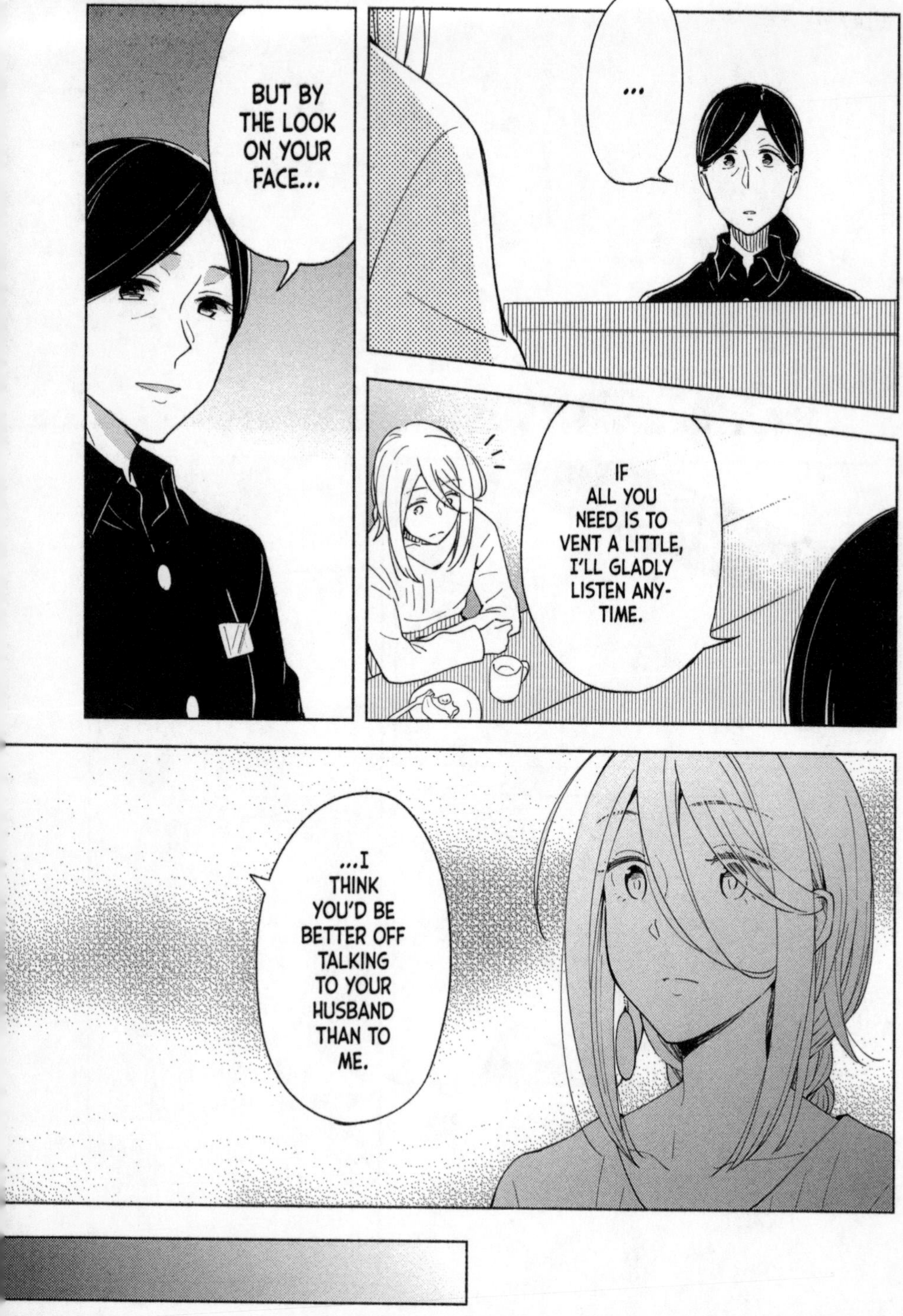
...
IF ALL YOU NEED IS TO VENT A LITTLE, I'LL GLADLY LISTEN ANY-TIME.
BUT BY THE LOOK ON YOUR FACE...
...I THINK YOU'D BE BETTER OFF TALKING TO YOUR HUSBAND THAN TO ME.

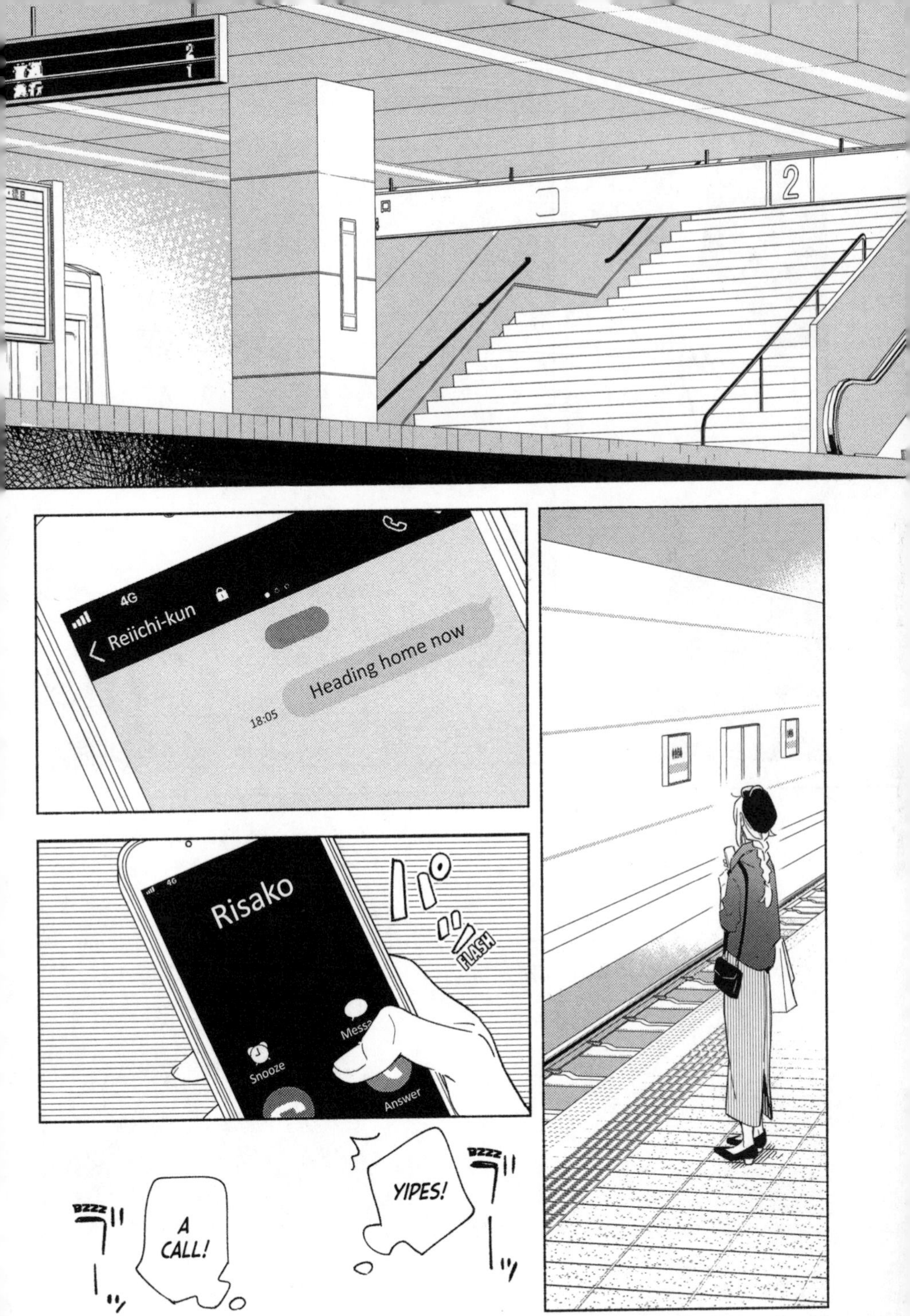
4G
Reiichi-kun
Heading home now
18:05
4G
Risako
Snooze
Answer
FLASH
BZZZ
YIPES!
BZZZ
A CALL!

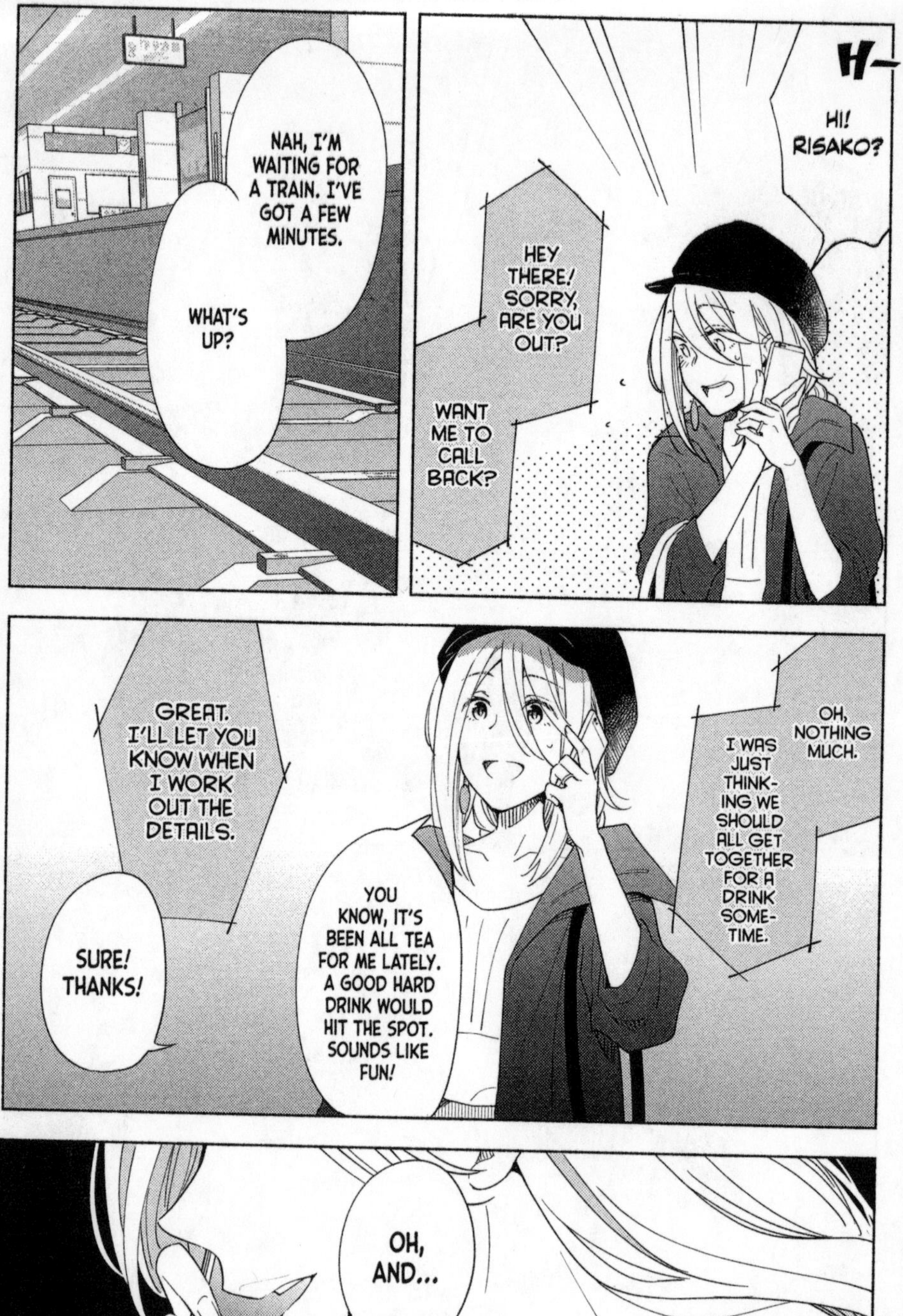
H—
HI! RISAKO?
HEY THERE! SORRY, ARE YOU OUT?
WANT ME TO CALL BACK?
NAH, I'M WAITING FOR A TRAIN. I'VE GOT A FEW MINUTES.
WHAT'S UP?
OH, NOTHING MUCH.
I WAS JUST THINKING WE SHOULD ALL GET TOGETHER FOR A DRINK SOMETIME.
YOU KNOW, IT'S BEEN ALL TEA FOR ME LATELY. A GOOD HARD DRINK WOULD HIT THE SPOT. SOUNDS LIKE FUN!
GREAT. I'LL LET YOU KNOW WHEN I WORK OUT THE DETAILS.
SURE! THANKS!
OH, AND...

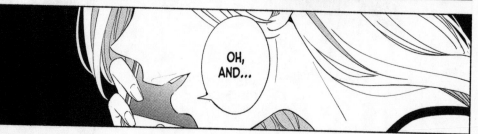

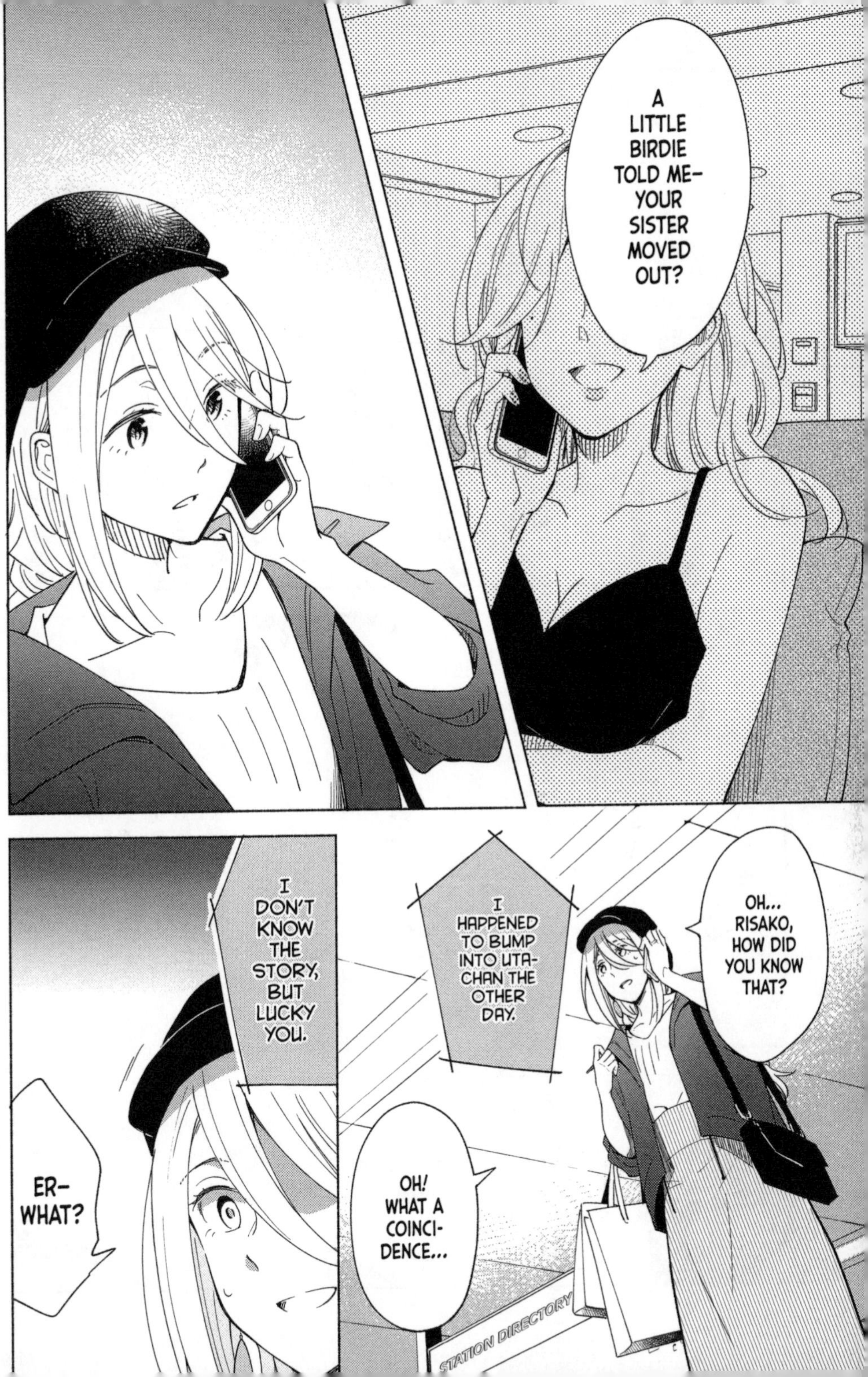
A LITTLE BIRDIE TOLD ME—YOUR SISTER MOVED OUT?
OH... RISAKO, HOW DID YOU KNOW THAT?
I HAPPENED TO BUMP INTO UTA-CHAN THE OTHER DAY.
STATION DIRECTORY
OH! WHAT A COINCI-DENCE...
I DON'T KNOW THE STORY, BUT LUCKY YOU.
ER—WHAT?

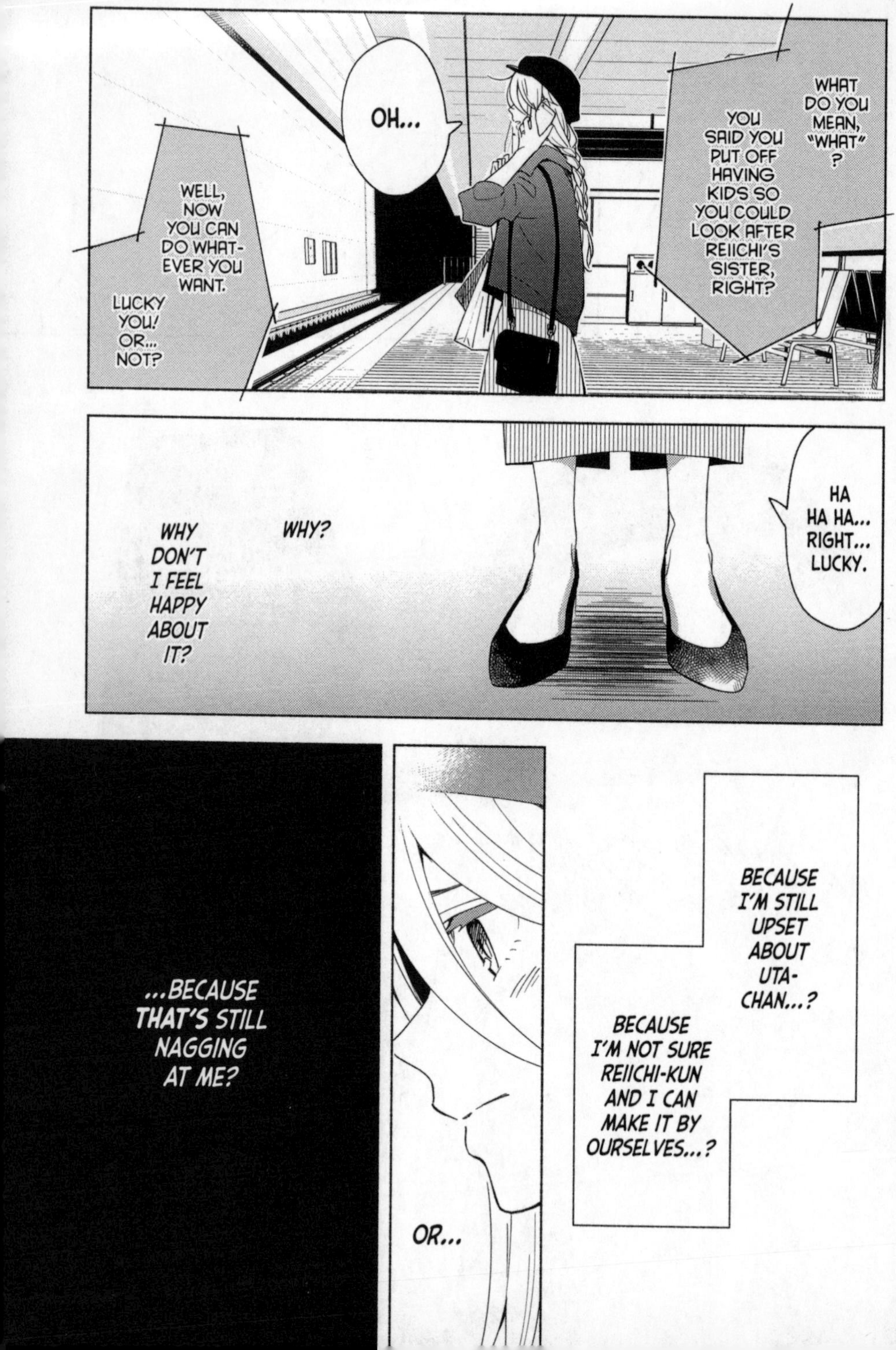

WHAT DO YOU MEAN, "WHAT"?
YOU SAID YOU PUT OFF HAVING KIDS SO YOU COULD LOOK AFTER REIICHI'S SISTER, RIGHT?
OH...
WELL, NOW YOU CAN DO WHATEVER YOU WANT.
LUCKY YOU! OR... NOT?
HA HA HA... RIGHT... LUCKY.
WHY?
WHY DON'T I FEEL HAPPY ABOUT IT?
BECAUSE I'M STILL UPSET ABOUT UTA-CHAN...?
BECAUSE I'M NOT SURE REIICHI-KUN AND I CAN MAKE IT BY OURSELVES...?
OR...
...BECAUSE THAT'S STILL NAGGING AT ME?

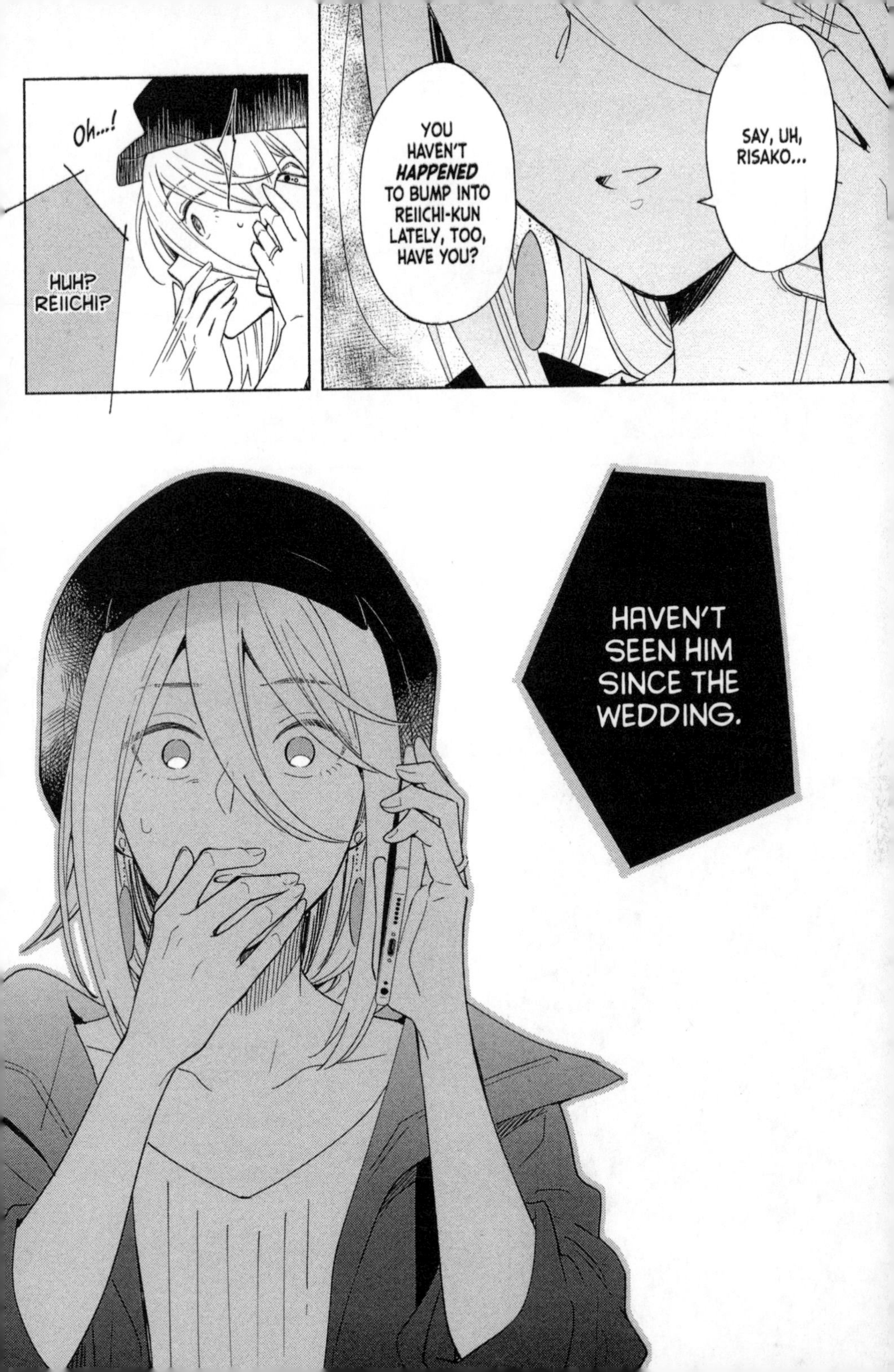
SAY, UH, RISAKO...
YOU HAVEN'T ***HAPPENED*** TO BUMP INTO REIICHI-KUN LATELY, TOO, HAVE YOU?
Oh...!
HUH? REIICHI?
HAVEN'T SEEN HIM SINCE THE WEDDING.

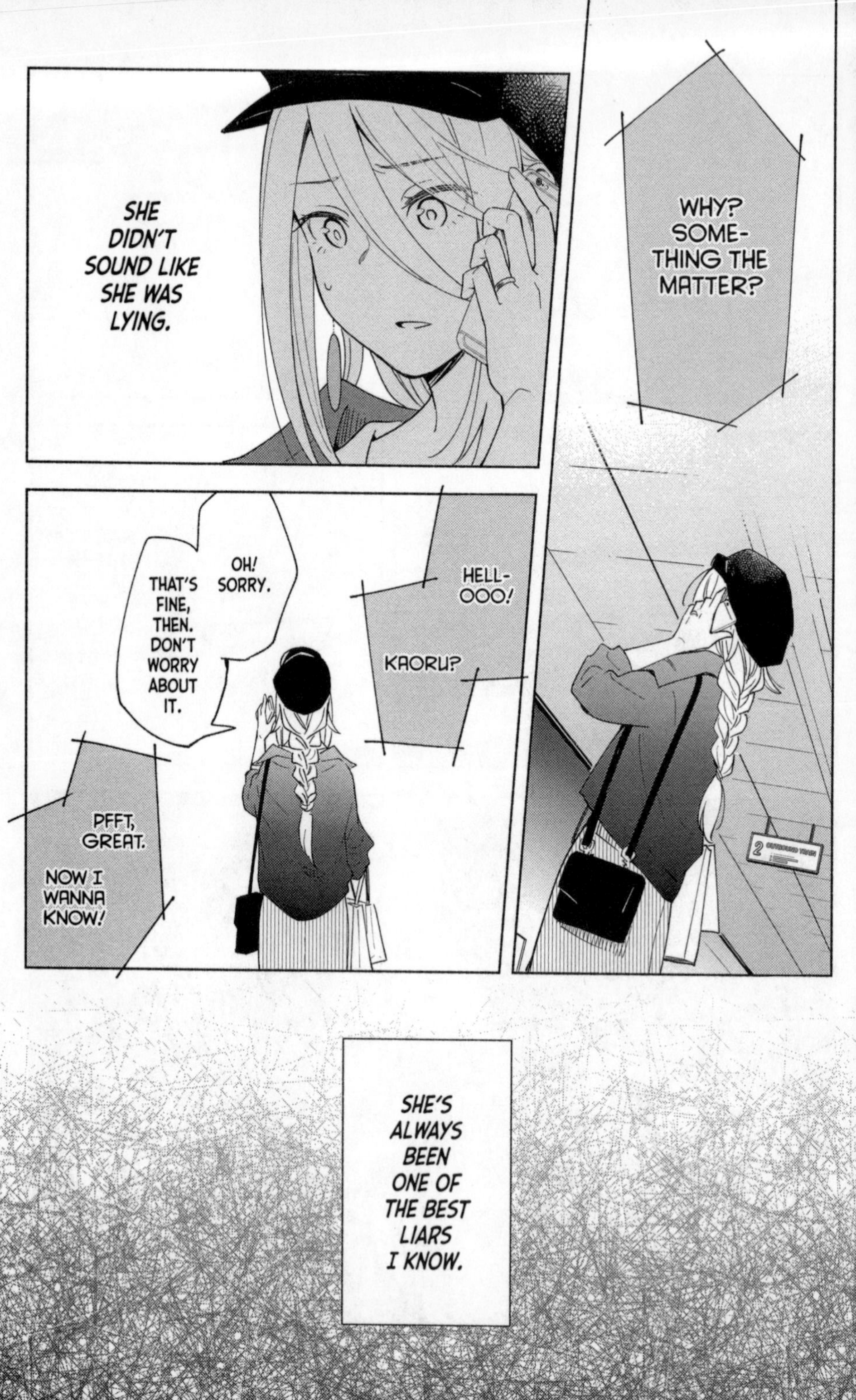
WHY? SOMETHING THE MATTER?
SHE DIDN'T SOUND LIKE SHE WAS LYING.
HELL-OOO!
OH! SORRY.
THAT'S FINE, THEN. DON'T WORRY ABOUT IT.
KAORU?
PFFT, GREAT.
NOW I WANNA KNOW!
SHE'S ALWAYS BEEN ONE OF THE BEST LIARS I KNOW.

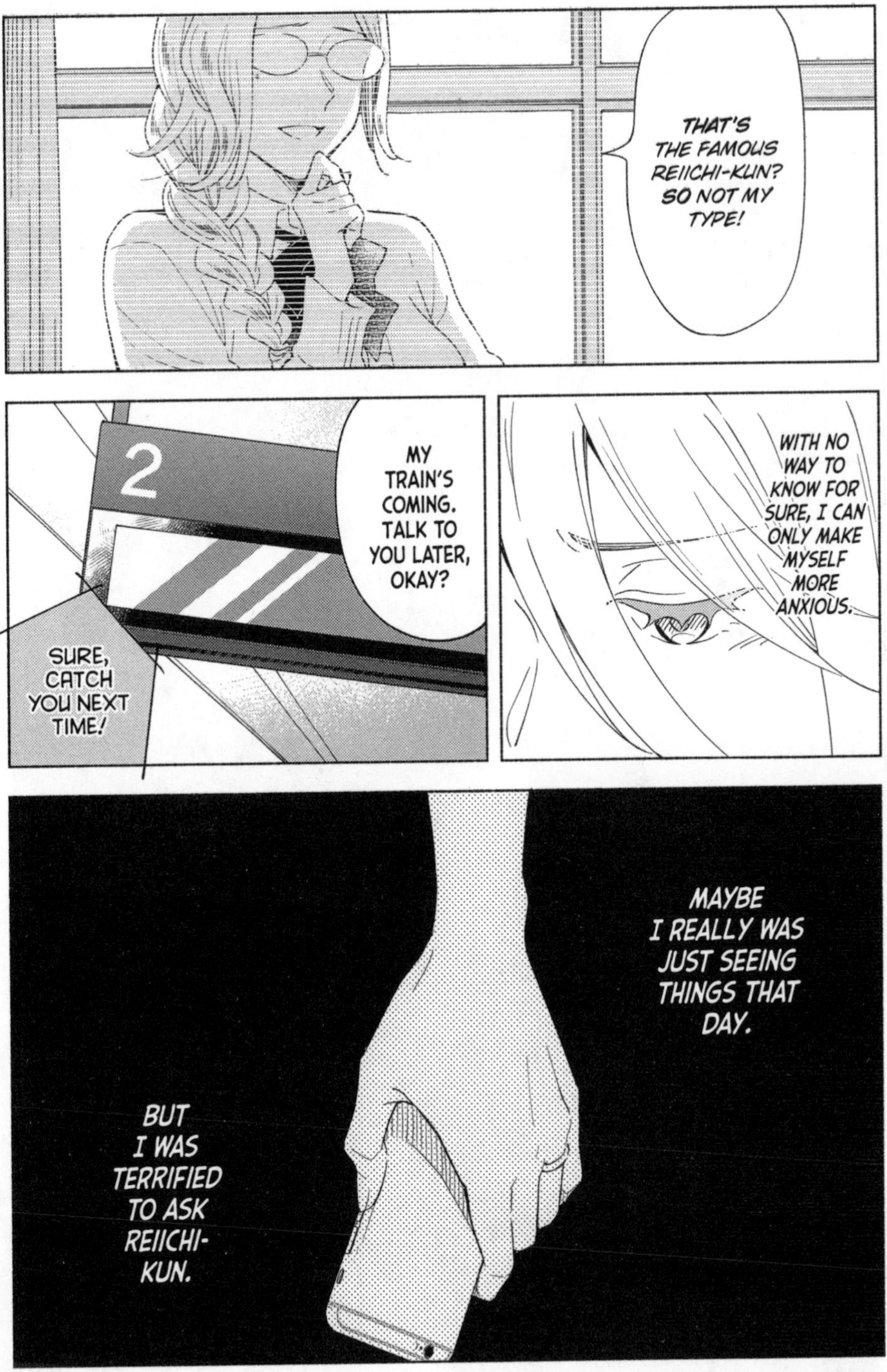
THAT'S THE FAMOUS REIICHI-KUN? SO NOT MY TYPE!
WITH NO WAY TO KNOW FOR SURE, I CAN ONLY MAKE MYSELF MORE ANXIOUS.
2
MY TRAIN'S COMING. TALK TO YOU LATER, OKAY?
SURE, CATCH YOU NEXT TIME!
MAYBE I REALLY WAS JUST SEEING THINGS THAT DAY.
BUT I WAS TERRIFIED TO ASK REIICHI-KUN.

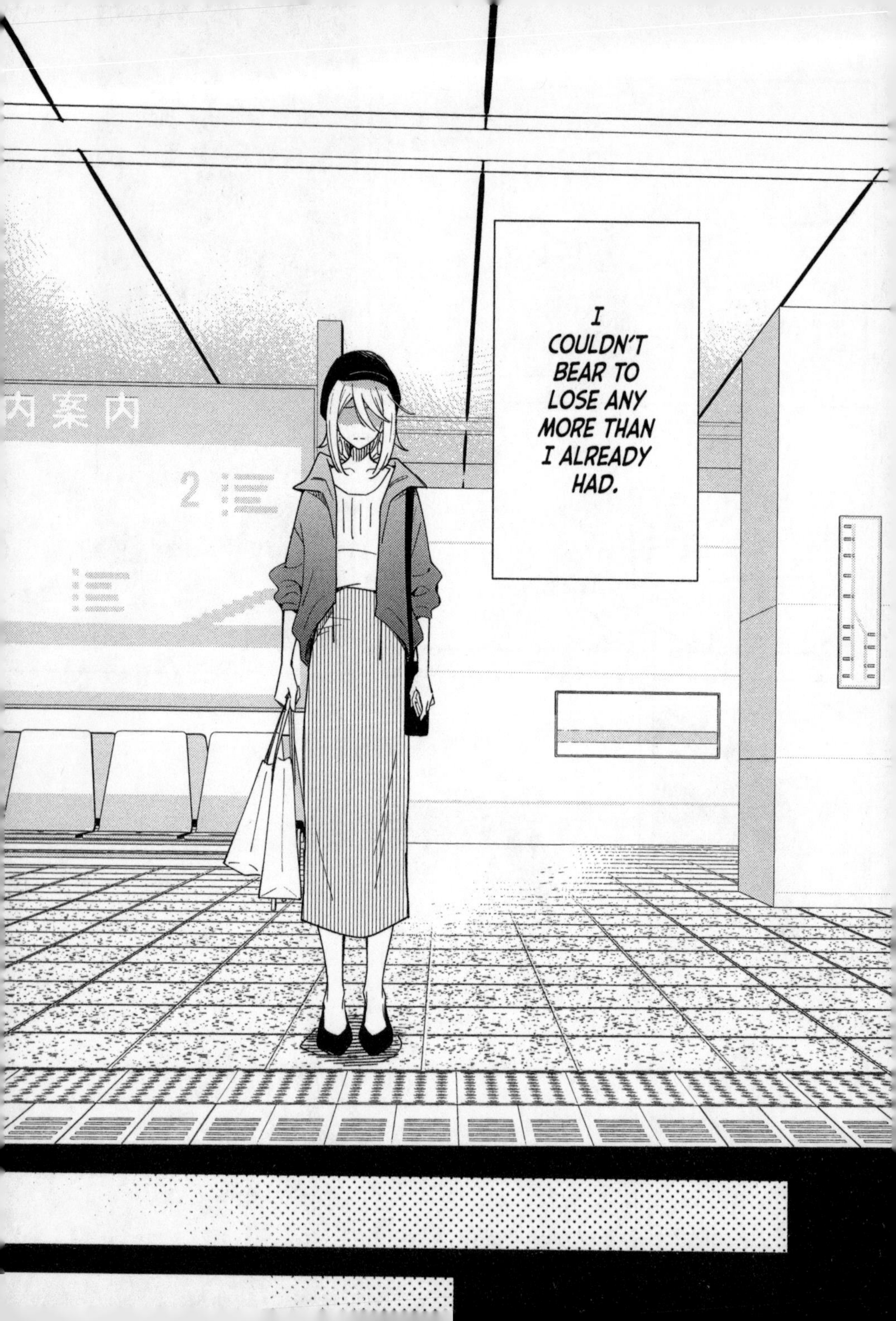
I COULDN'T BEAR TO LOSE ANY MORE THAN I ALREADY HAD.
内案内

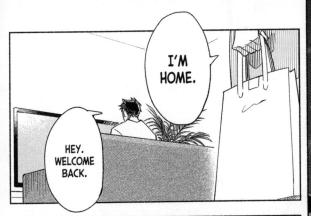

I'M HOME.

HEY. WELCOME BACK.

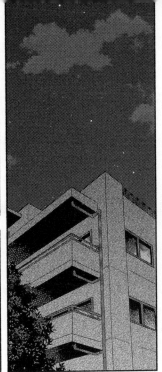

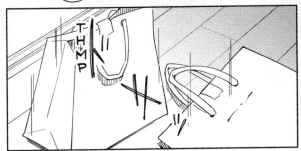

T-H-M-P

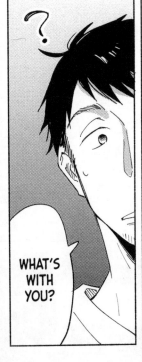

WHAT'S WITH YOU?

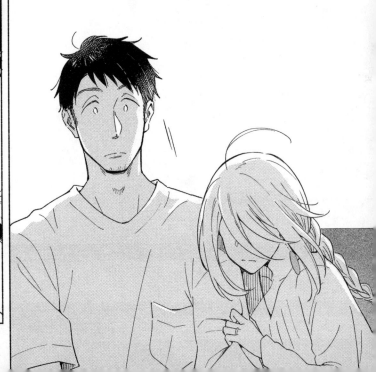

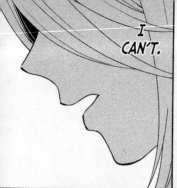

...
I CAN'T.
I SHOULDN'T SAY ANY-THING...
KAORU?
...NOT WHEN I'M STILL FEELING SO VULNER-ABLE .
HEY, LISTEN...
I...

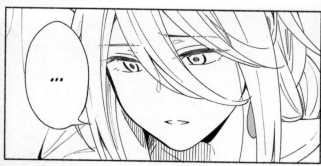

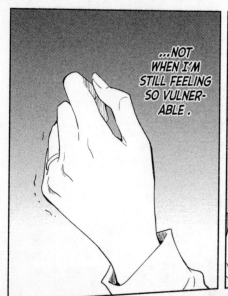

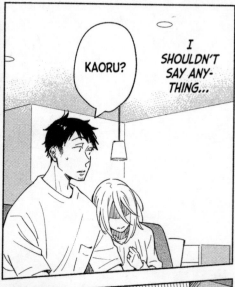

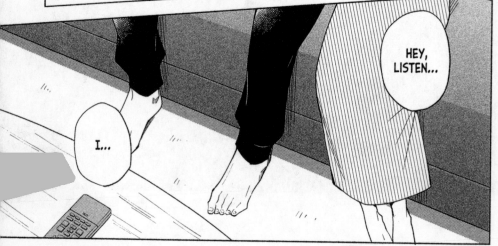

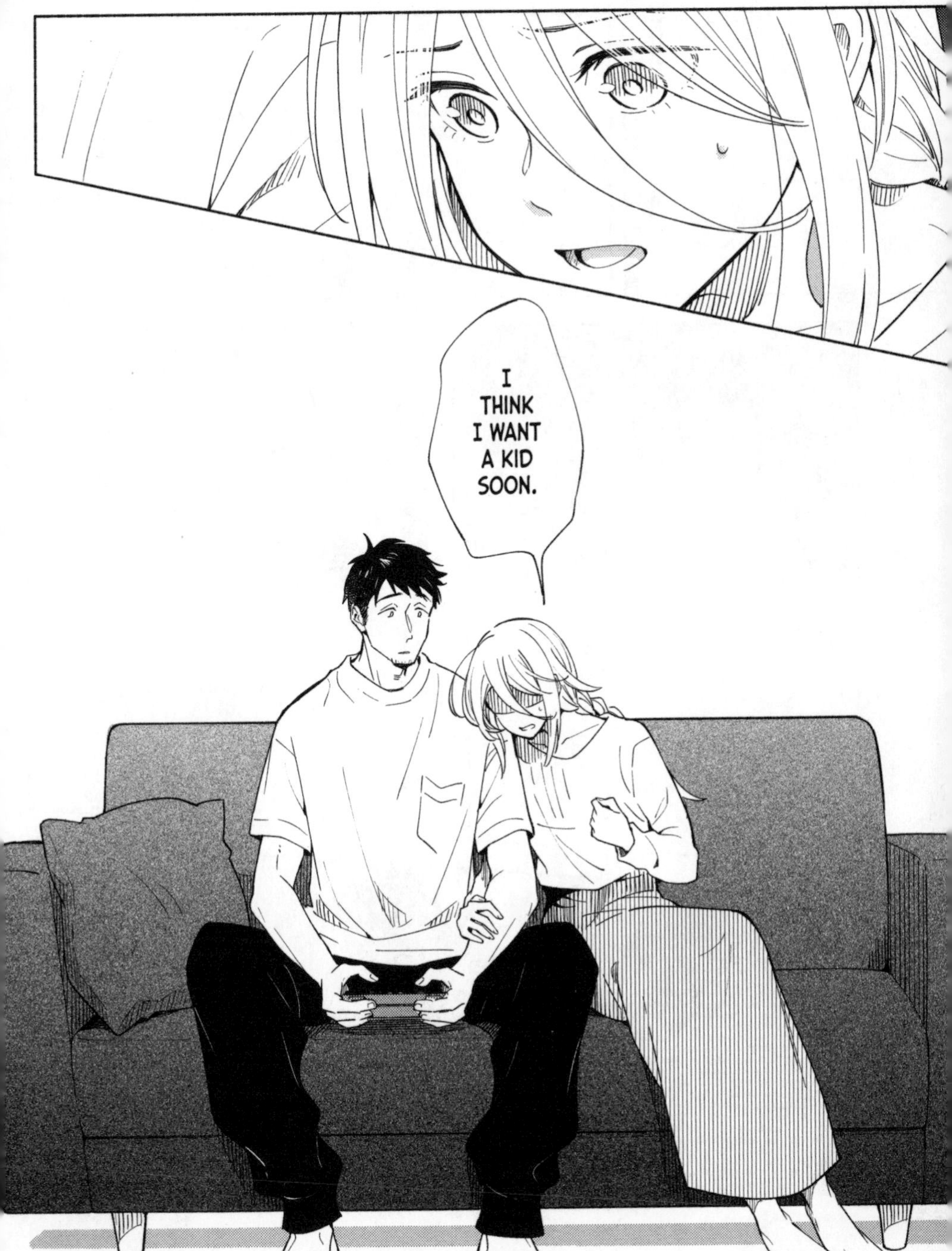
I THINK I WANT A KID SOON.

If I Could
Reach You

If I Could
Reach You

Chapter 27

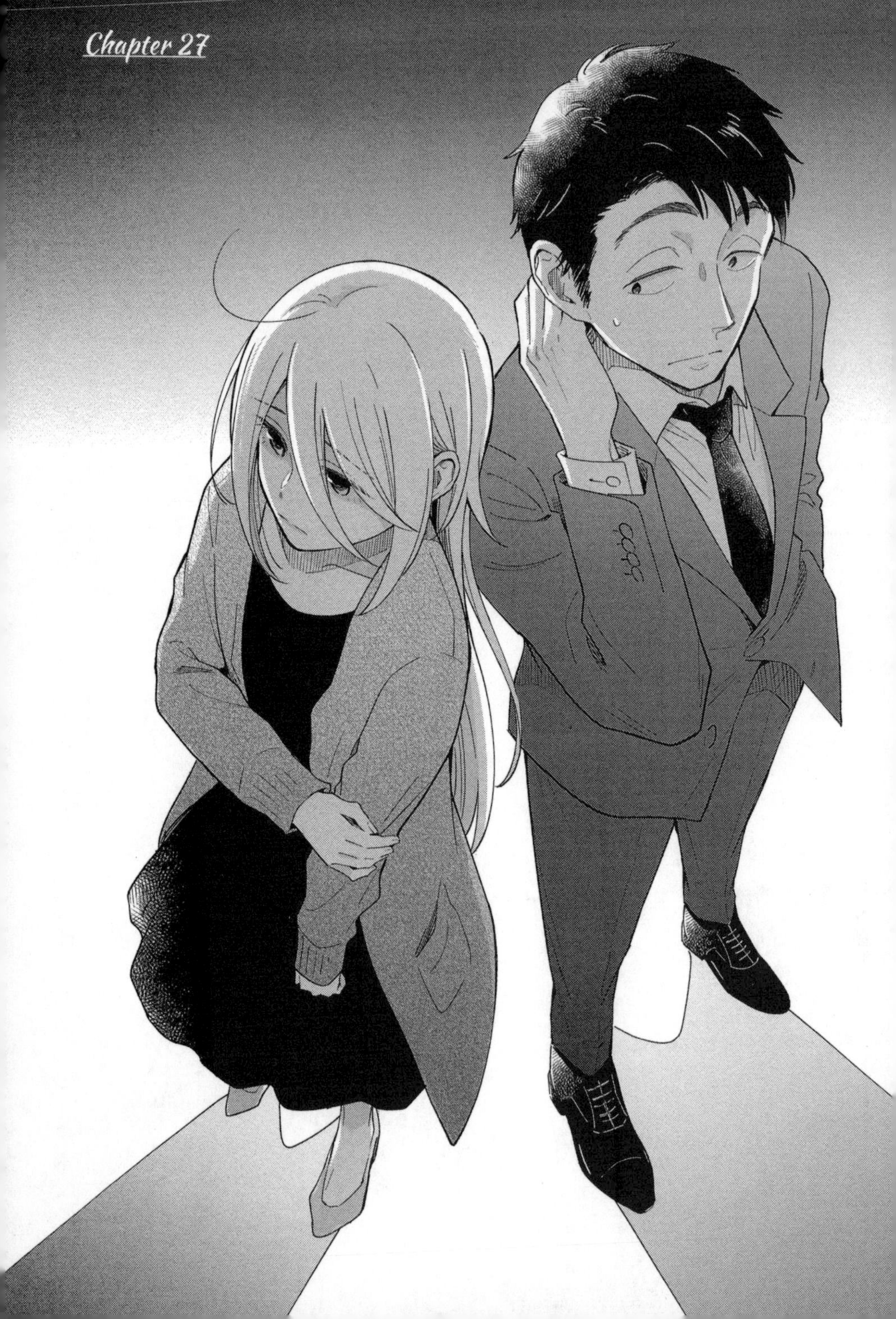

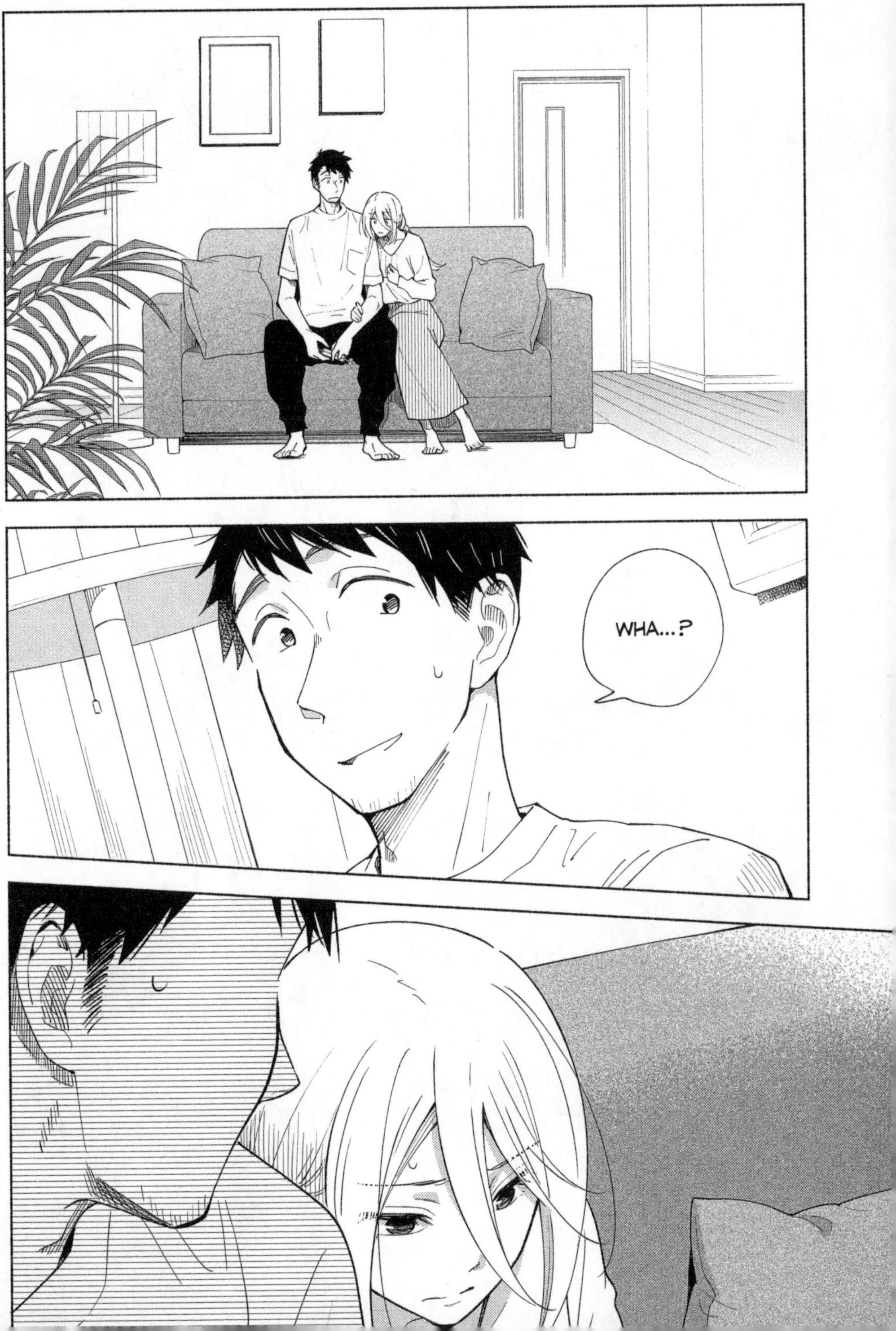
WHA...?

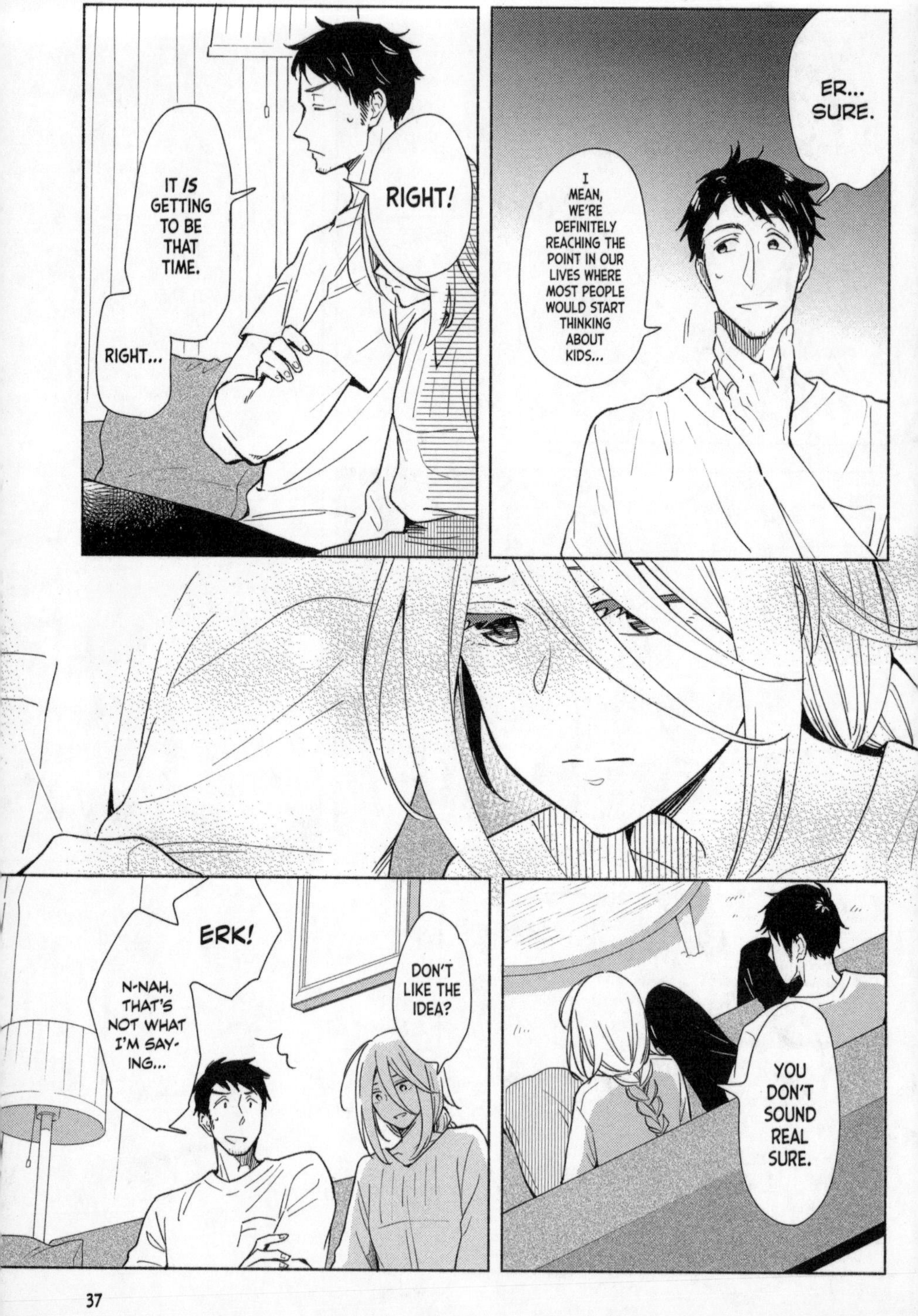
ER... SURE.
I MEAN, WE'RE DEFINITELY REACHING THE POINT IN OUR LIVES WHERE MOST PEOPLE WOULD START THINKING ABOUT KIDS...
RIGHT!
IT *IS* GETTING TO BE THAT TIME.
RIGHT...
YOU DON'T SOUND REAL SURE.
DON'T LIKE THE IDEA?
ERK!
N-NAH, THAT'S NOT WHAT I'M SAY-ING...

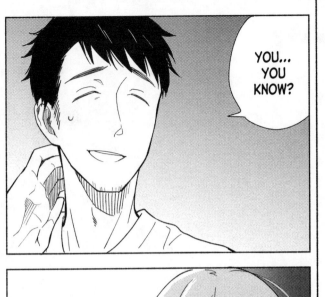

YOU... YOU KNOW?

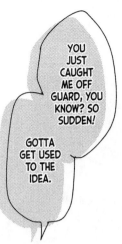

YOU JUST CAUGHT ME OFF GUARD, YOU KNOW? SO SUDDEN!

GOTTA GET USED TO THE IDEA.

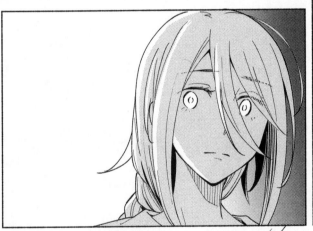

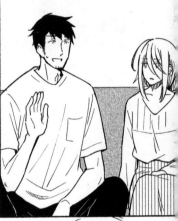

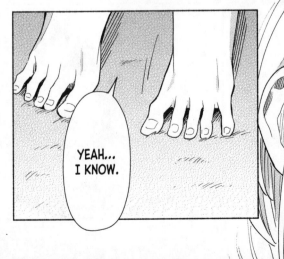

YEAH... I KNOW.

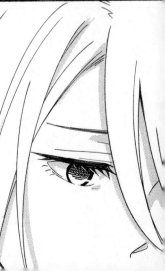

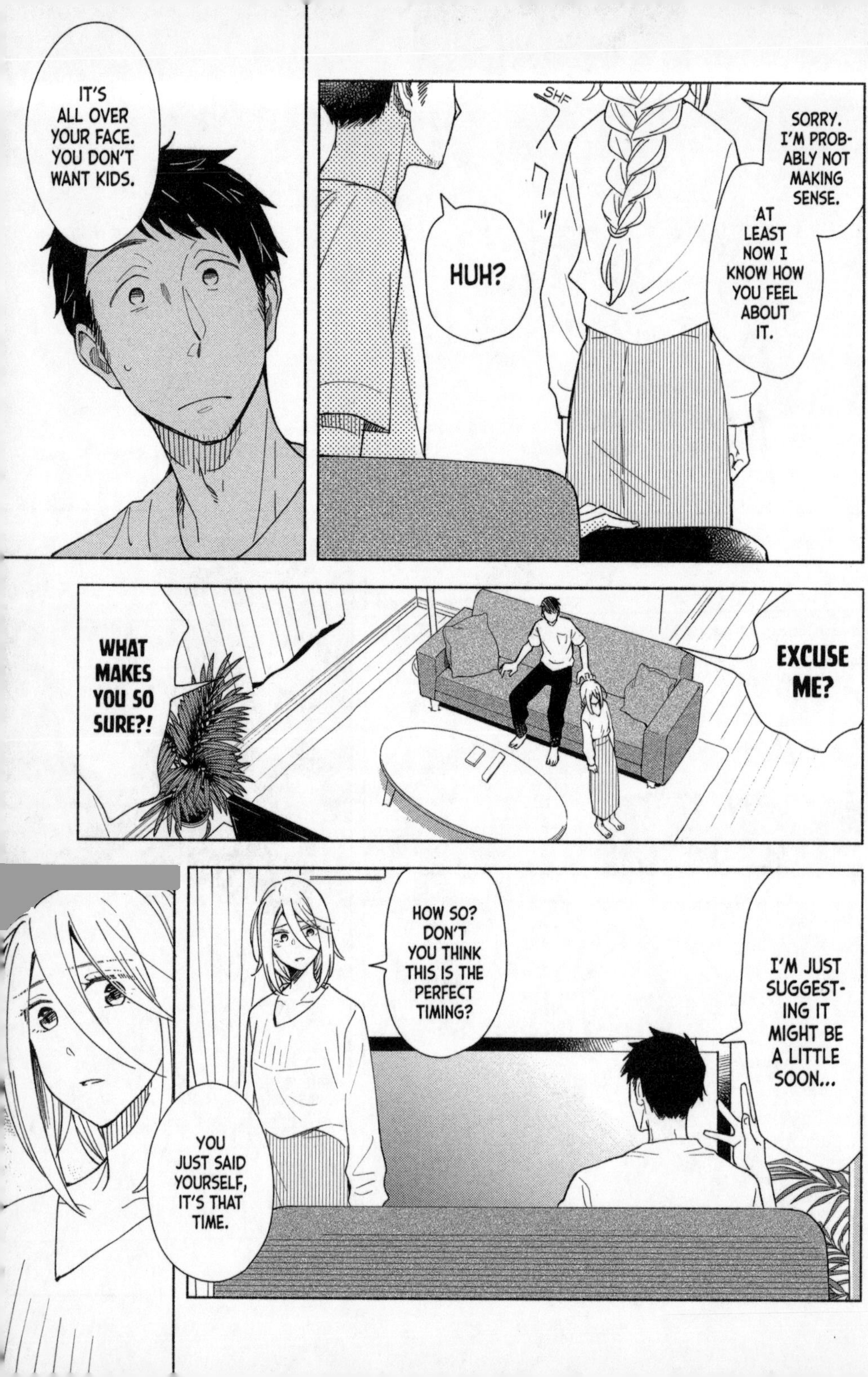
SORRY. I'M PROB-ABLY NOT MAKING SENSE.
AT LEAST NOW I KNOW HOW YOU FEEL ABOUT IT.
SHF
HUH?
IT'S ALL OVER YOUR FACE. YOU DON'T WANT KIDS.
EXCUSE ME?
WHAT MAKES YOU SO SURE?!
I'M JUST SUGGEST-ING IT MIGHT BE A LITTLE SOON...
HOW SO? DON'T YOU THINK THIS IS THE PERFECT TIMING?
YOU JUST SAID YOURSELF, IT'S THAT TIME.

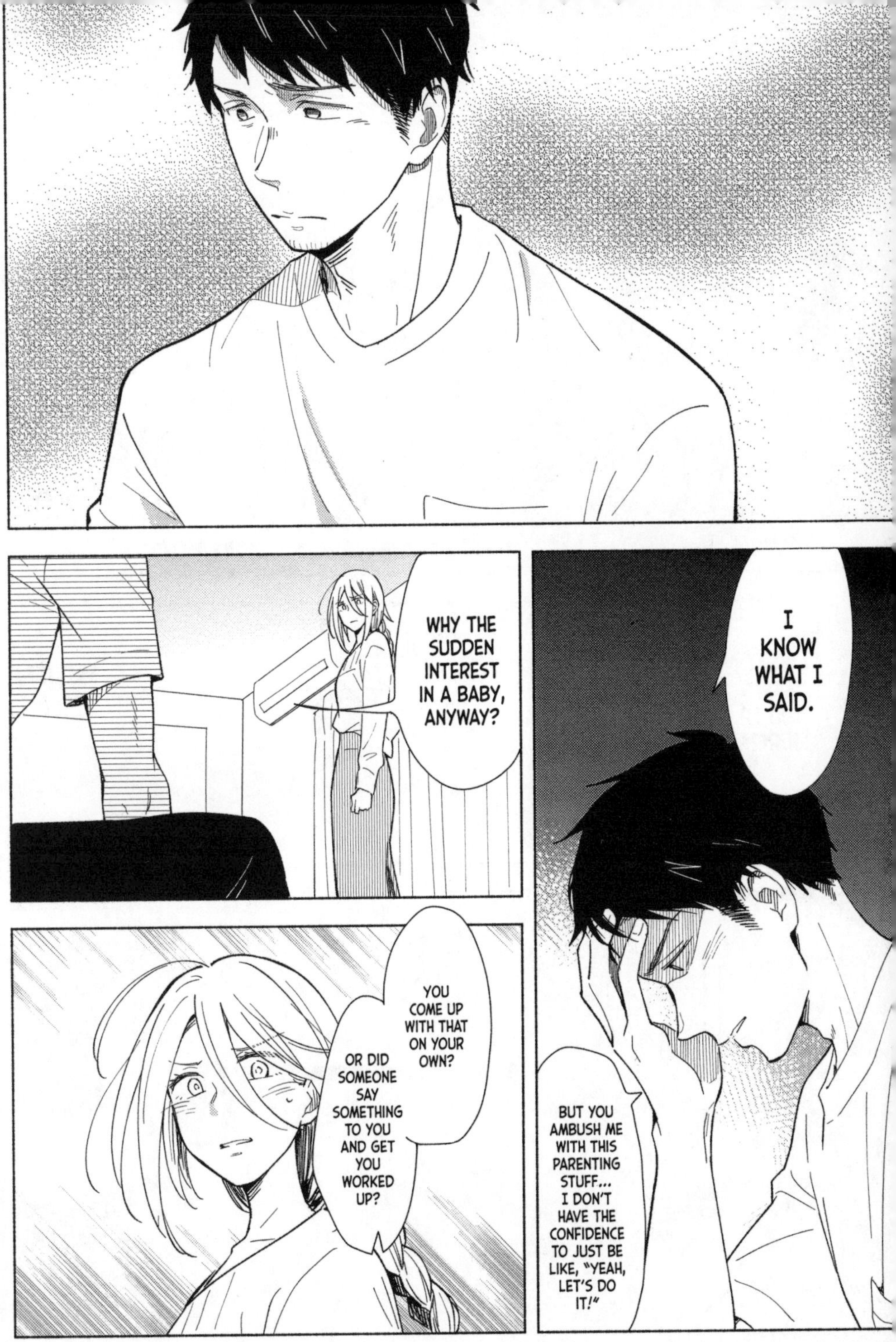
WHY THE SUDDEN INTEREST IN A BABY, ANYWAY?
YOU COME UP WITH THAT ON YOUR OWN?
OR DID SOMEONE SAY SOMETHING TO YOU AND GET YOU WORKED UP?
I KNOW WHAT I SAID.
BUT YOU AMBUSH ME WITH THIS PARENTING STUFF... I DON'T HAVE THE CONFIDENCE TO JUST BE LIKE, "YEAH, LET'S DO IT!"

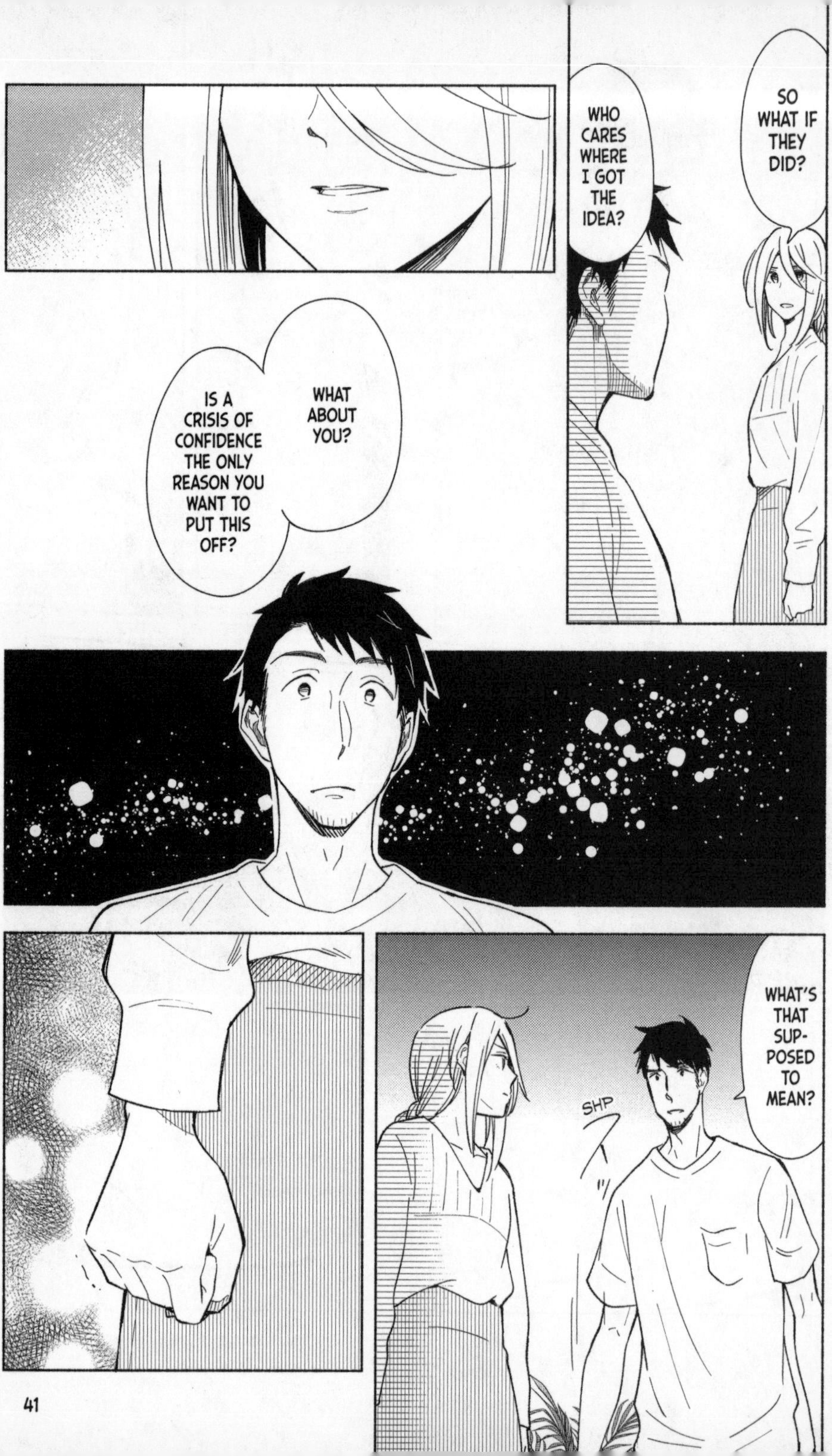
SO WHAT IF THEY DID?
WHO CARES WHERE I GOT THE IDEA?
WHAT ABOUT YOU?
IS A CRISIS OF CONFIDENCE THE ONLY REASON YOU WANT TO PUT THIS OFF?
WHAT'S THAT SUP-POSED TO MEAN?
SHP

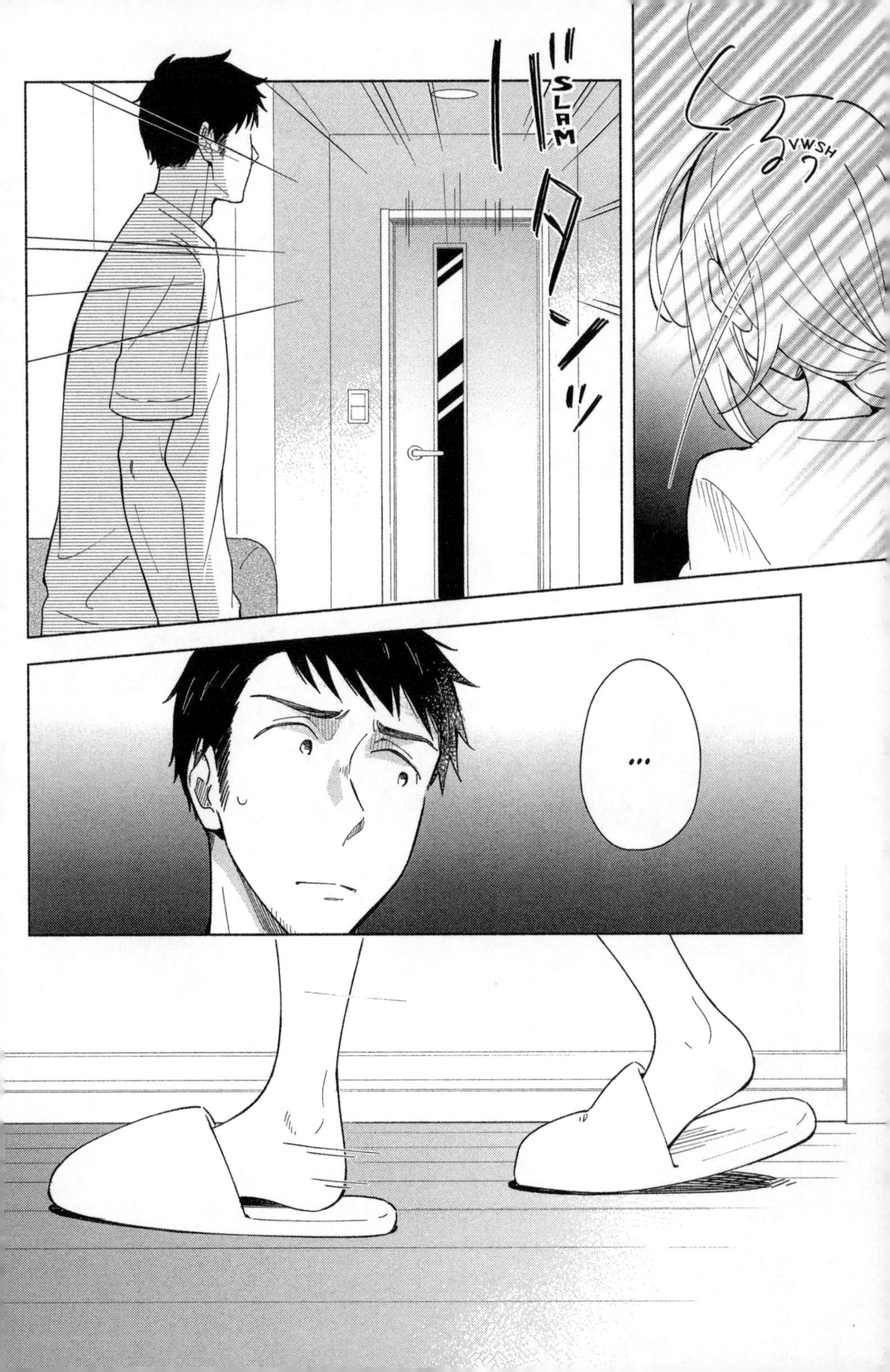
VWSH
SLAM
...

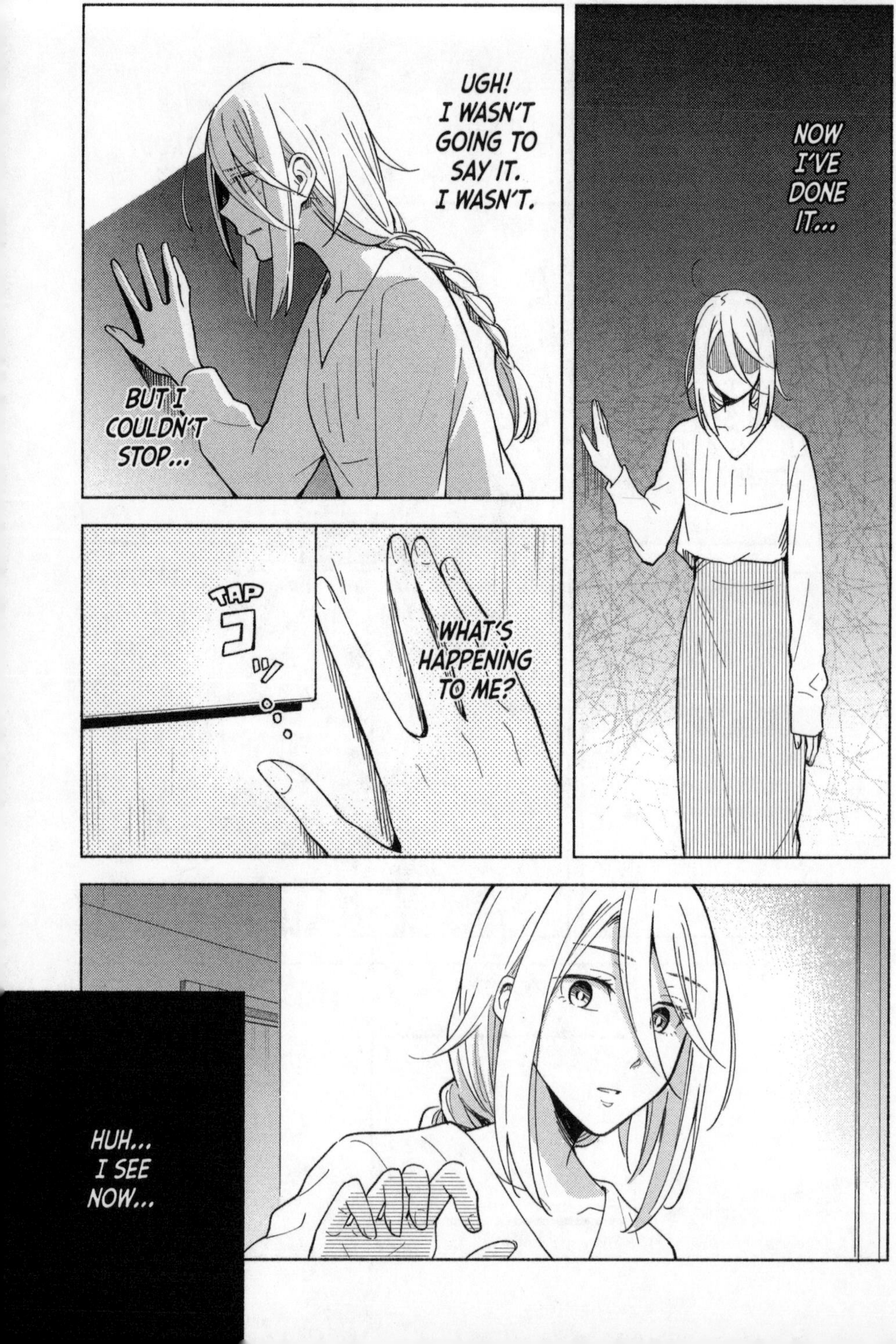
NOW I'VE DONE IT...
UGH! I WASN'T GOING TO SAY IT. I WASN'T.
BUT I COULDN'T STOP...
TAP
コッ
WHAT'S HAPPENING TO ME?
HUH... I SEE NOW...

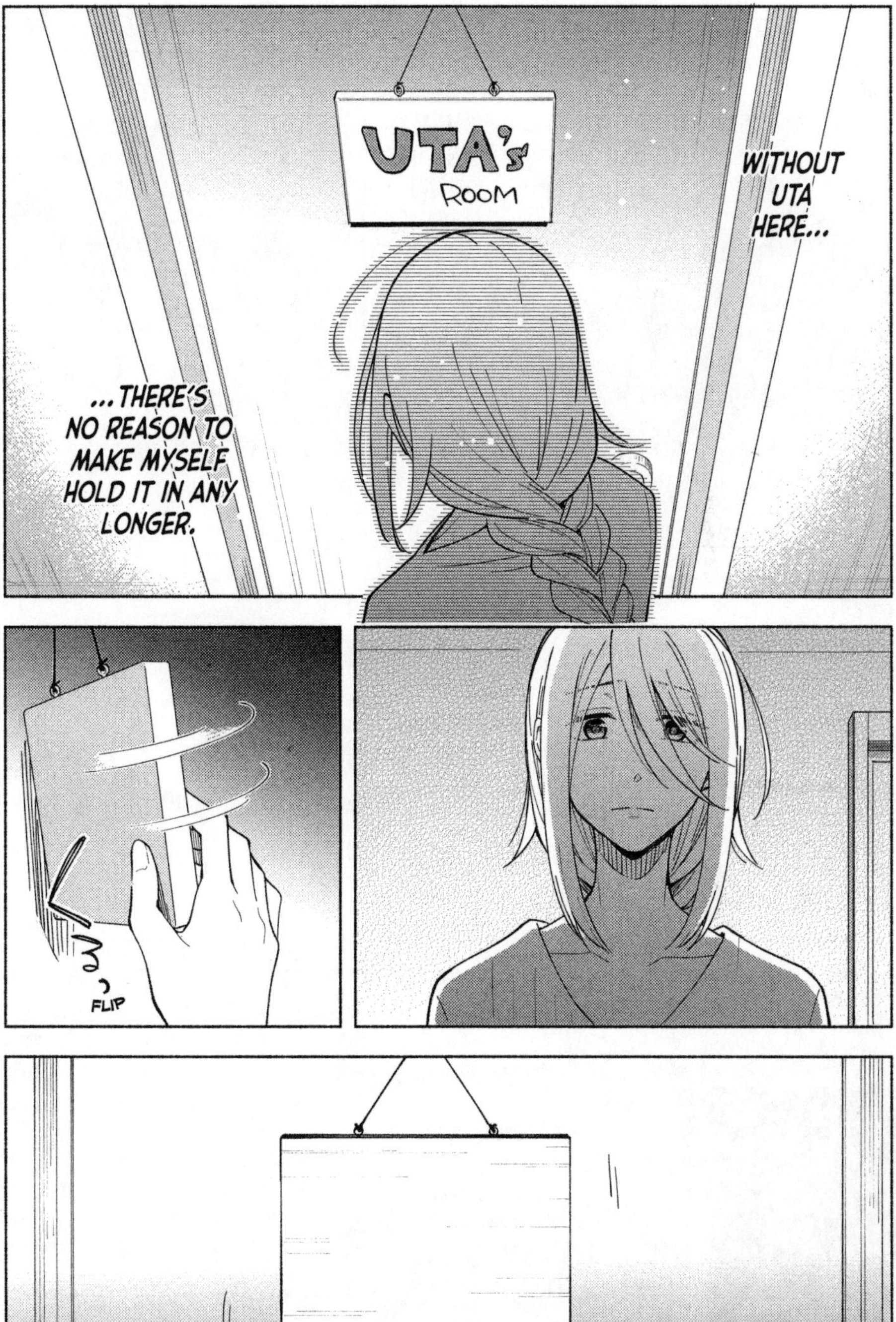
UTA's ROOM
WITHOUT UTA HERE...
...THERE'S NO REASON TO MAKE MYSELF HOLD IT IN ANY LONGER.
FLIP

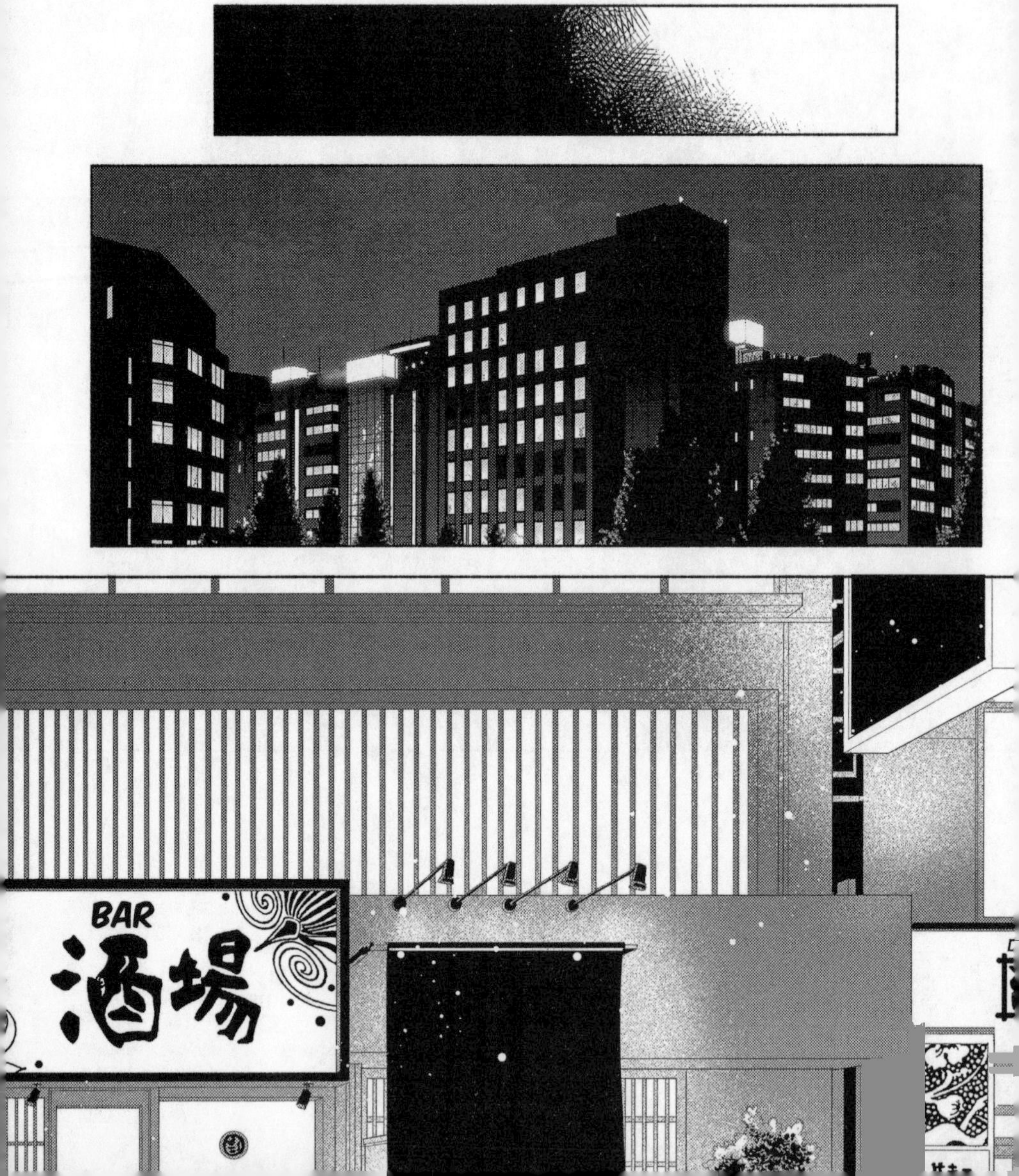
BAR
酒場

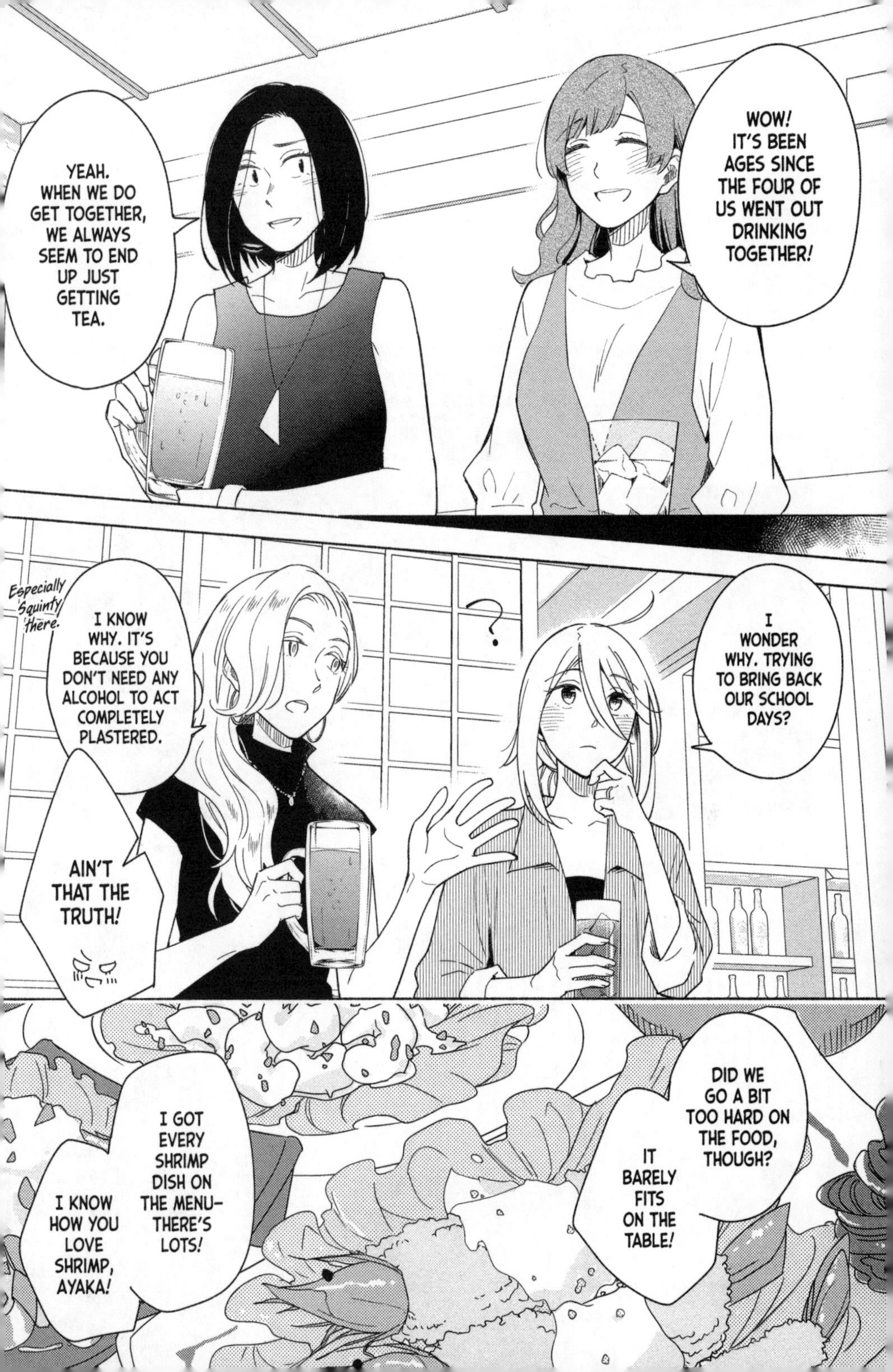
WOW! IT'S BEEN AGES SINCE THE FOUR OF US WENT OUT DRINKING TOGETHER!
YEAH. WHEN WE DO GET TOGETHER, WE ALWAYS SEEM TO END UP JUST GETTING TEA.
I WONDER WHY. TRYING TO BRING BACK OUR SCHOOL DAYS?
I KNOW WHY. IT'S BECAUSE YOU DON'T NEED ANY ALCOHOL TO ACT COMPLETELY PLASTERED.
Especially Squinty there.
AIN'T THAT THE TRUTH!
DID WE GO A BIT TOO HARD ON THE FOOD, THOUGH?
IT BARELY FITS ON THE TABLE!
I GOT EVERY SHRIMP DISH ON THE MENU— THERE'S LOTS!
I KNOW HOW YOU LOVE SHRIMP, AYAKA!

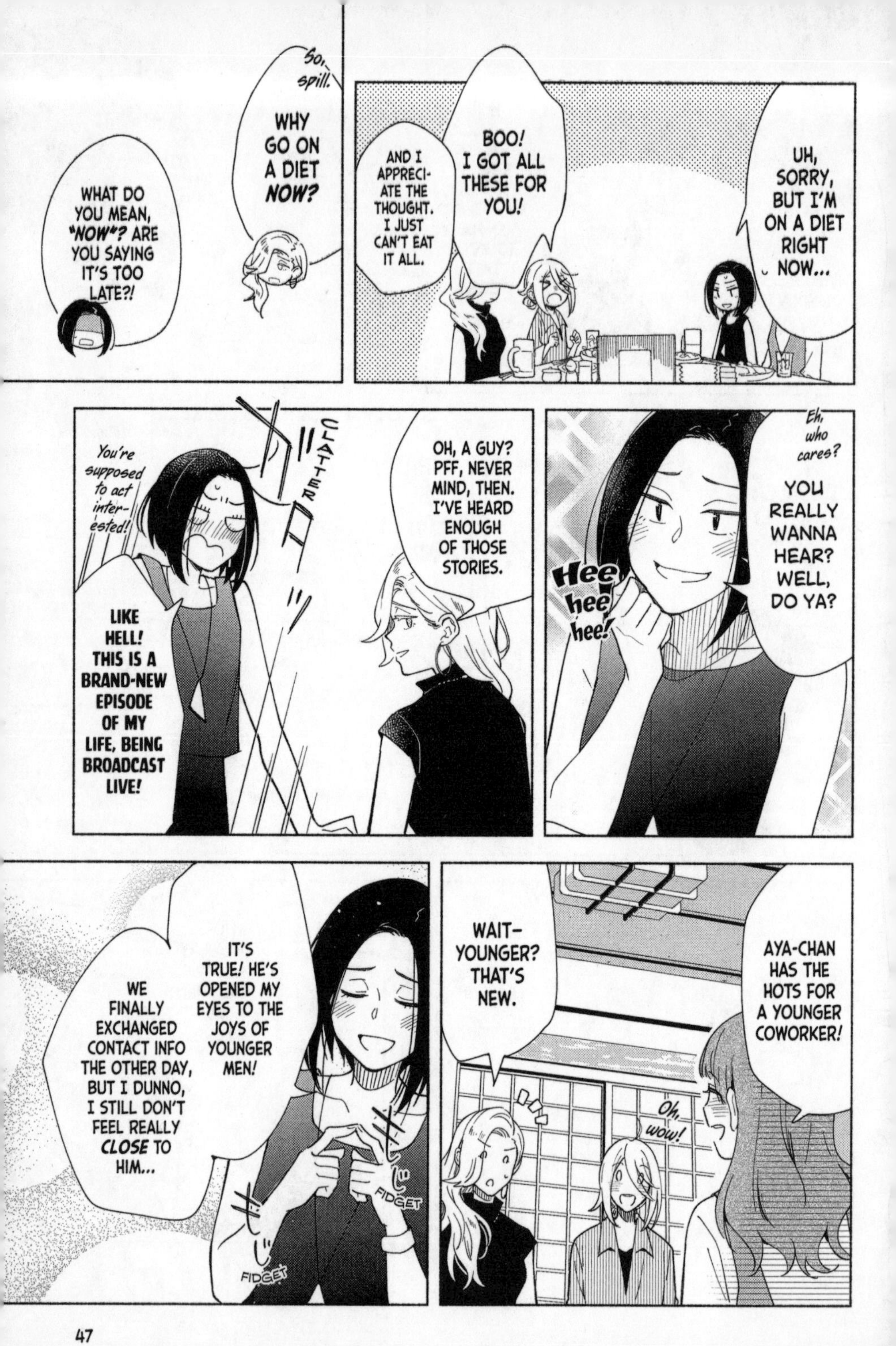
UH, SORRY, BUT I'M ON A DIET RIGHT NOW...
BOO! I GOT ALL THESE FOR YOU!
AND I APPRECIATE THE THOUGHT. I JUST CAN'T EAT IT ALL.
So, spill.
WHY GO ON A DIET NOW?
WHAT DO YOU MEAN, "NOW"? ARE YOU SAYING IT'S TOO LATE?!
Eh, who cares?
YOU REALLY WANNA HEAR? WELL, DO YA?
Hee hee hee!
OH, A GUY? PFF, NEVER MIND, THEN. I'VE HEARD ENOUGH OF THOSE STORIES.
CLATTER
You're supposed to act interested!
LIKE HELL! THIS IS A BRAND-NEW EPISODE OF MY LIFE, BEING BROADCAST LIVE!
AYA-CHAN HAS THE HOTS FOR A YOUNGER COWORKER!
WAIT—YOUNGER? THAT'S NEW.
Oh, wow!
IT'S TRUE! HE'S OPENED MY EYES TO THE JOYS OF YOUNGER MEN!
WE FINALLY EXCHANGED CONTACT INFO THE OTHER DAY, BUT I DUNNO, I STILL DON'T FEEL REALLY CLOSE TO HIM...
FIDGET
FIDGET

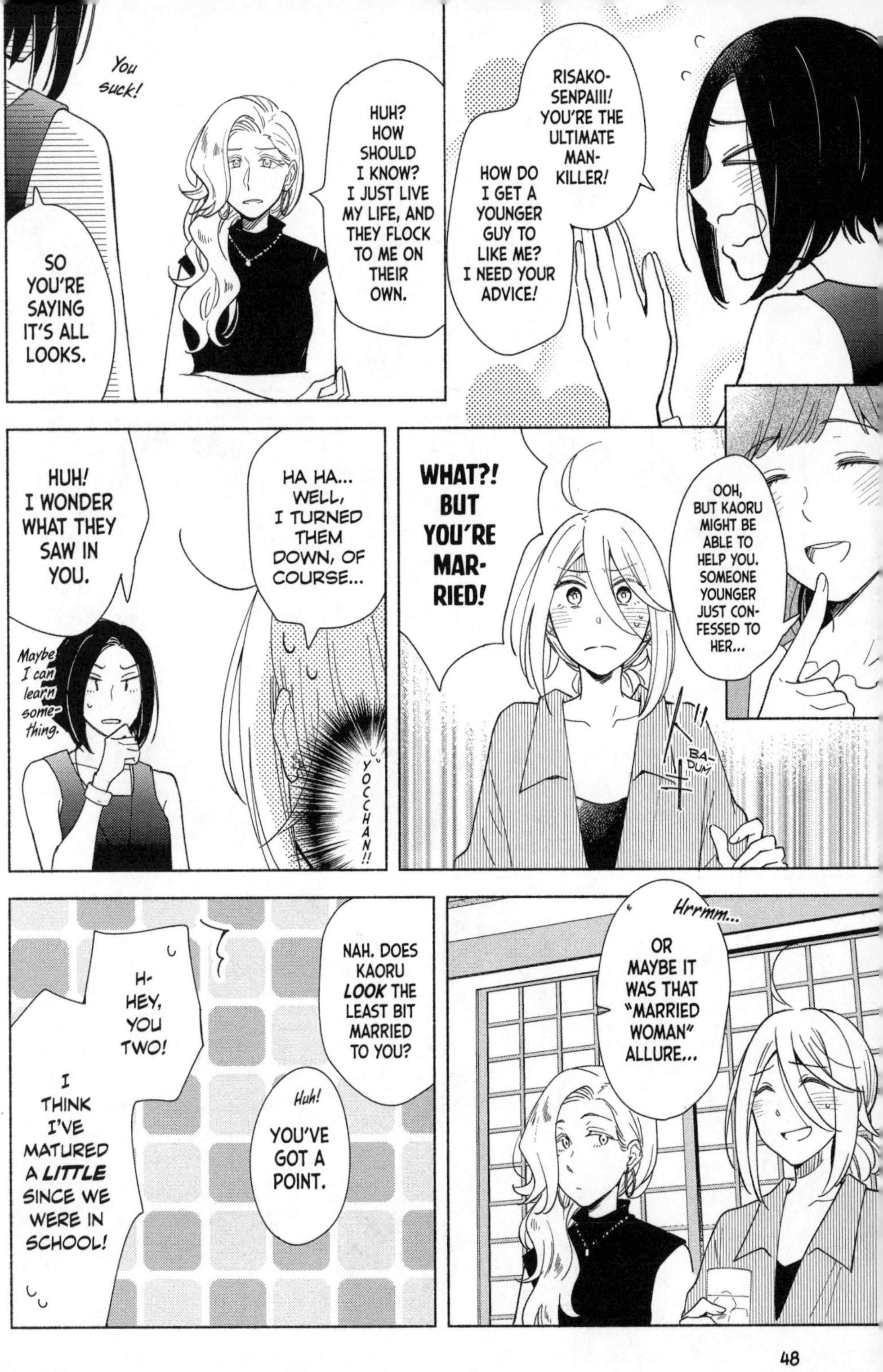
RISAKO-SENPAIII! YOU'RE THE ULTIMATE MAN-KILLER!
HOW DO I GET A YOUNGER GUY TO LIKE ME? I NEED YOUR ADVICE!
HUH? HOW SHOULD I KNOW? I JUST LIVE MY LIFE, AND THEY FLOCK TO ME ON THEIR OWN.
You suck!
SO YOU'RE SAYING IT'S ALL LOOKS.
OOH, BUT KAORU MIGHT BE ABLE TO HELP YOU. SOMEONE YOUNGER JUST CONFESSED TO HER...
WHAT?! BUT YOU'RE MARRIED!
BA-DUM
HA HA... WELL, I TURNED THEM DOWN, OF COURSE...
YOCCHAN!!
HUH! I WONDER WHAT THEY SAW IN YOU.
Maybe I can learn something.
Hrrmm...
OR MAYBE IT WAS THAT "MARRIED WOMAN" ALLURE...
NAH. DOES KAORU *LOOK* THE LEAST BIT MARRIED TO YOU?
Huh!
YOU'VE GOT A POINT.
H-HEY, YOU TWO!
I THINK I'VE MATURED A *LITTLE* SINCE WE WERE IN SCHOOL!

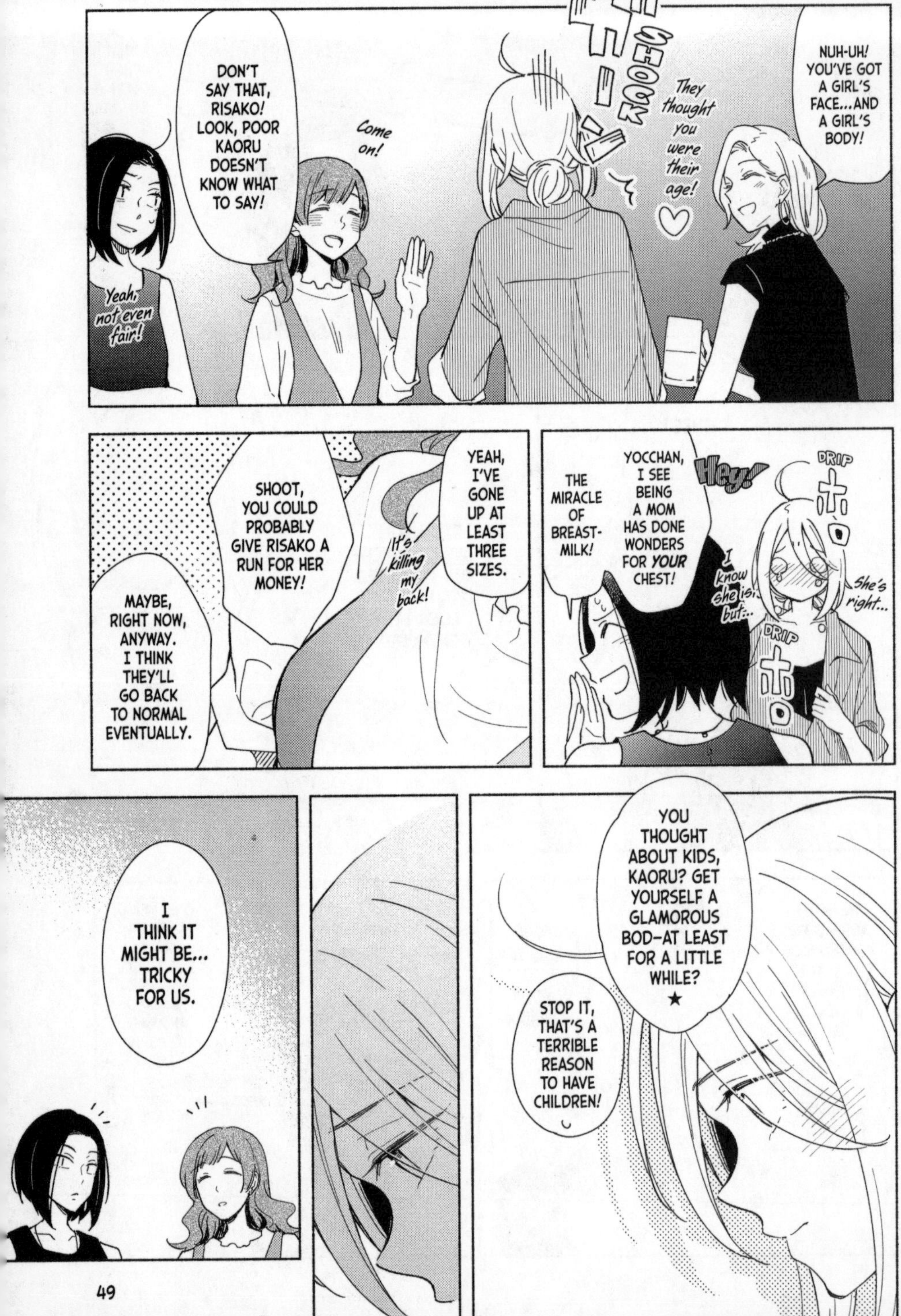
NUH-UH! YOU'VE GOT A GIRL'S FACE...AND A GIRL'S BODY!
They thought you were their age! ♥
SHOCK
Come on!
DON'T SAY THAT, RISAKO! LOOK, POOR KAORU DOESN'T KNOW WHAT TO SAY!
Yeah, not even fair!
Hey!
YOCCHAN, I SEE BEING A MOM HAS DONE WONDERS FOR *YOUR* CHEST!
THE MIRACLE OF BREAST-MILK!
DRIP
I know she is, but...
She's right...
DRIP
YEAH, I'VE GONE UP AT LEAST THREE SIZES.
It's killing my back!
SHOOT, YOU COULD PROBABLY GIVE RISAKO A RUN FOR HER MONEY!
MAYBE, RIGHT NOW, ANYWAY. I THINK THEY'LL GO BACK TO NORMAL EVENTUALLY.
YOU THOUGHT ABOUT KIDS, KAORU? GET YOURSELF A GLAMOROUS BOD—AT LEAST FOR A LITTLE WHILE? ★
STOP IT, THAT'S A TERRIBLE REASON TO HAVE CHILDREN!
I THINK IT MIGHT BE... TRICKY FOR US.

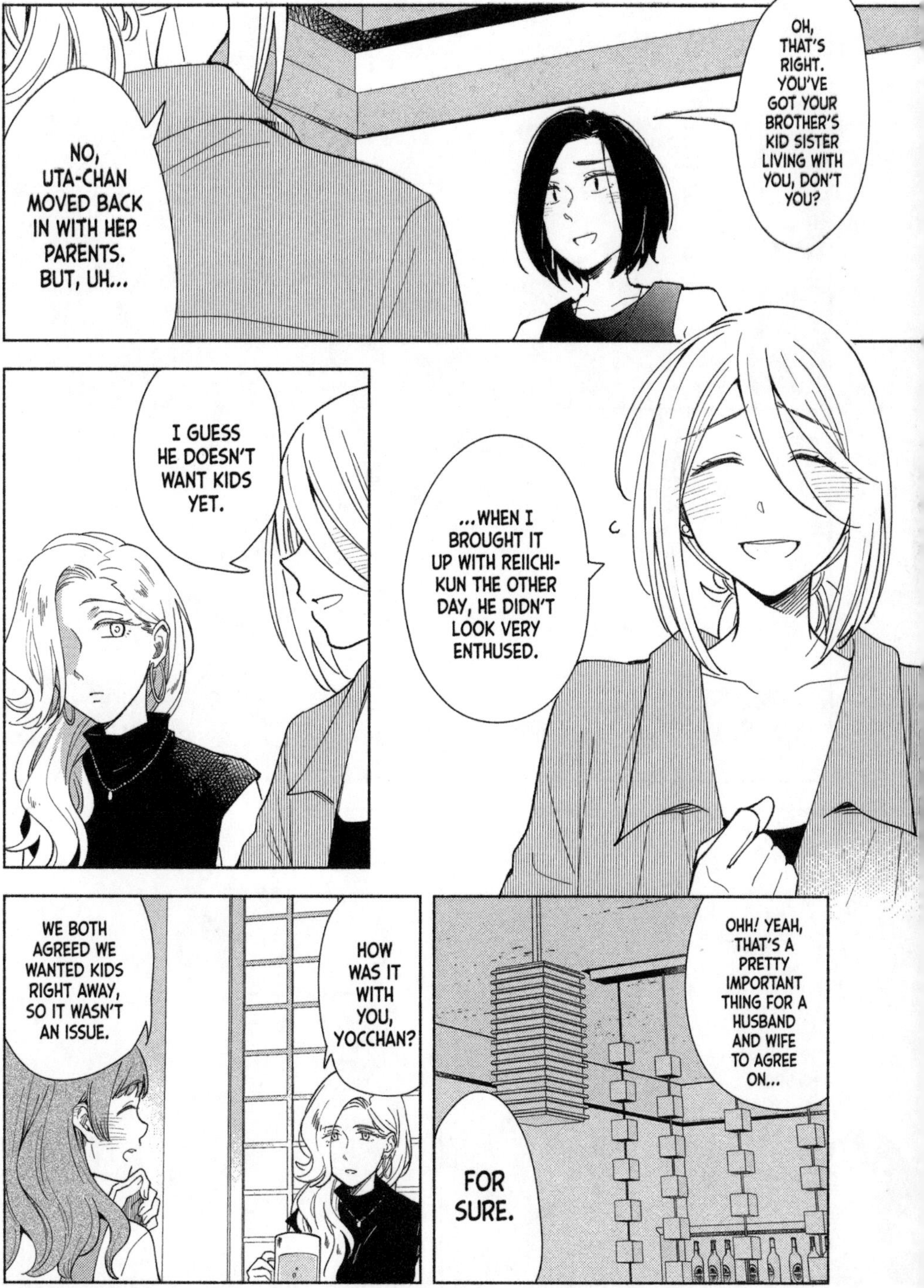
OH, THAT'S RIGHT. YOU'VE GOT YOUR BROTHER'S KID SISTER LIVING WITH YOU, DON'T YOU?
NO, UTA-CHAN MOVED BACK IN WITH HER PARENTS. BUT, UH...
...WHEN I BROUGHT IT UP WITH REIICHI-KUN THE OTHER DAY, HE DIDN'T LOOK VERY ENTHUSED.
I GUESS HE DOESN'T WANT KIDS YET.
OHH! YEAH, THAT'S A PRETTY IMPORTANT THING FOR A HUSBAND AND WIFE TO AGREE ON...
FOR SURE.
HOW WAS IT WITH YOU, YOCCHAN?
WE BOTH AGREED WE WANTED KIDS RIGHT AWAY, SO IT WASN'T AN ISSUE.

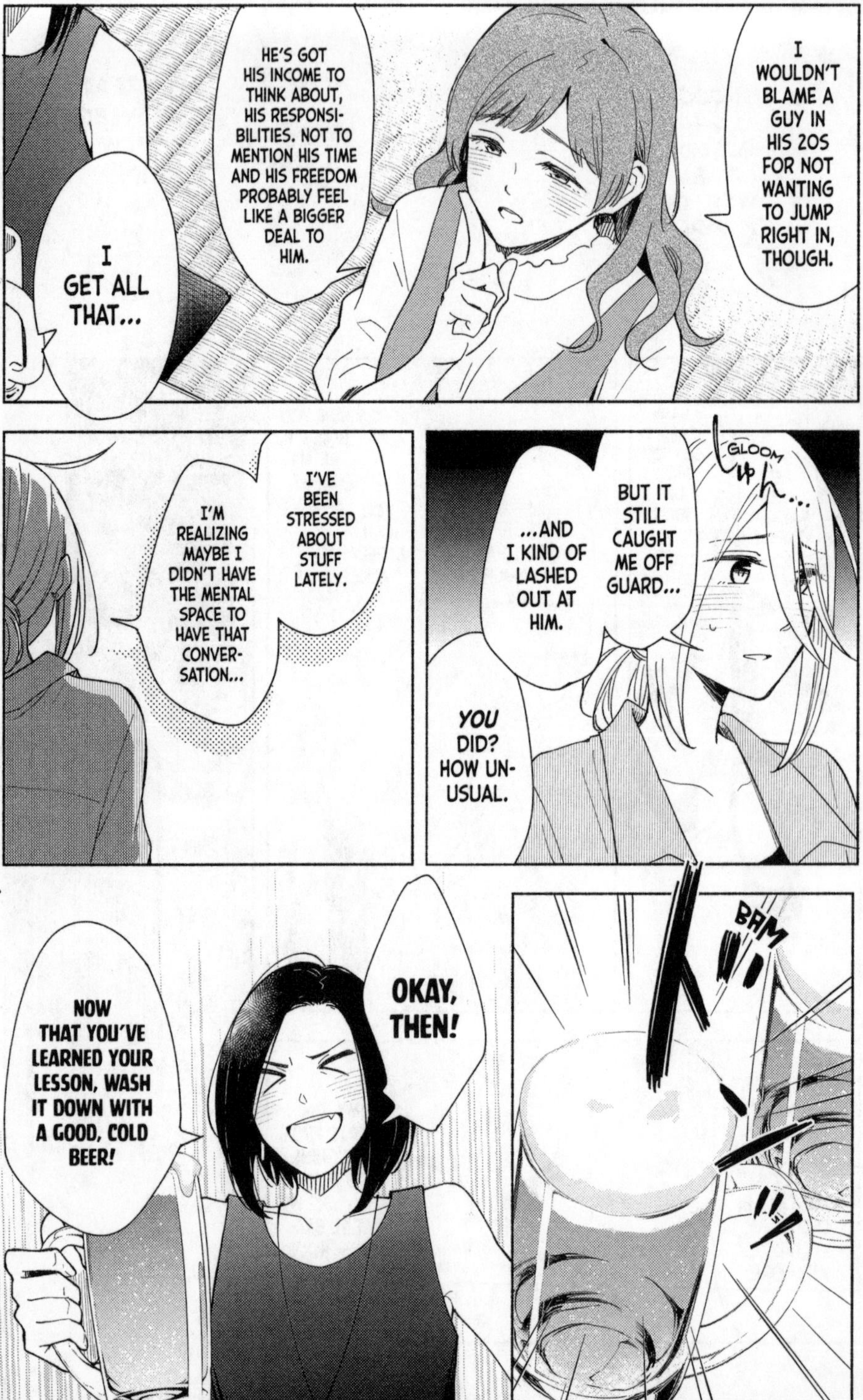
I WOULDN'T BLAME A GUY IN HIS 20S FOR NOT WANTING TO JUMP RIGHT IN, THOUGH.
HE'S GOT HIS INCOME TO THINK ABOUT, HIS RESPONSI-BILITIES. NOT TO MENTION HIS TIME AND HIS FREEDOM PROBABLY FEEL LIKE A BIGGER DEAL TO HIM.
I GET ALL THAT...
しゅん…
GLOOM
BUT IT STILL CAUGHT ME OFF GUARD...
...AND I KIND OF LASHED OUT AT HIM.
YOU DID? HOW UN-USUAL.
I'VE BEEN STRESSED ABOUT STUFF LATELY.
I'M REALIZING MAYBE I DIDN'T HAVE THE MENTAL SPACE TO HAVE THAT CONVER-SATION...
BAM
OKAY, THEN!
NOW THAT YOU'VE LEARNED YOUR LESSON, WASH IT DOWN WITH A GOOD, COLD BEER!

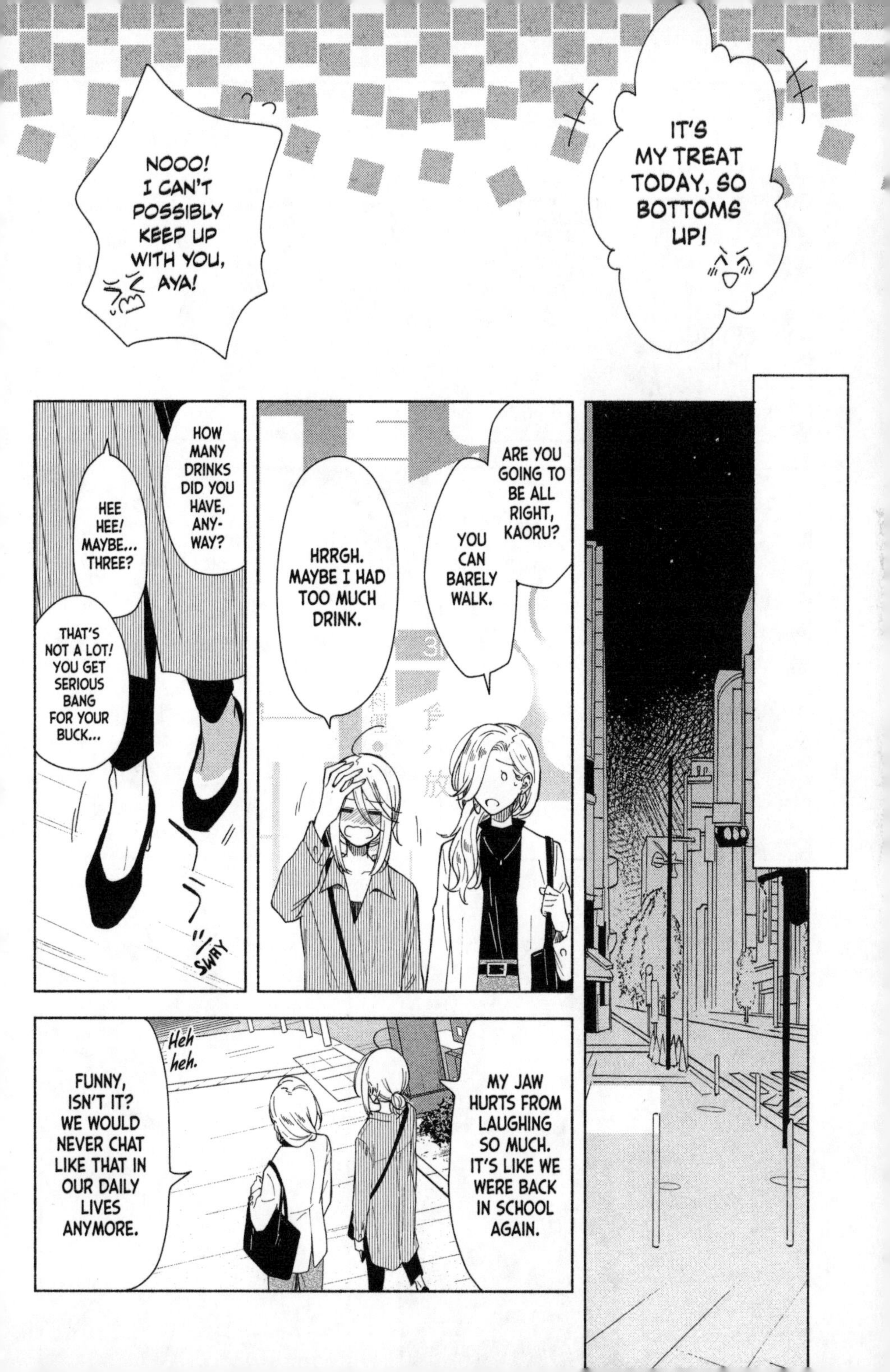
IT'S MY TREAT TODAY, SO BOTTOMS UP!
NOOO! I CAN'T POSSIBLY KEEP UP WITH YOU, AYA!
ARE YOU GOING TO BE ALL RIGHT, KAORU?
YOU CAN BARELY WALK.
HRRGH. MAYBE I HAD TOO MUCH DRINK.
HOW MANY DRINKS DID YOU HAVE, ANY-WAY?
HEE HEE! MAYBE... THREE?
THAT'S NOT A LOT! YOU GET SERIOUS BANG FOR YOUR BUCK...
SWAY
MY JAW HURTS FROM LAUGHING SO MUCH. IT'S LIKE WE WERE BACK IN SCHOOL AGAIN.
Heh heh.
FUNNY, ISN'T IT? WE WOULD NEVER CHAT LIKE THAT IN OUR DAILY LIVES ANYMORE.

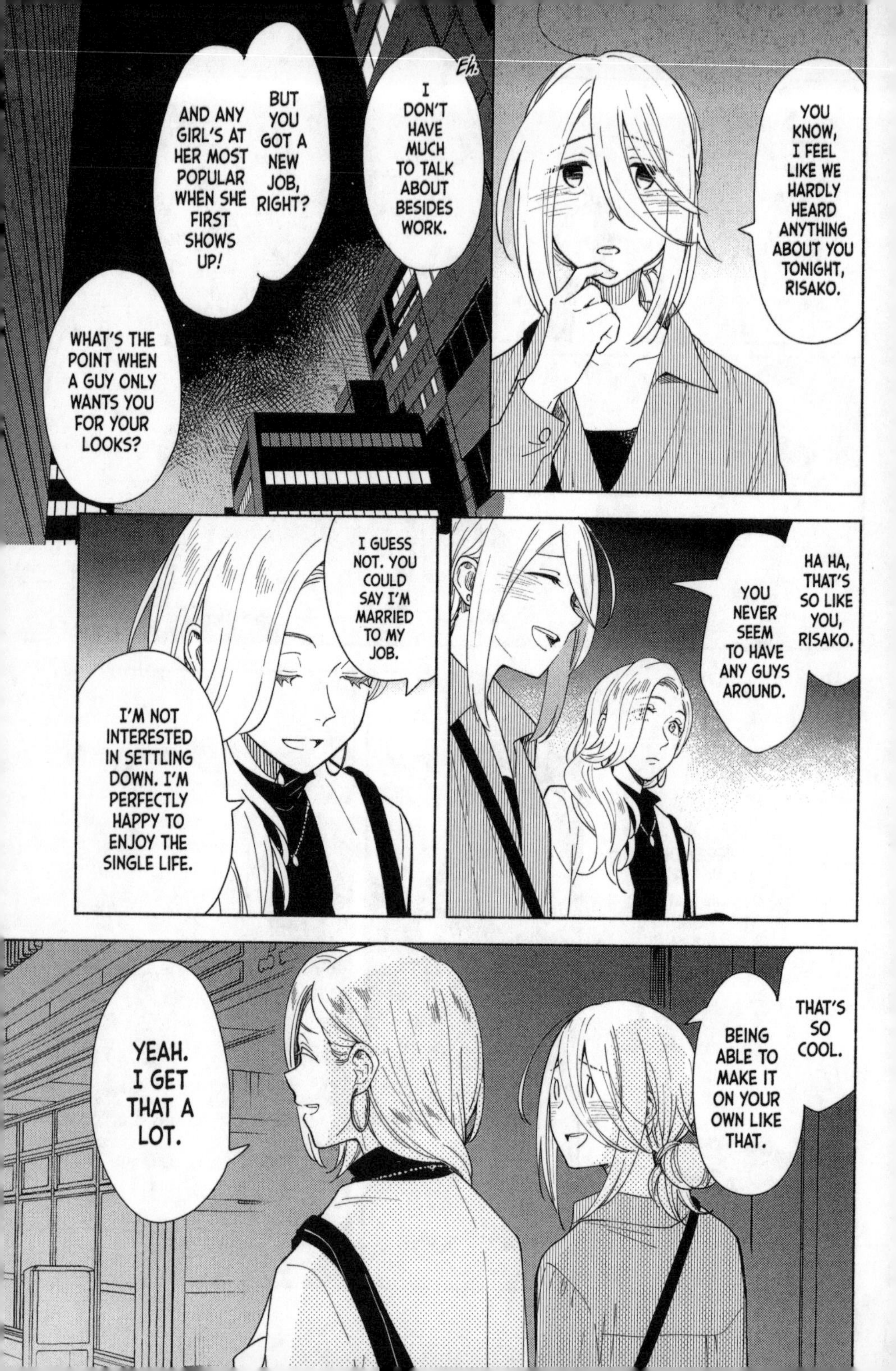
YOU KNOW, I FEEL LIKE WE HARDLY HEARD ANYTHING ABOUT YOU TONIGHT, RISAKO.
Eh.
I DON'T HAVE MUCH TO TALK ABOUT BESIDES WORK.
BUT YOU GOT A NEW JOB, RIGHT?
AND ANY GIRL'S AT HER MOST POPULAR WHEN SHE FIRST SHOWS UP!
WHAT'S THE POINT WHEN A GUY ONLY WANTS YOU FOR YOUR LOOKS?
HA HA, THAT'S SO LIKE YOU, RISAKO.
YOU NEVER SEEM TO HAVE ANY GUYS AROUND.
I GUESS NOT. YOU COULD SAY I'M MARRIED TO MY JOB.
I'M NOT INTERESTED IN SETTLING DOWN. I'M PERFECTLY HAPPY TO ENJOY THE SINGLE LIFE.
THAT'S SO COOL.
BEING ABLE TO MAKE IT ON YOUR OWN LIKE THAT.
YEAH. I GET THAT A LOT.

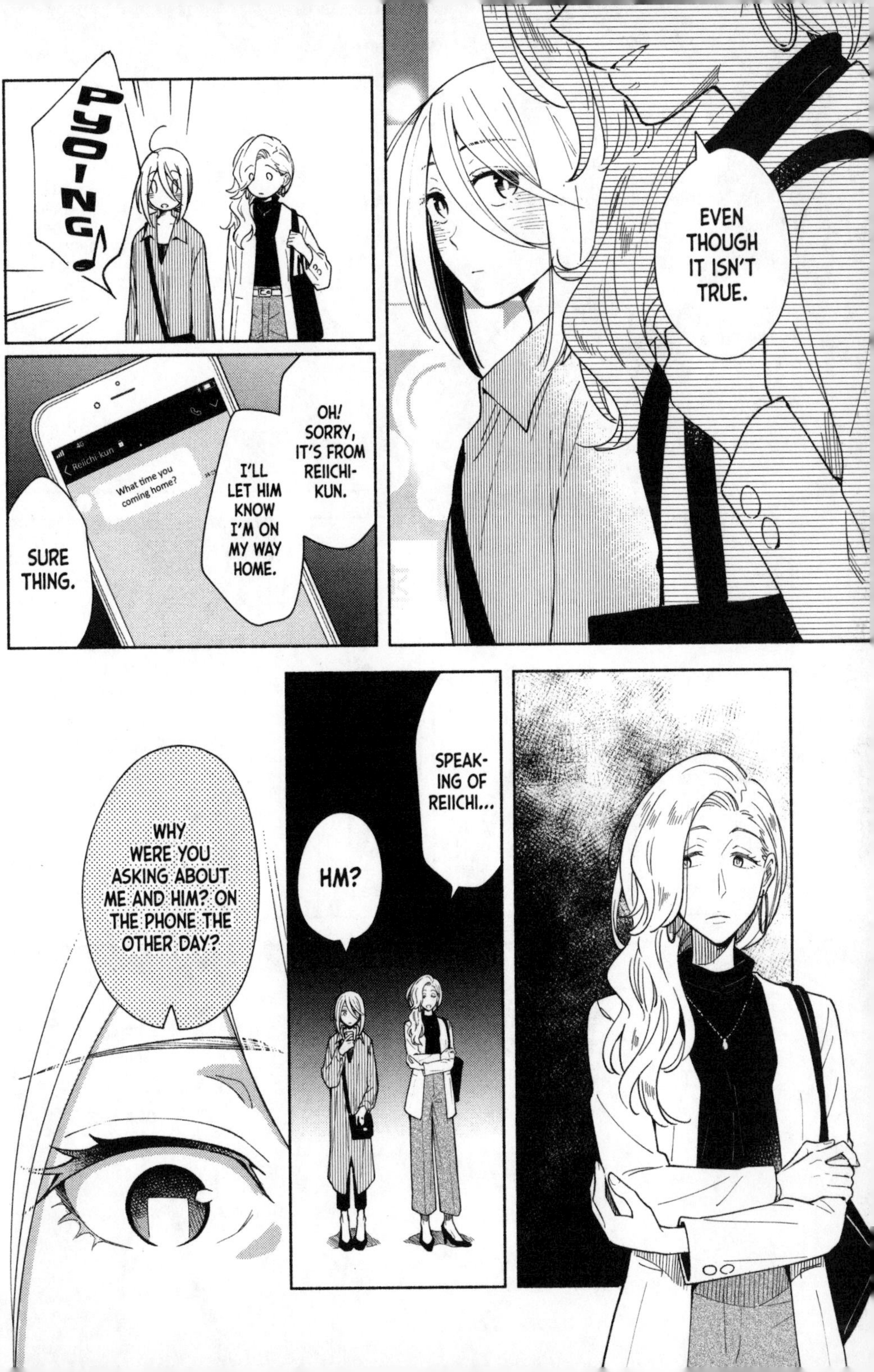
EVEN THOUGH IT ISN'T TRUE.
PYOING♪
OH! SORRY, IT'S FROM REIICHI-KUN.
Reiichi-kun
What time you coming home?
I'LL LET HIM KNOW I'M ON MY WAY HOME.
SURE THING.
SPEAK-ING OF REIICHI...
HM?
WHY WERE YOU ASKING ABOUT ME AND HIM? ON THE PHONE THE OTHER DAY?

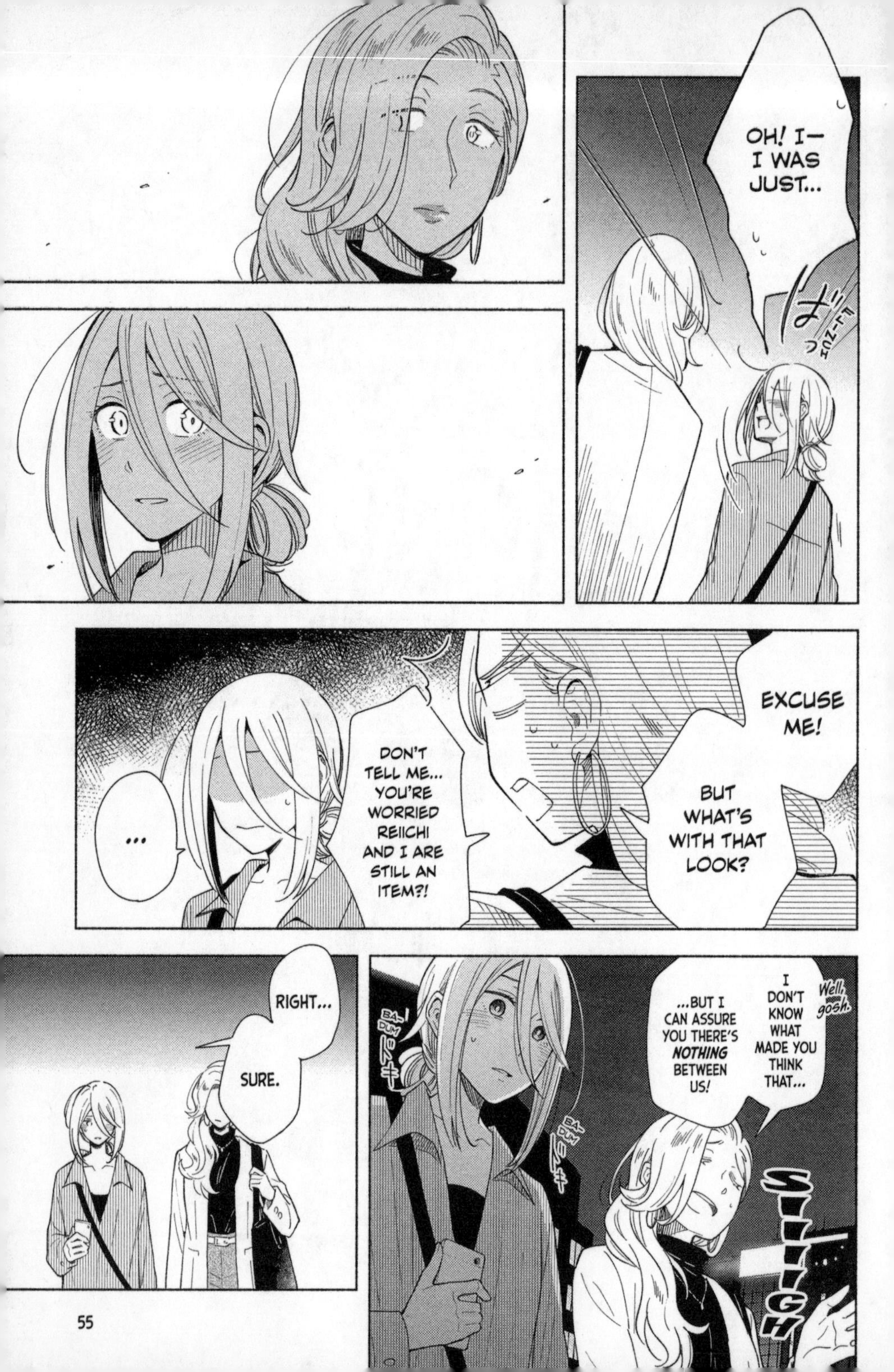
OH! I—
I WAS JUST...
HUP
...
EXCUSE ME!
BUT WHAT'S WITH THAT LOOK?
DON'T TELL ME... YOU'RE WORRIED REIICHI AND I ARE STILL AN ITEM?!
...
Well, gosh.
I DON'T KNOW WHAT MADE YOU THINK THAT...
...BUT I CAN ASSURE YOU THERE'S *NOTHING* BETWEEN US!
SIIIIGH
BA-DUM
BA-DUM
RIGHT...
SURE.

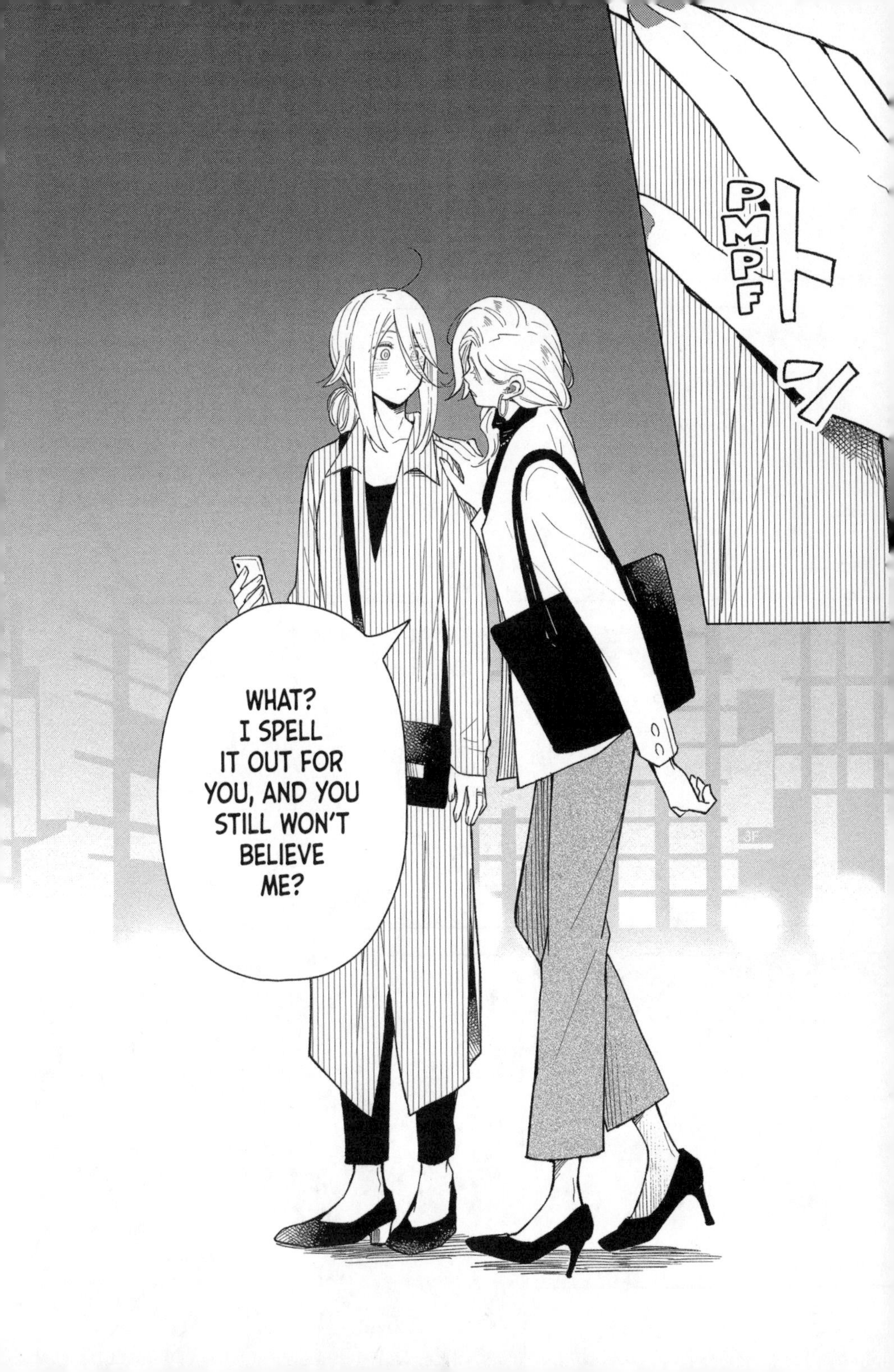
PMPF
WHAT? I SPELL IT OUT FOR YOU, AND YOU STILL WON'T BELIEVE ME?

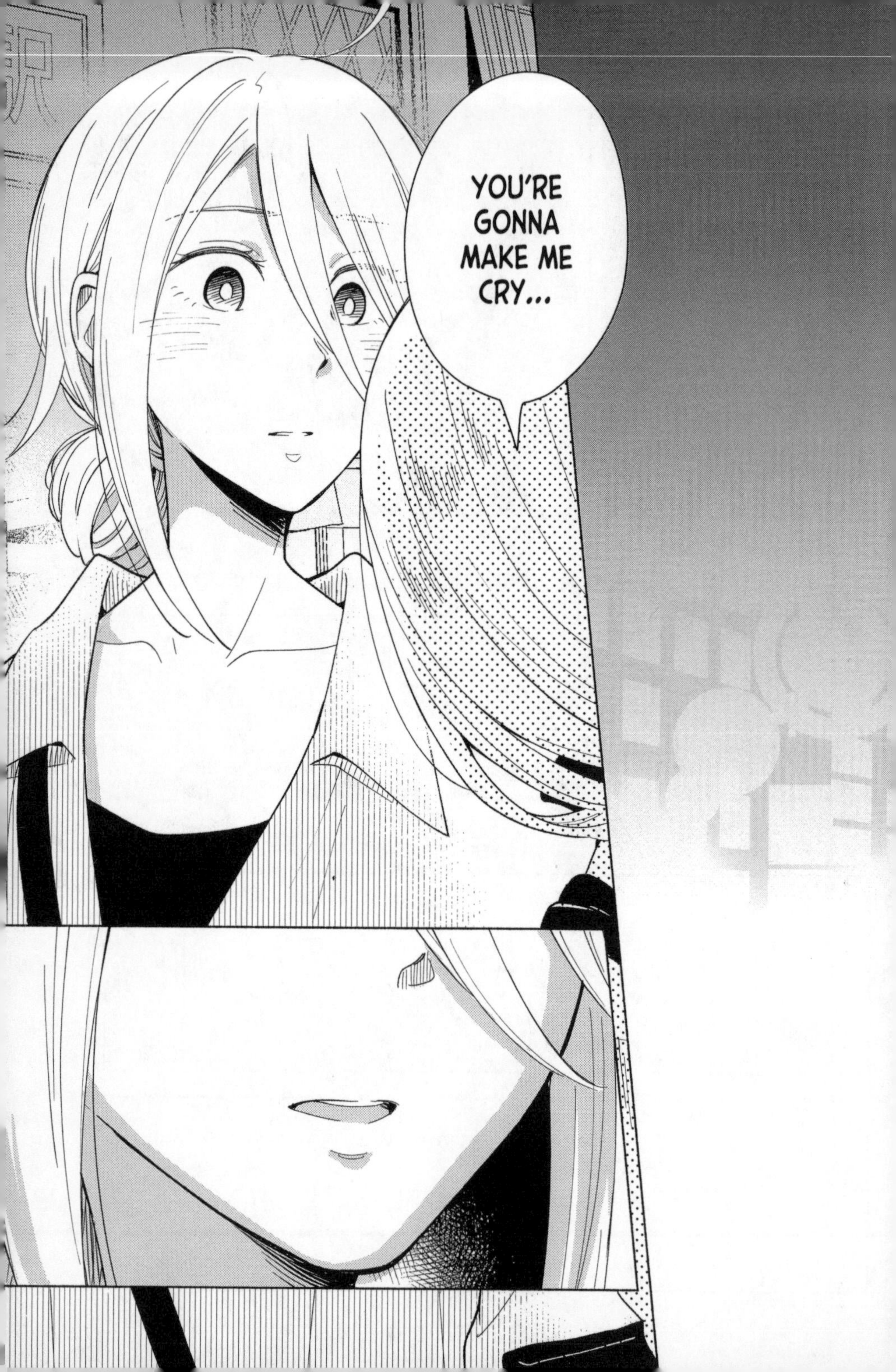
YOU'RE GONNA MAKE ME CRY...

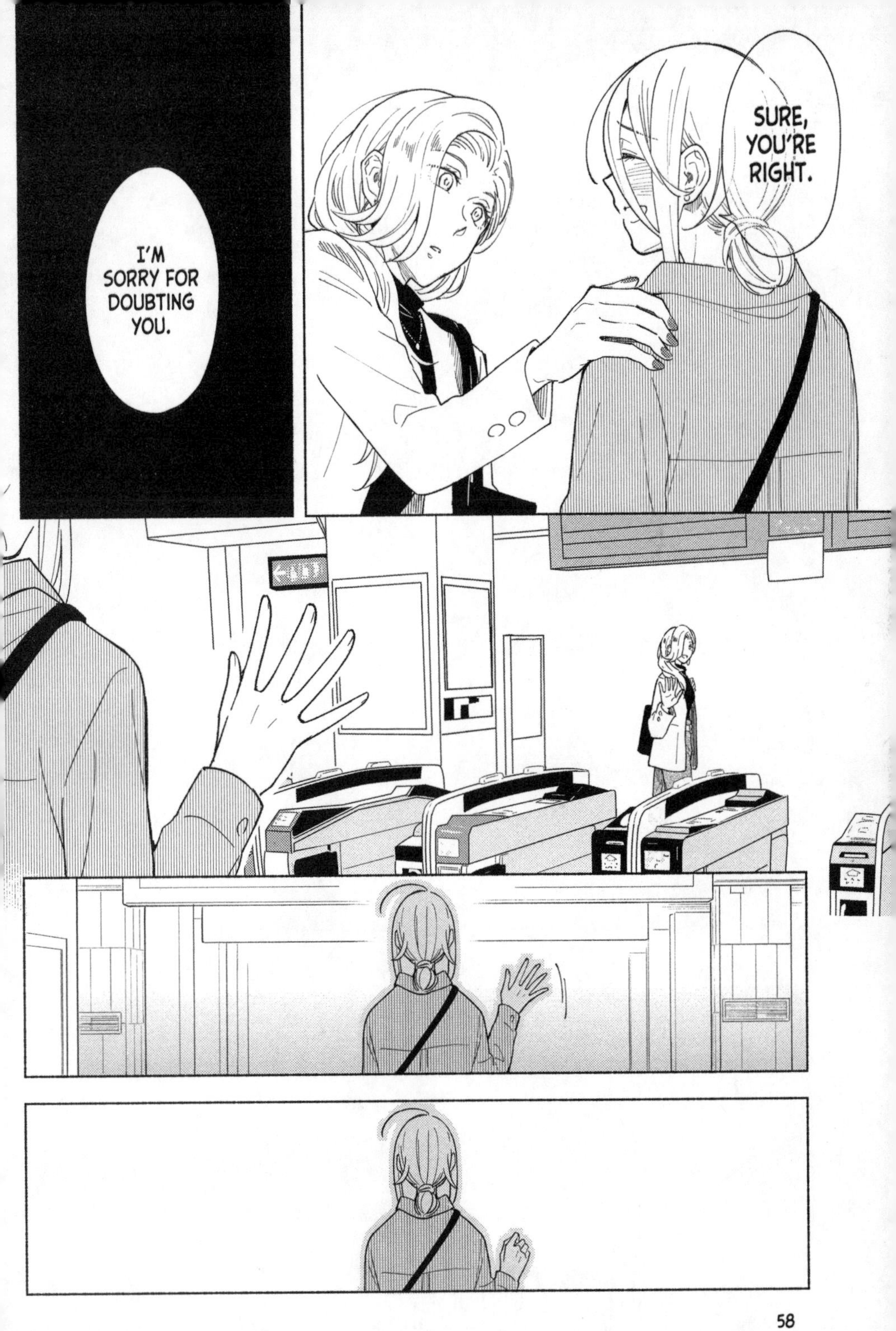
SURE, YOU'RE RIGHT.
I'M SORRY FOR DOUBTING YOU.

I SHOULD TRUST RISAKO MORE THAN MY OWN FUZZY MEMORIES.

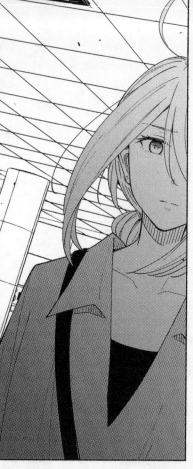

AT LEAST...

...IT WOULD BE NICE IF I COULD CONVINCE MYSELF OF THAT.

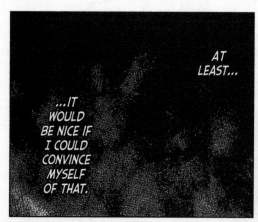

I WANT TO BE ABLE TO TRUST THE PEOPLE I CARE ABOUT.

AND YET IT FEELS LIKE THAT TRUST IS STILL JUST OUT OF REACH FOR ME...

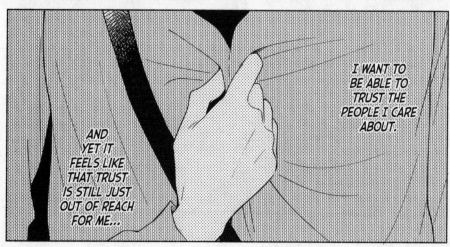

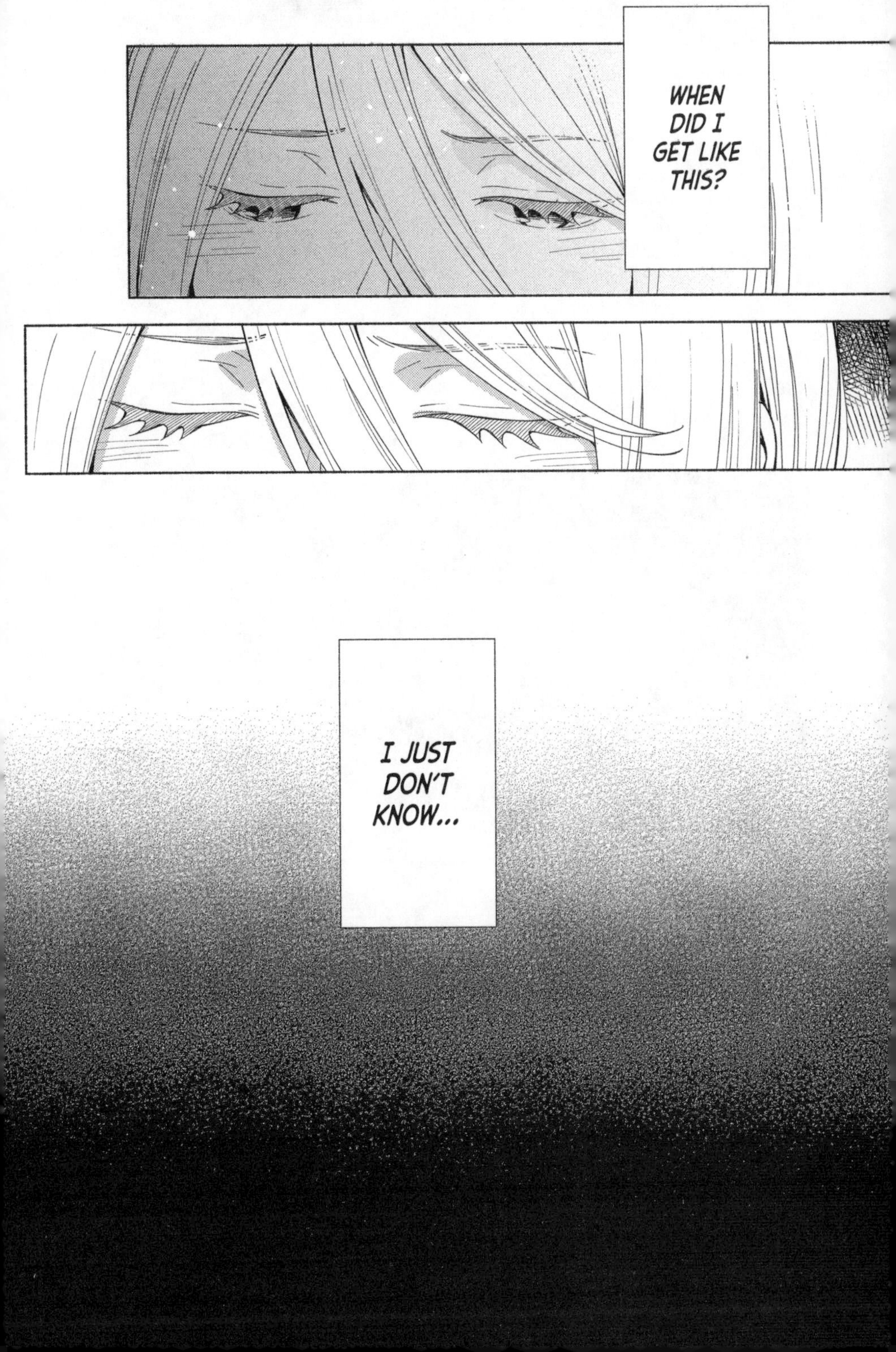
WHEN DID I GET LIKE THIS?
I JUST DON'T KNOW...

If I Could
Reach You

If I Could
Reach You

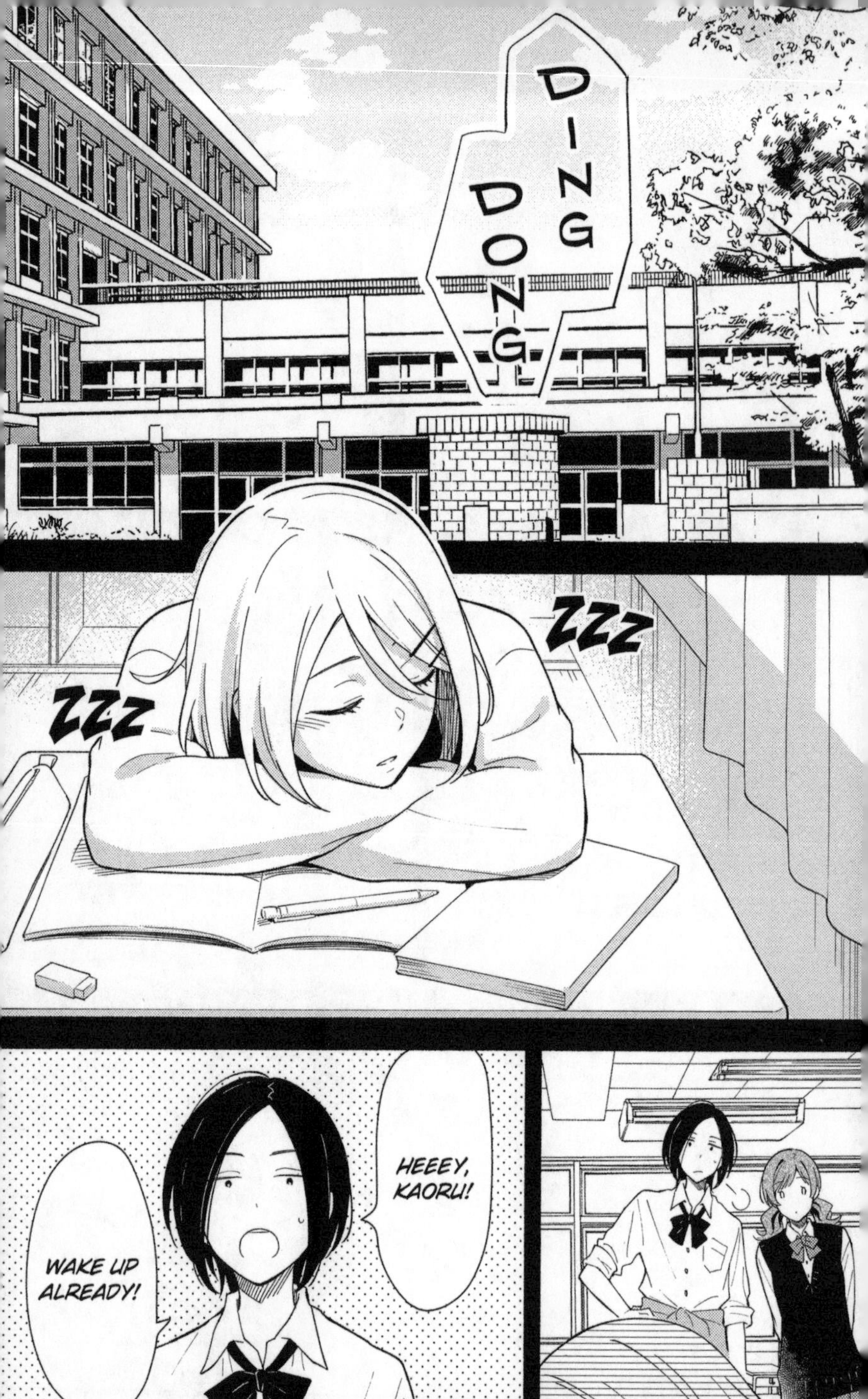
DING DONG
ZZZ
ZZZ
HEEEY, KAORU!
WAKE UP ALREADY!

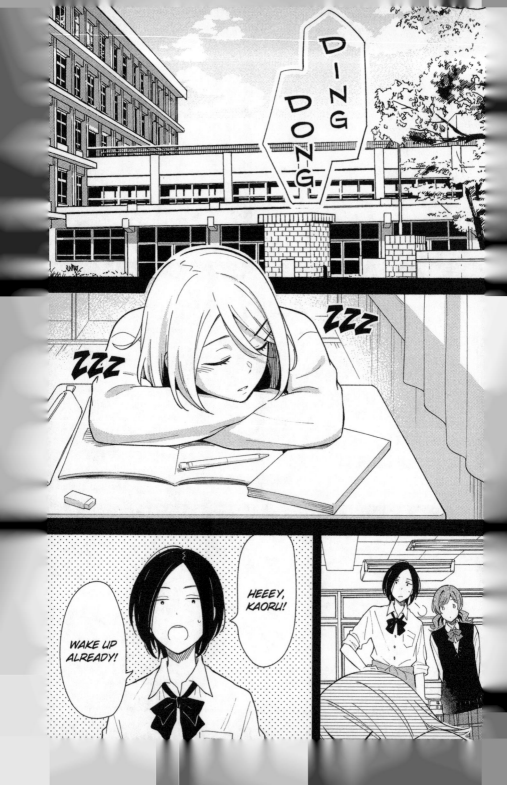

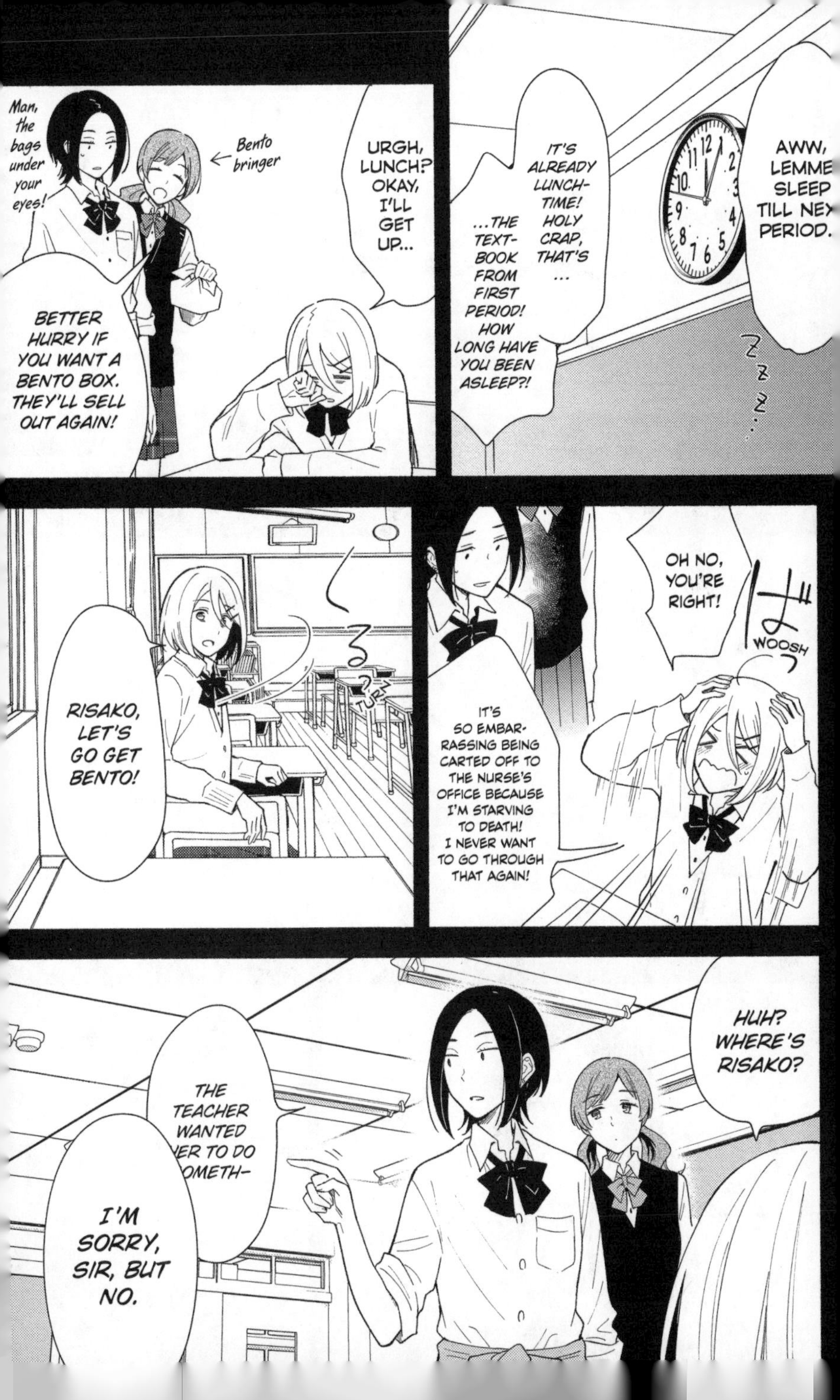
AWW, LEMME SLEEP TILL NEX PERIOD.
Z Z Z...
IT'S ALREADY LUNCHTIME! HOLY CRAP, THAT'S ...
...THE TEXTBOOK FROM FIRST PERIOD! HOW LONG HAVE YOU BEEN ASLEEP?!
URGH, LUNCH? OKAY, I'LL GET UP...
Man, the bags under your eyes!
Bento bringer
BETTER HURRY IF YOU WANT A BENTO BOX. THEY'LL SELL OUT AGAIN!
OH NO, YOU'RE RIGHT!
WOOSH
IT'S SO EMBARRASSING BEING CARTED OFF TO THE NURSE'S OFFICE BECAUSE I'M STARVING TO DEATH! I NEVER WANT TO GO THROUGH THAT AGAIN!
TURN
RISAKO, LET'S GO GET BENTO!
HUH? WHERE'S RISAKO?
THE TEACHER WANTED ER TO DO OMETH-
I'M SORRY, SIR, BUT NO.

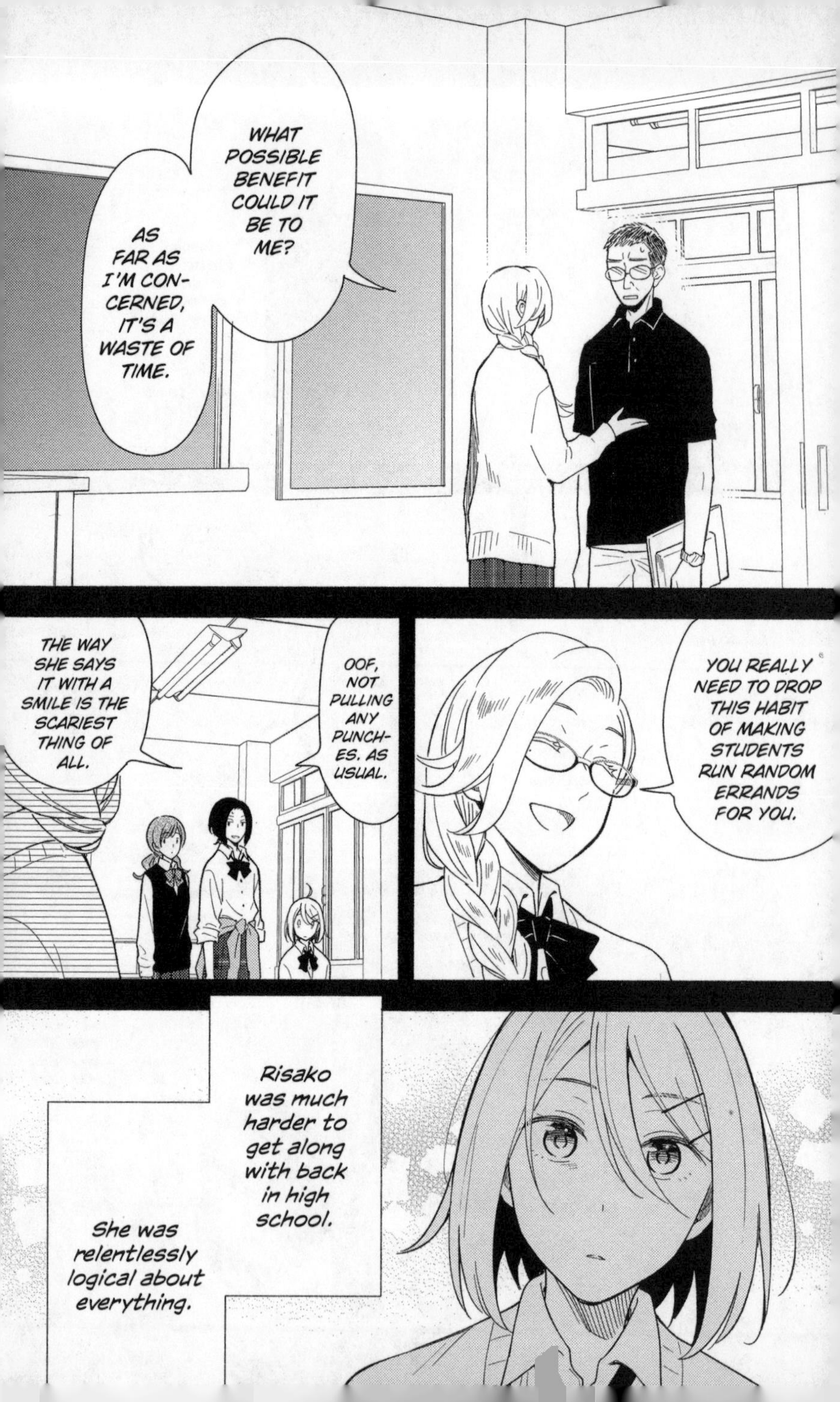
WHAT POSSIBLE BENEFIT COULD IT BE TO ME?
AS FAR AS I'M CON-CERNED, IT'S A WASTE OF TIME.
YOU REALLY NEED TO DROP THIS HABIT OF MAKING STUDENTS RUN RANDOM ERRANDS FOR YOU.
OOF, NOT PULLING ANY PUNCH-ES. AS USUAL.
THE WAY SHE SAYS IT WITH A SMILE IS THE SCARIEST THING OF ALL.
Risako was much harder to get along with back in high school.
She was relentlessly logical about everything.

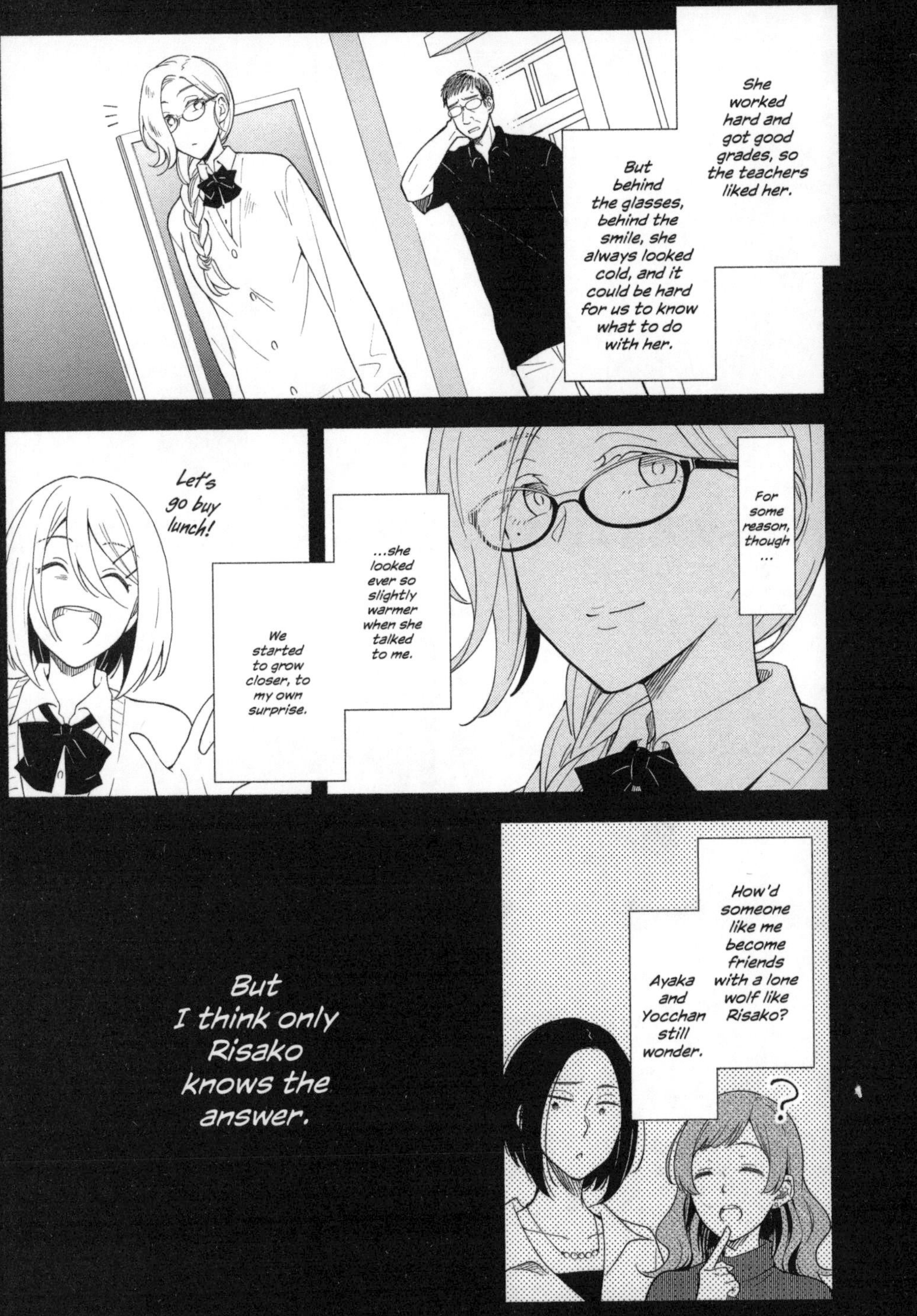
She worked hard and got good grades, so the teachers liked her.
But behind the glasses, behind the smile, she always looked cold, and it could be hard for us to know what to do with her.
For some reason, though…
…she looked ever so slightly warmer when she talked to me.
Let's go buy lunch!
We started to grow closer, to my own surprise.
How'd someone like me become friends with a lone wolf like Risako?
Ayaka and Yocchan still wonder.
But I think only Risako knows the answer.

Chapter 28

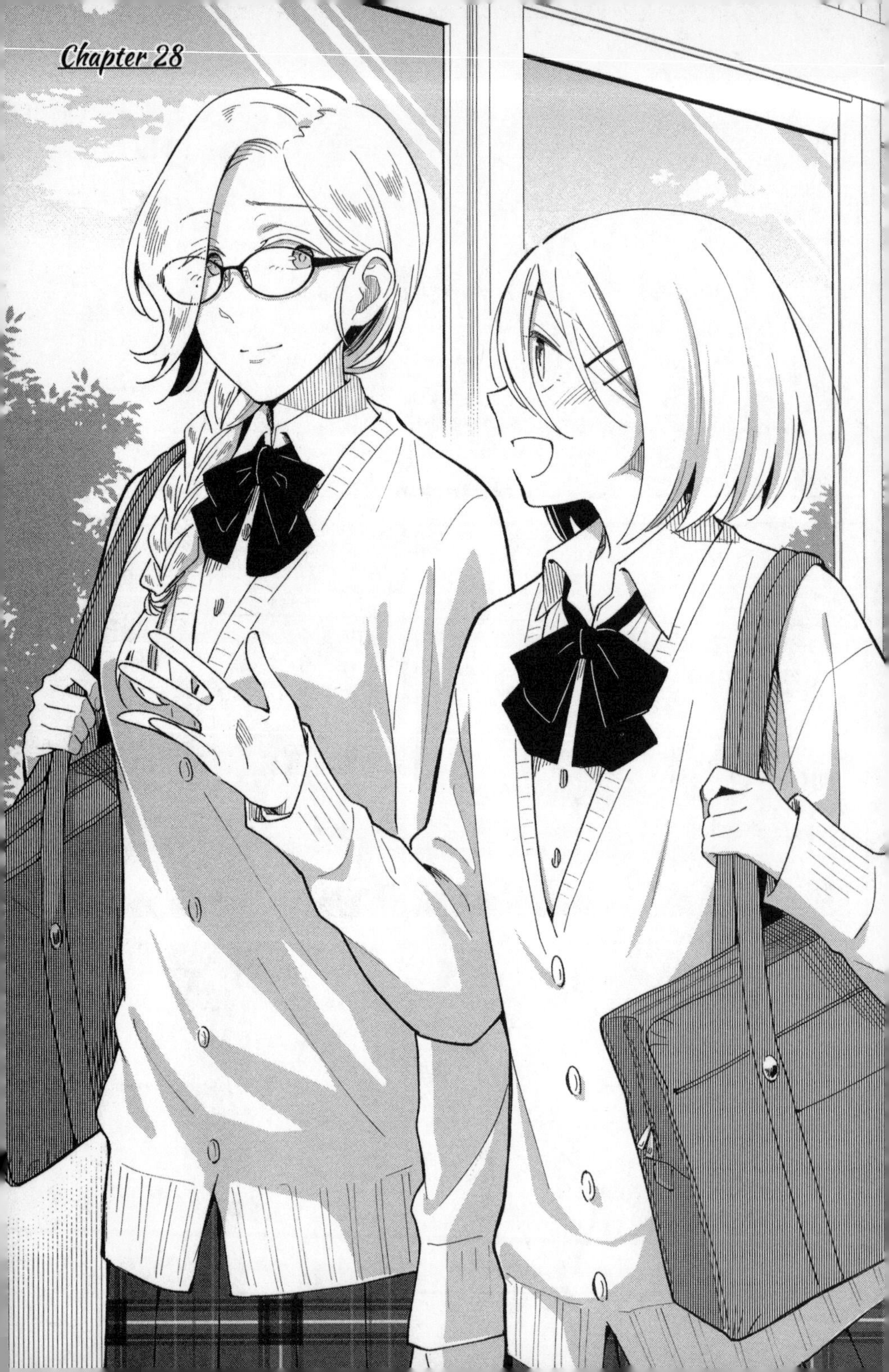

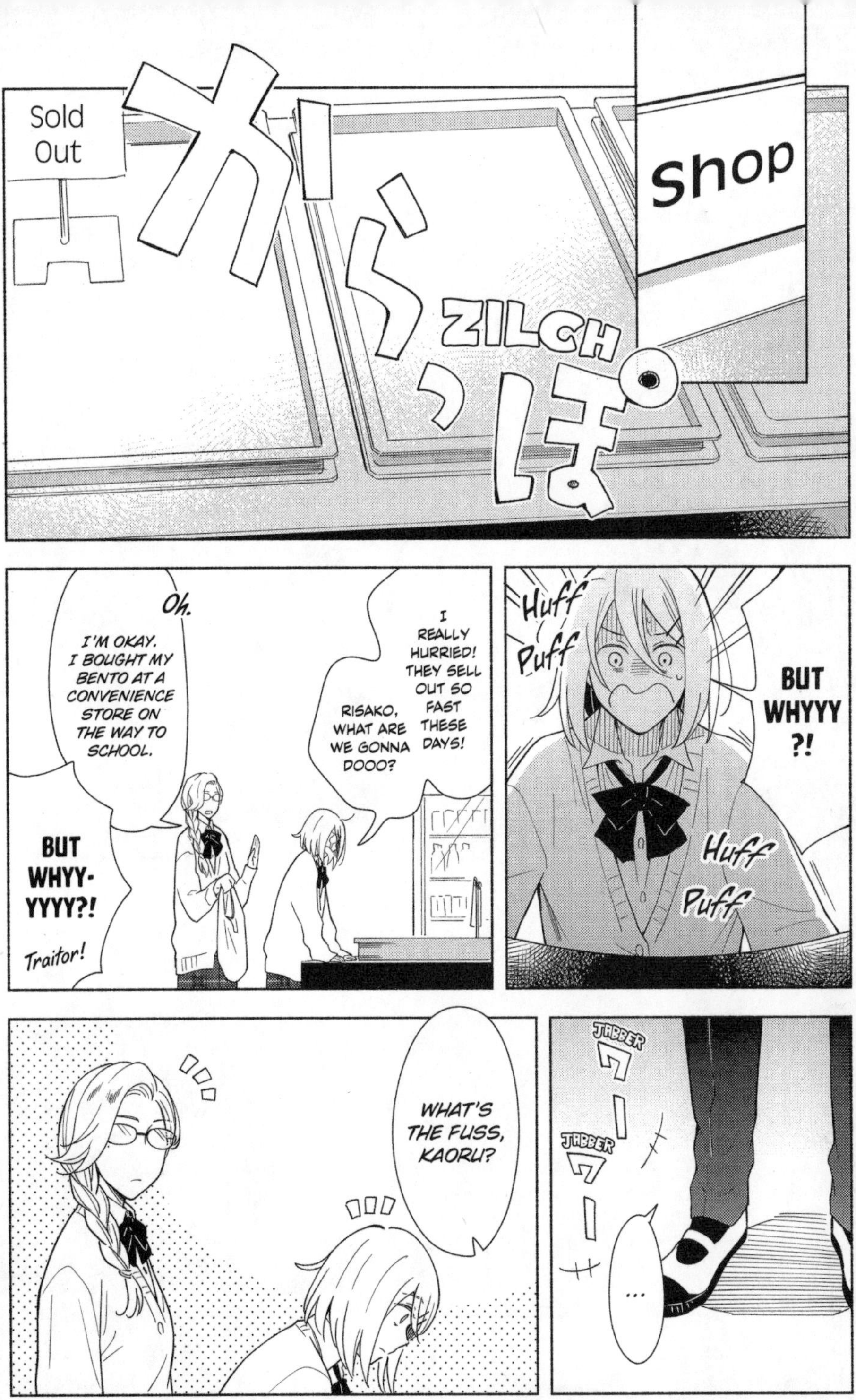
Shop
Sold Out
からっぽ
ZILCH
Huff Puff
BUT WHYYY?!
Huff Puff
I REALLY HURRIED! THEY SELL OUT SO FAST THESE DAYS!
RISAKO, WHAT ARE WE GONNA DOOO?
Oh.
I'M OKAY. I BOUGHT MY BENTO AT A CONVENIENCE STORE ON THE WAY TO SCHOOL.
BUT WHYY-YYYY?!
Traitor!
JABBER ワー
JABBER ワー
...
WHAT'S THE FUSS, KAORU?

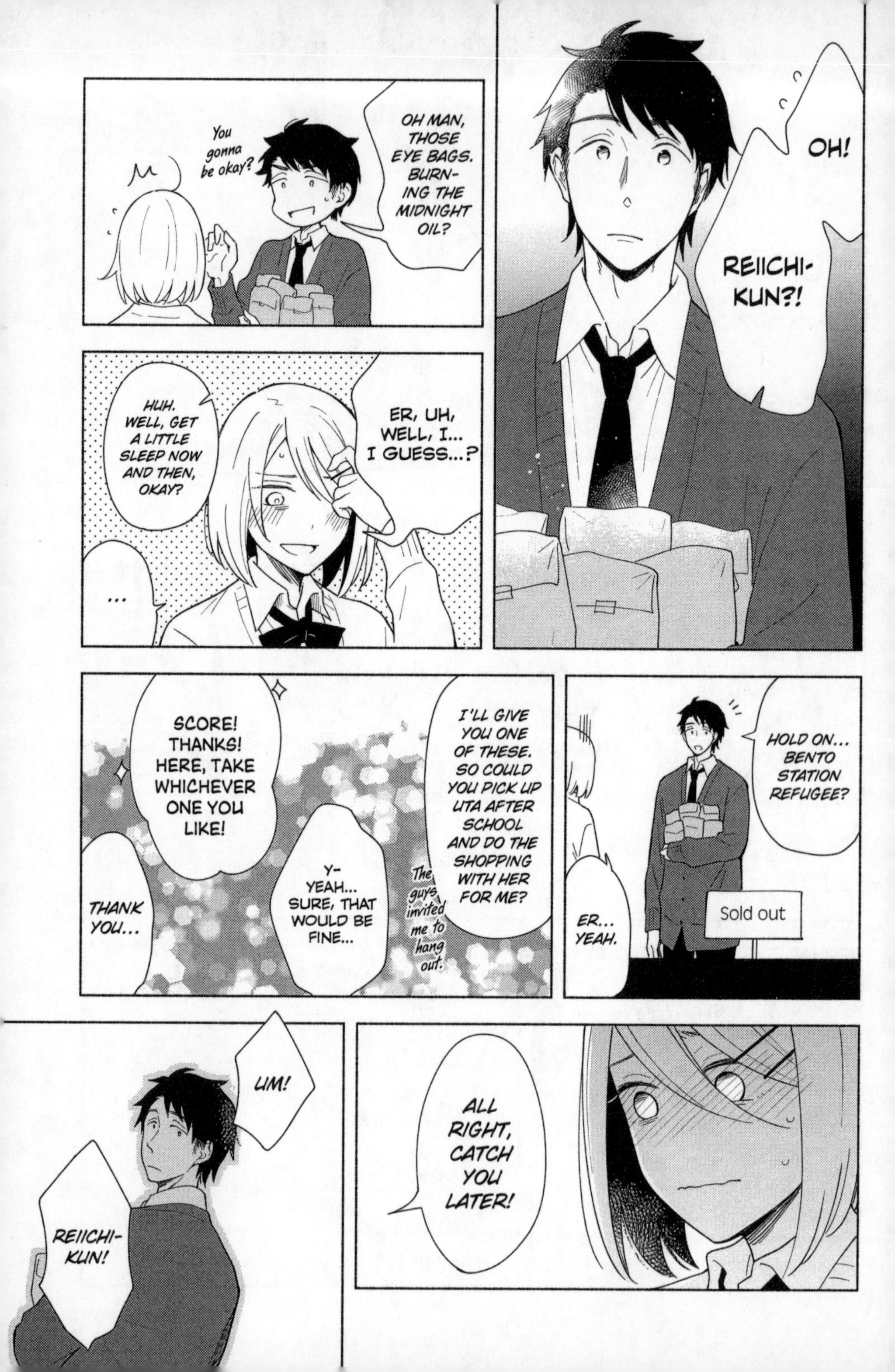
OH!
REIICHI-KUN?!
OH MAN, THOSE EYE BAGS. BURNING THE MIDNIGHT OIL?
You gonna be okay?
ER, UH, WELL, I... I GUESS...?
HUH. WELL, GET A LITTLE SLEEP NOW AND THEN, OKAY?
...
HOLD ON... BENTO STATION REFUGEE?
Sold out
ER... YEAH.
I'LL GIVE YOU ONE OF THESE. SO COULD YOU PICK UP UTA AFTER SCHOOL AND DO THE SHOPPING WITH HER FOR ME?
The guys invited me to hang out.
Y-YEAH... SURE, THAT WOULD BE FINE...
SCORE! THANKS! HERE, TAKE WHICHEVER ONE YOU LIKE!
THANK YOU...
ALL RIGHT, CATCH YOU LATER!
UM!
REIICHI-KUN!

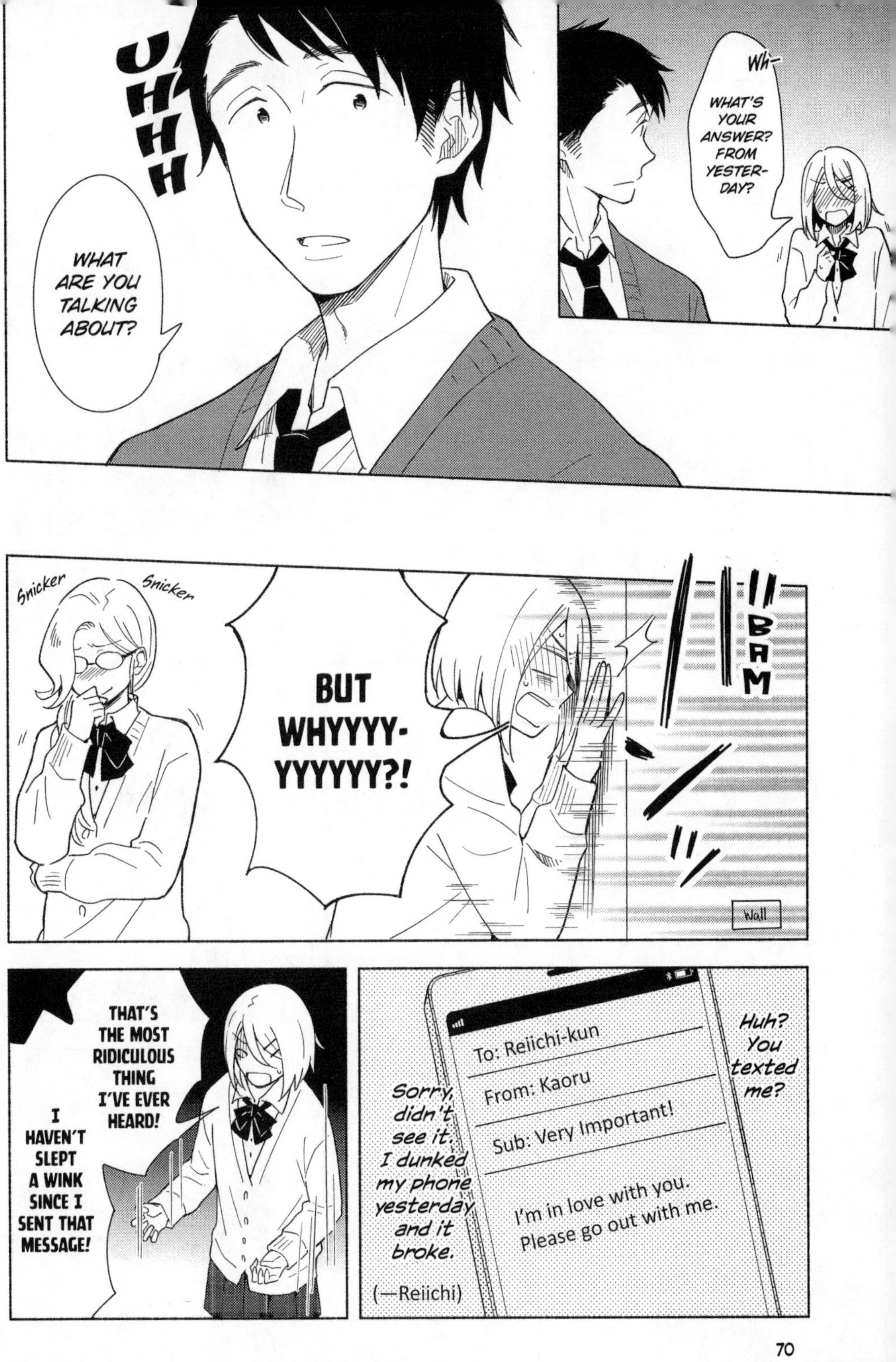
Wh-
WHAT'S YOUR ANSWER? FROM YESTER-DAY?
UHHH
WHAT ARE YOU TALKING ABOUT?
BAM
BUT WHYYYY-YYYYYY?!
Snicker
Snicker
Wall
Huh? You texted me?
To: Reiichi-kun
From: Kaoru
Sub: Very Important!
I'm in love with you. Please go out with me.
Sorry, didn't see it. I dunked my phone yesterday and it broke.
(—Reiichi)
THAT'S THE MOST RIDICULOUS THING I'VE EVER HEARD!
I HAVEN'T SLEPT A WINK SINCE I SENT THAT MESSAGE!

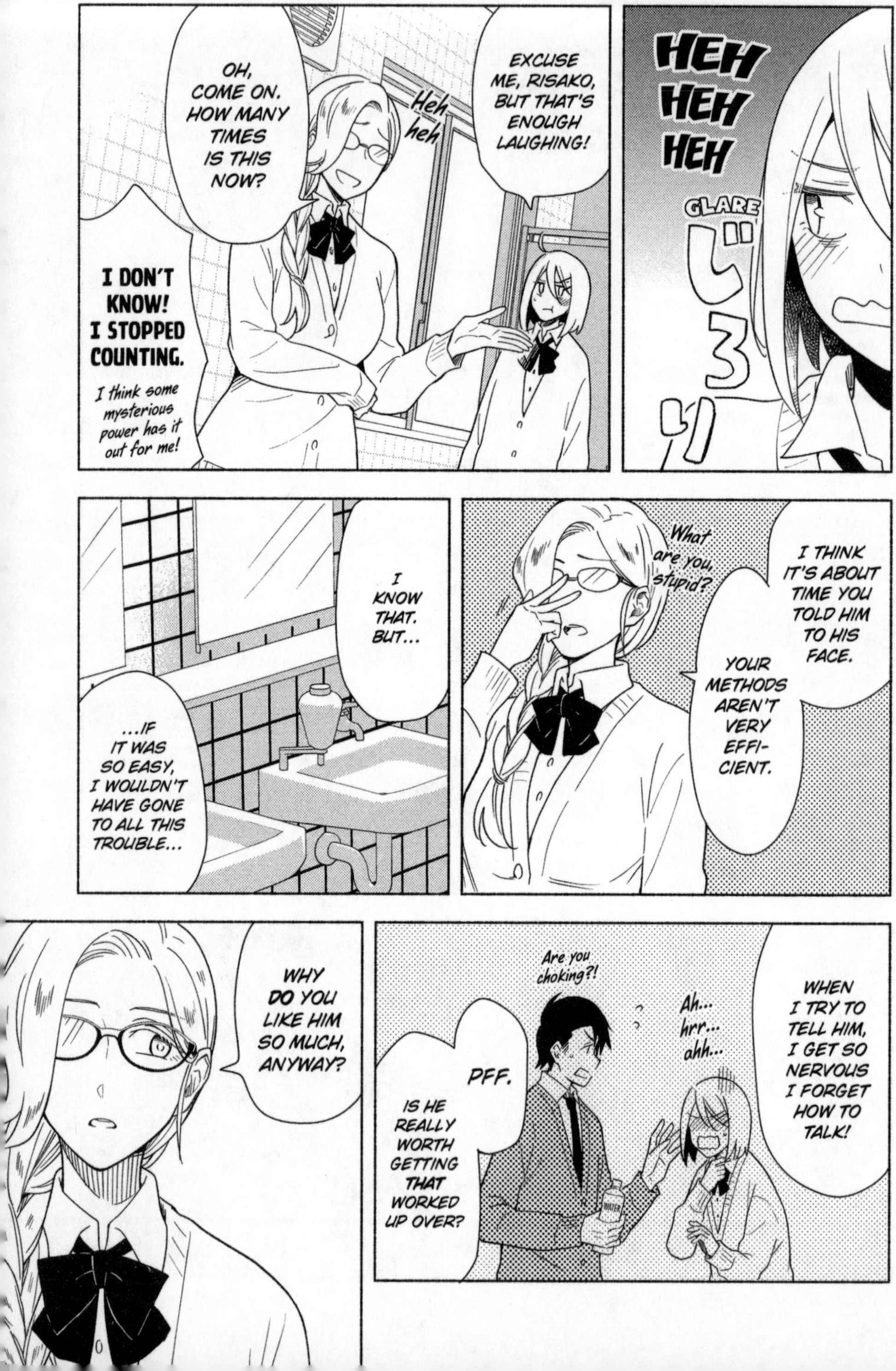
HEH HEH HEH
GLARE
EXCUSE ME, RISAKO, BUT THAT'S ENOUGH LAUGHING!
Heh heh
OH, COME ON. HOW MANY TIMES IS THIS NOW?
I DON'T KNOW! I STOPPED COUNTING.
I think some mysterious power has it out for me!
I THINK IT'S ABOUT TIME YOU TOLD HIM TO HIS FACE.
What are you, stupid?
YOUR METHODS AREN'T VERY EFFI- CIENT.
I KNOW THAT. BUT...
...IF IT WAS SO EASY, I WOULDN'T HAVE GONE TO ALL THIS TROUBLE...
WHEN I TRY TO TELL HIM, I GET SO NERVOUS I FORGET HOW TO TALK!
Ah... hrr... ahh...
Are you choking?!
WATER
PFF.
IS HE REALLY WORTH GETTING THAT WORKED UP OVER?
WHY DO YOU LIKE HIM SO MUCH, ANYWAY?

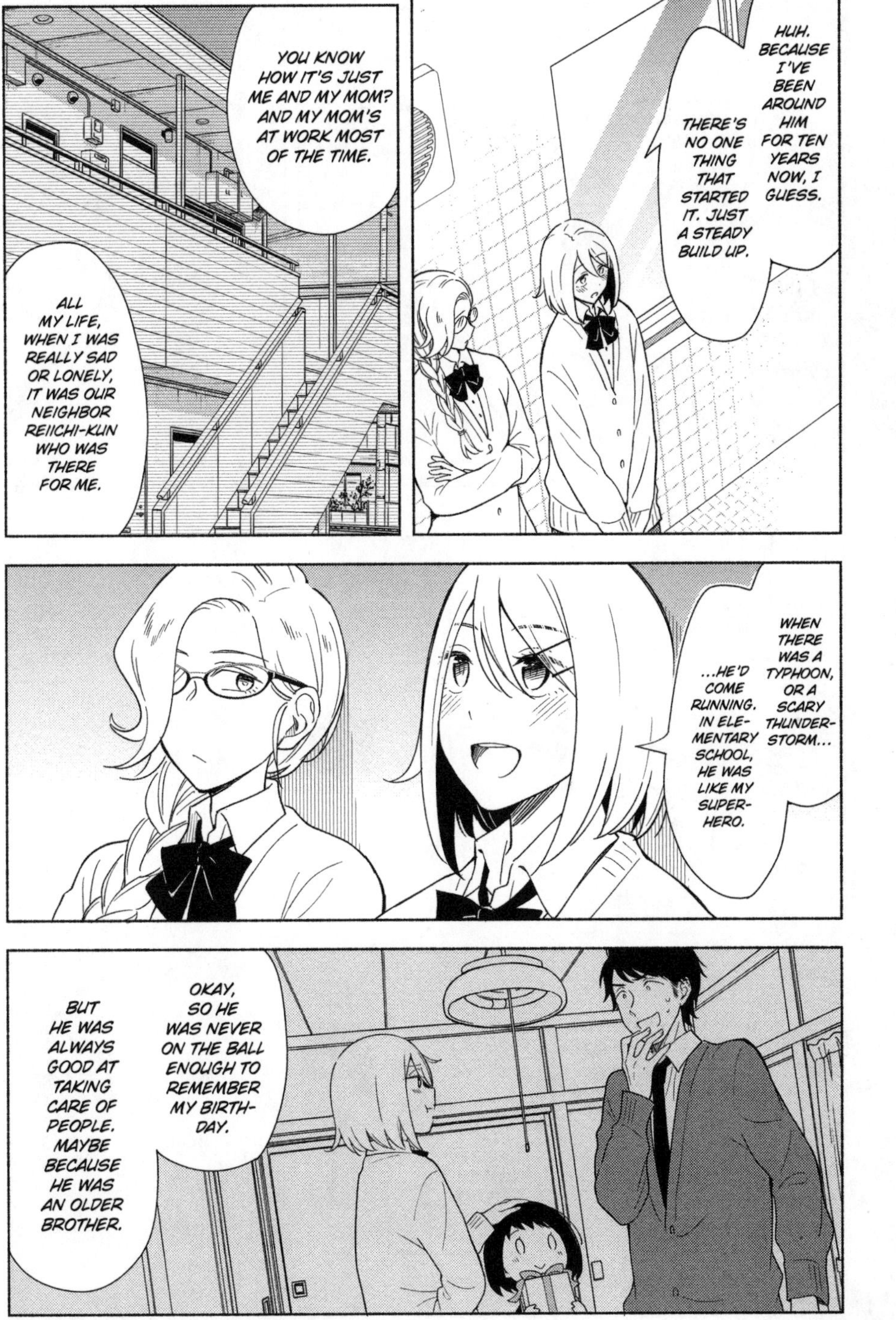
HUH. BECAUSE I'VE BEEN AROUND HIM FOR TEN YEARS NOW, I GUESS.
THERE'S NO ONE THING THAT STARTED IT. JUST A STEADY BUILD UP.
YOU KNOW HOW IT'S JUST ME AND MY MOM? AND MY MOM'S AT WORK MOST OF THE TIME.
ALL MY LIFE, WHEN I WAS REALLY SAD OR LONELY, IT WAS OUR NEIGHBOR REIICHI-KUN WHO WAS THERE FOR ME.
WHEN THERE WAS A TYPHOON, OR A SCARY THUNDER-STORM...
...HE'D COME RUNNING. IN ELE-MENTARY SCHOOL, HE WAS LIKE MY SUPER-HERO.
OKAY, SO HE WAS NEVER ON THE BALL ENOUGH TO REMEMBER MY BIRTH-DAY.
BUT HE WAS ALWAYS GOOD AT TAKING CARE OF PEOPLE. MAYBE BECAUSE HE WAS AN OLDER BROTHER.

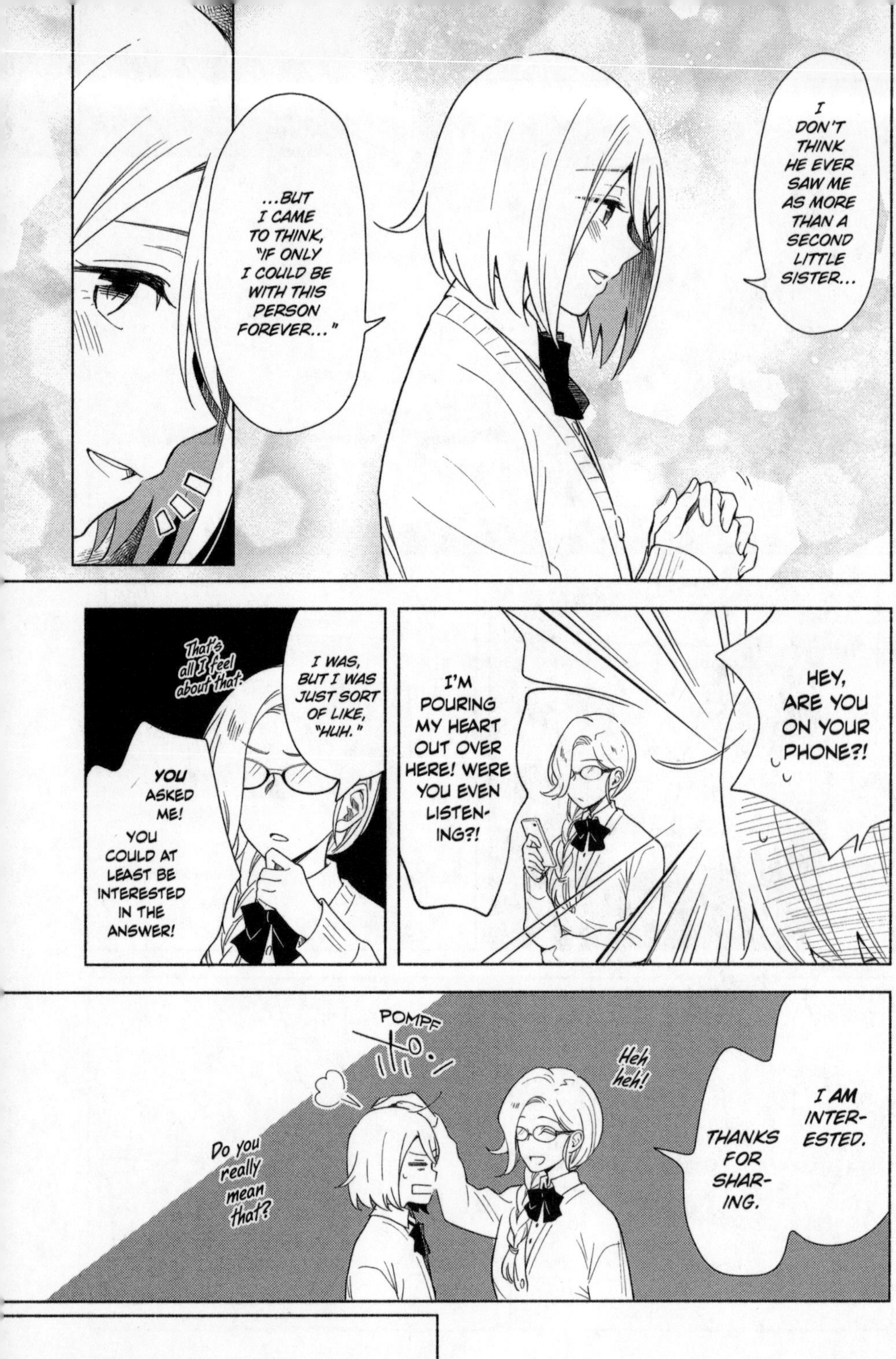
I DON'T THINK HE EVER SAW ME AS MORE THAN A SECOND LITTLE SISTER...
...BUT I CAME TO THINK, "IF ONLY I COULD BE WITH THIS PERSON FOREVER..."
HEY, ARE YOU ON YOUR PHONE?!
I'M POURING MY HEART OUT OVER HERE! WERE YOU EVEN LISTENING?!
I WAS, BUT I WAS JUST SORT OF LIKE, "HUH."
That's all I feel about that.
YOU ASKED ME! YOU COULD AT LEAST BE INTERESTED IN THE ANSWER!
I AM INTERESTED.
THANKS FOR SHARING.
Heh heh!
POMPF
Do you really mean that?

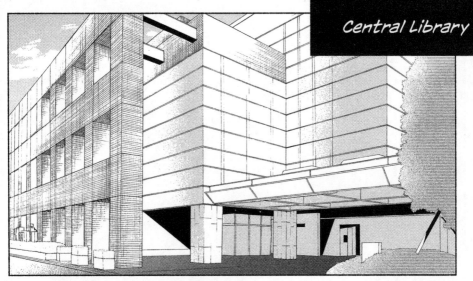

Central Library

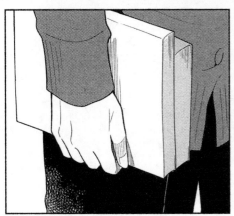

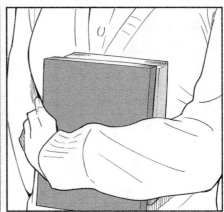

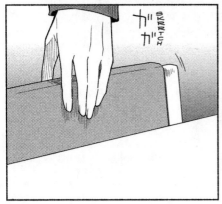

SKETCH

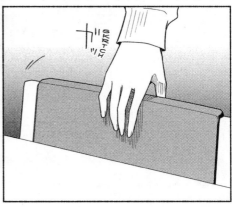

SKETCH

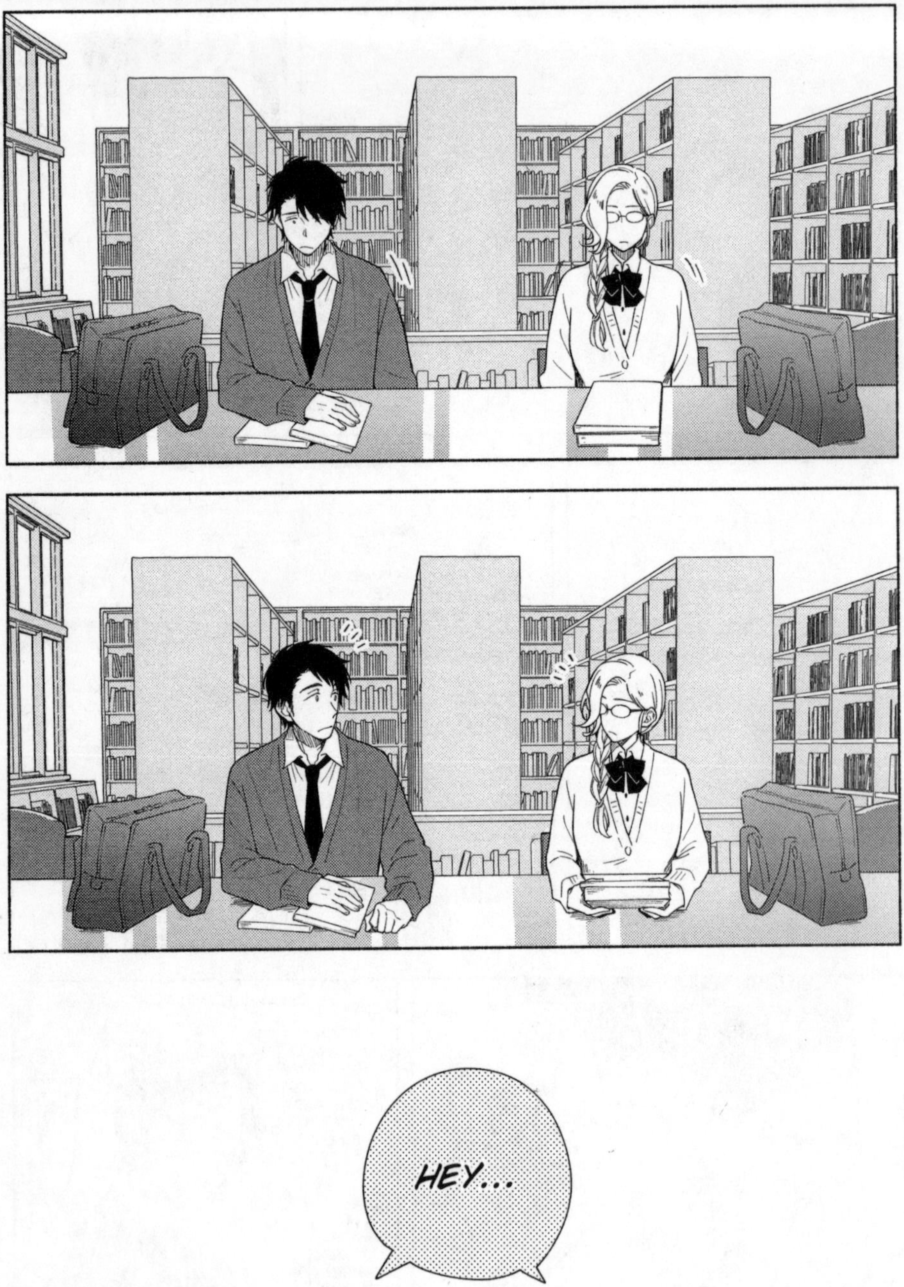
HEY...

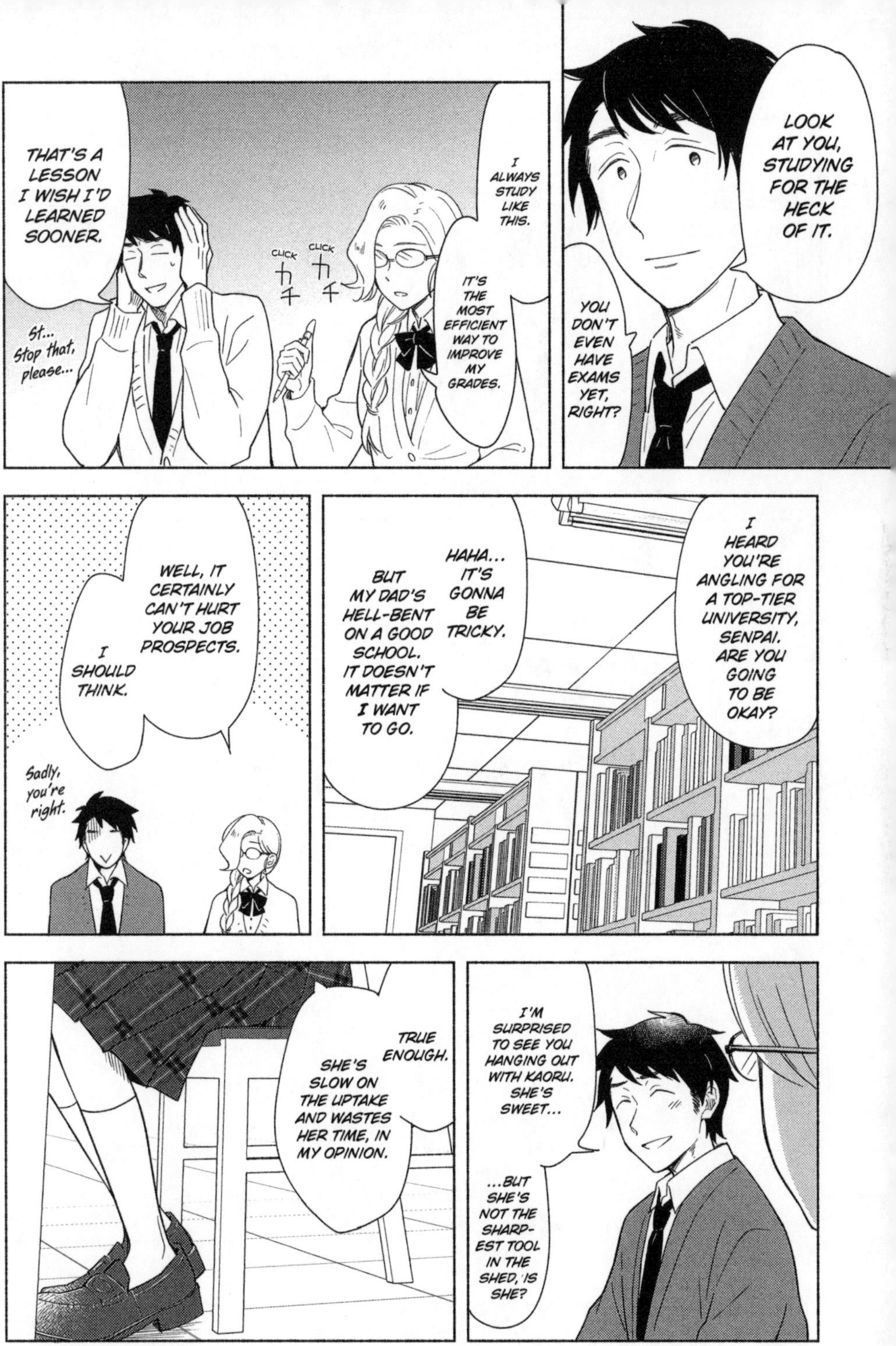
LOOK AT YOU, STUDYING FOR THE HECK OF IT.
YOU DON'T EVEN HAVE EXAMS YET, RIGHT?
I ALWAYS STUDY LIKE THIS.
CLICK CLICK カチ カチ
IT'S THE MOST EFFICIENT WAY TO IMPROVE MY GRADES.
THAT'S A LESSON I WISH I'D LEARNED SOONER.
St... Stop that, please...
I HEARD YOU'RE ANGLING FOR A TOP-TIER UNIVERSITY, SENPAI. ARE YOU GOING TO BE OKAY?
HAHA... IT'S GONNA BE TRICKY.
BUT MY DAD'S HELL-BENT ON A GOOD SCHOOL. IT DOESN'T MATTER IF I WANT TO GO.
WELL, IT CERTAINLY CAN'T HURT YOUR JOB PROSPECTS.
I SHOULD THINK.
Sadly, you're right.
I'M SURPRISED TO SEE YOU HANGING OUT WITH KAORU. SHE'S SWEET...
...BUT SHE'S NOT THE SHARP-EST TOOL IN THE SHED, IS SHE?
TRUE ENOUGH.
SHE'S SLOW ON THE UPTAKE AND WASTES HER TIME, IN MY OPINION.

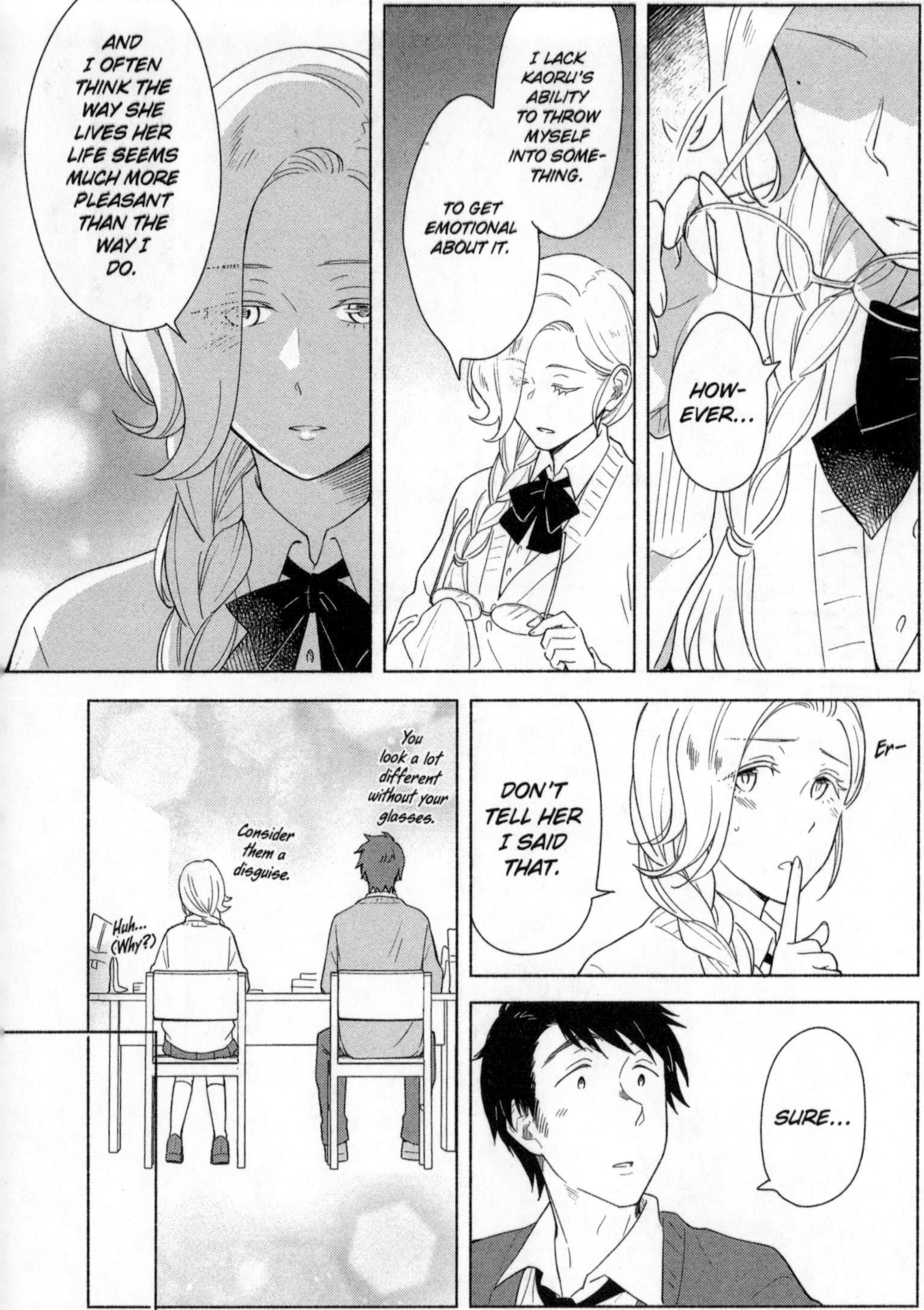
HOW-EVER...
I LACK KAORU'S ABILITY TO THROW MYSELF INTO SOME-THING.
TO GET EMOTIONAL ABOUT IT.
AND I OFTEN THINK THE WAY SHE LIVES HER LIFE SEEMS MUCH MORE PLEASANT THAN THE WAY I DO.
Er—
DON'T TELL HER I SAID THAT.
SURE...
You look a lot different without your glasses.
Consider them a disguise.
Huh... (Why?)

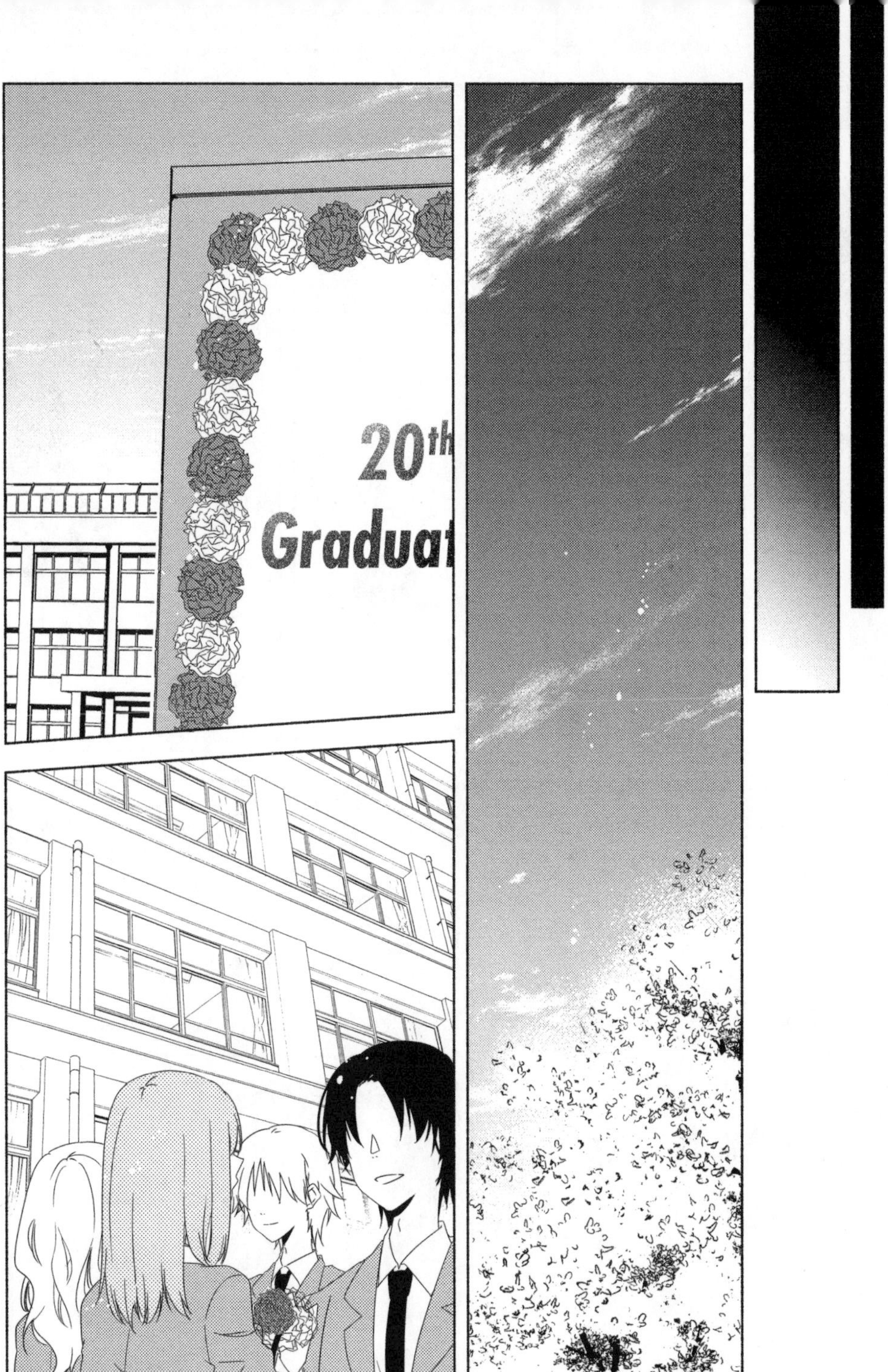
20th
Graduat

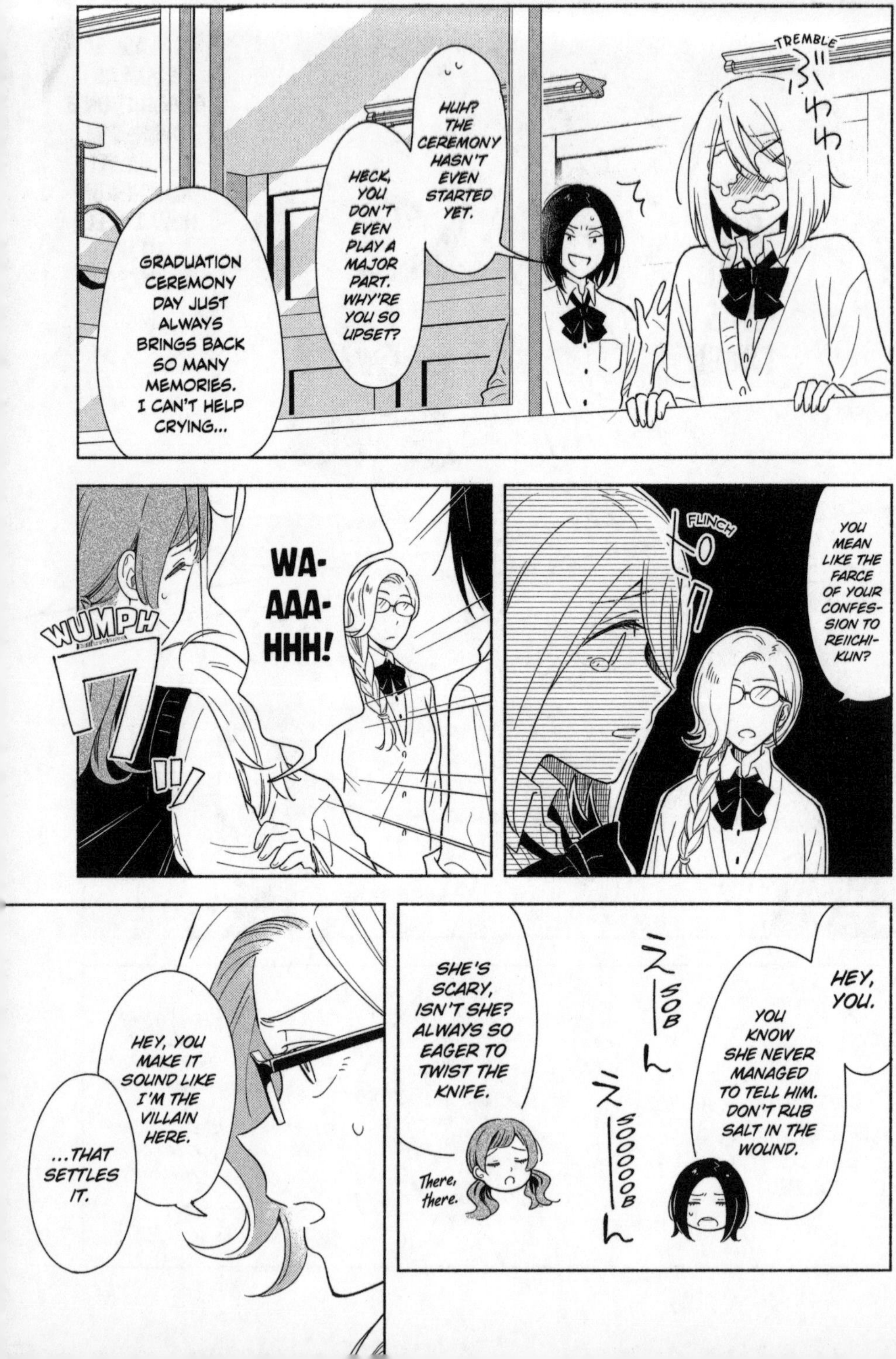
TREMBLE
HUH? THE CEREMONY HASN'T EVEN STARTED YET.
HECK, YOU DON'T EVEN PLAY A MAJOR PART. WHY'RE YOU SO UPSET?
GRADUATION CEREMONY DAY JUST ALWAYS BRINGS BACK SO MANY MEMORIES. I CAN'T HELP CRYING...
YOU MEAN LIKE THE FARCE OF YOUR CONFESSION TO REIICHI-KUN?
FLINCH
WA-AAA-HHH!
WUMPH
HEY, YOU.
YOU KNOW SHE NEVER MANAGED TO TELL HIM. DON'T RUB SALT IN THE WOUND.
SOB
SOOOOOB
SHE'S SCARY, ISN'T SHE? ALWAYS SO EAGER TO TWIST THE KNIFE.
There, there.
HEY, YOU MAKE IT SOUND LIKE I'M THE VILLAIN HERE.
...THAT SETTLES IT.

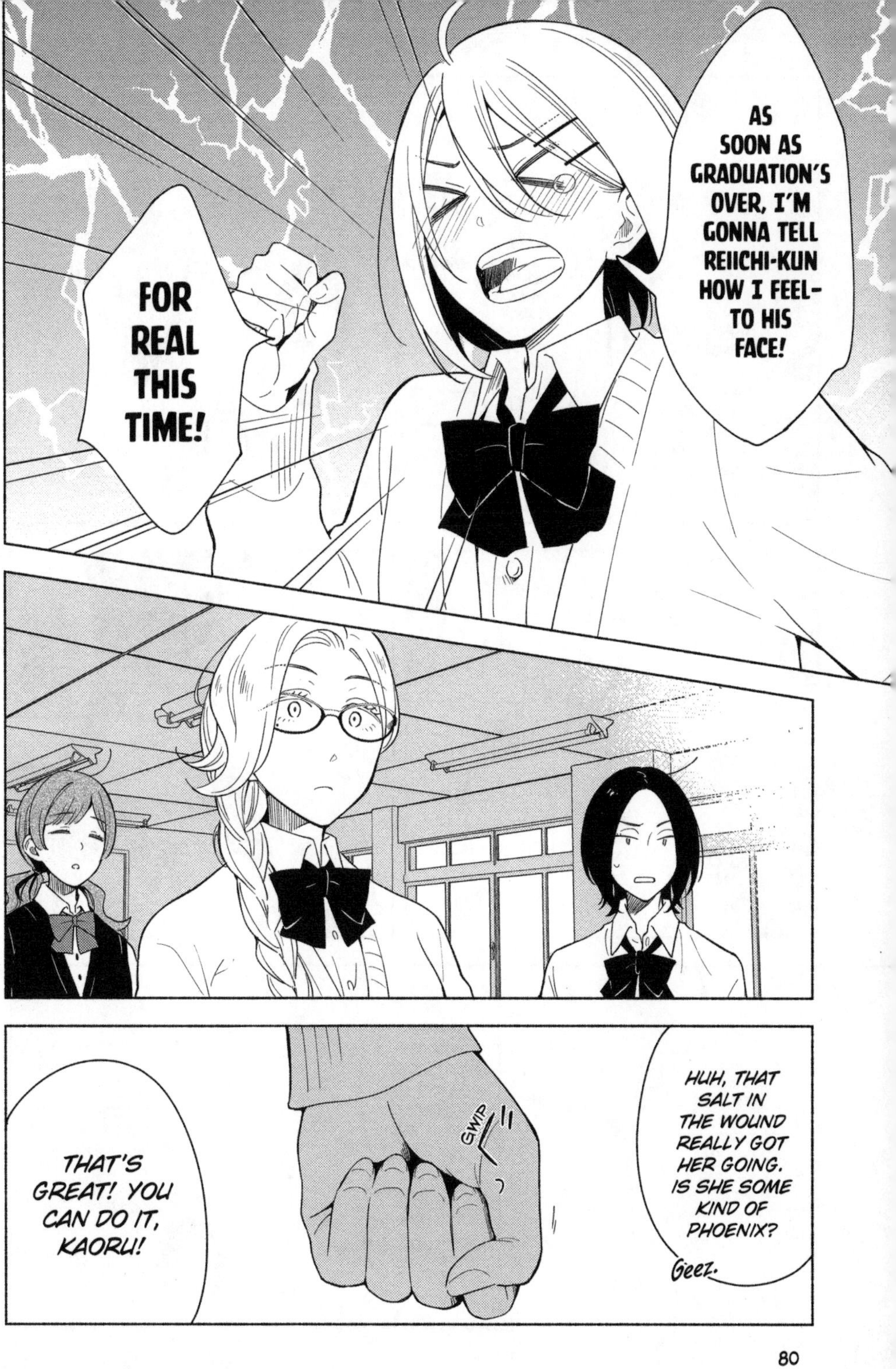
AS SOON AS GRADUATION'S OVER, I'M GONNA TELL REIICHI-KUN HOW I FEEL–TO HIS FACE!
FOR REAL THIS TIME!
HUH, THAT SALT IN THE WOUND REALLY GOT HER GOING. IS SHE SOME KIND OF PHOENIX?
Geez.
GWIP
THAT'S GREAT! YOU CAN DO IT, KAORU!

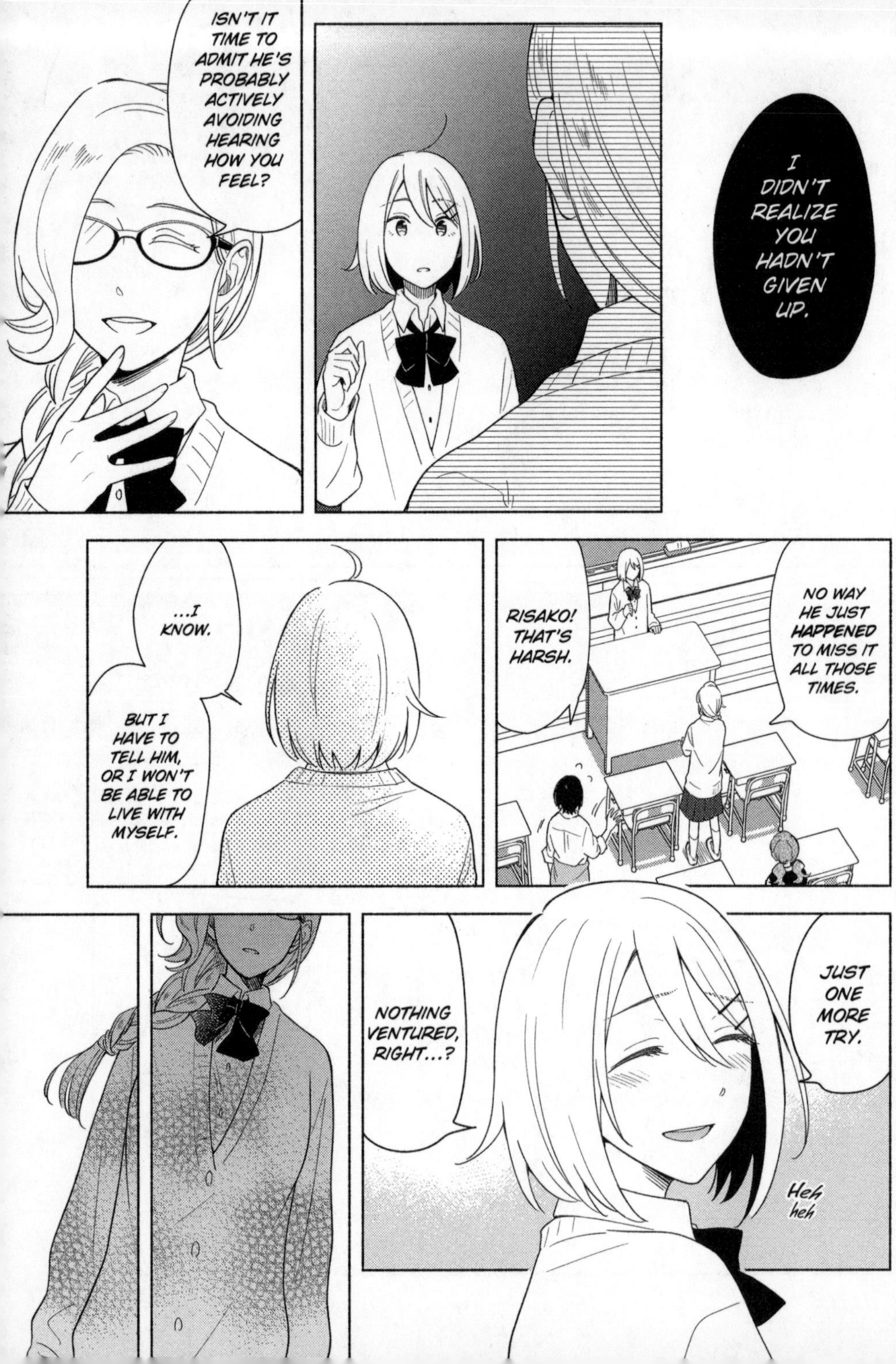
I DIDN'T REALIZE YOU HADN'T GIVEN UP.
ISN'T IT TIME TO ADMIT HE'S PROBABLY ACTIVELY AVOIDING HEARING HOW YOU FEEL?
NO WAY HE JUST HAPPENED TO MISS IT ALL THOSE TIMES.
RISAKO! THAT'S HARSH.
...I KNOW.
BUT I HAVE TO TELL HIM, OR I WON'T BE ABLE TO LIVE WITH MYSELF.
JUST ONE MORE TRY.
Heh heh
NOTHING VENTURED, RIGHT...?

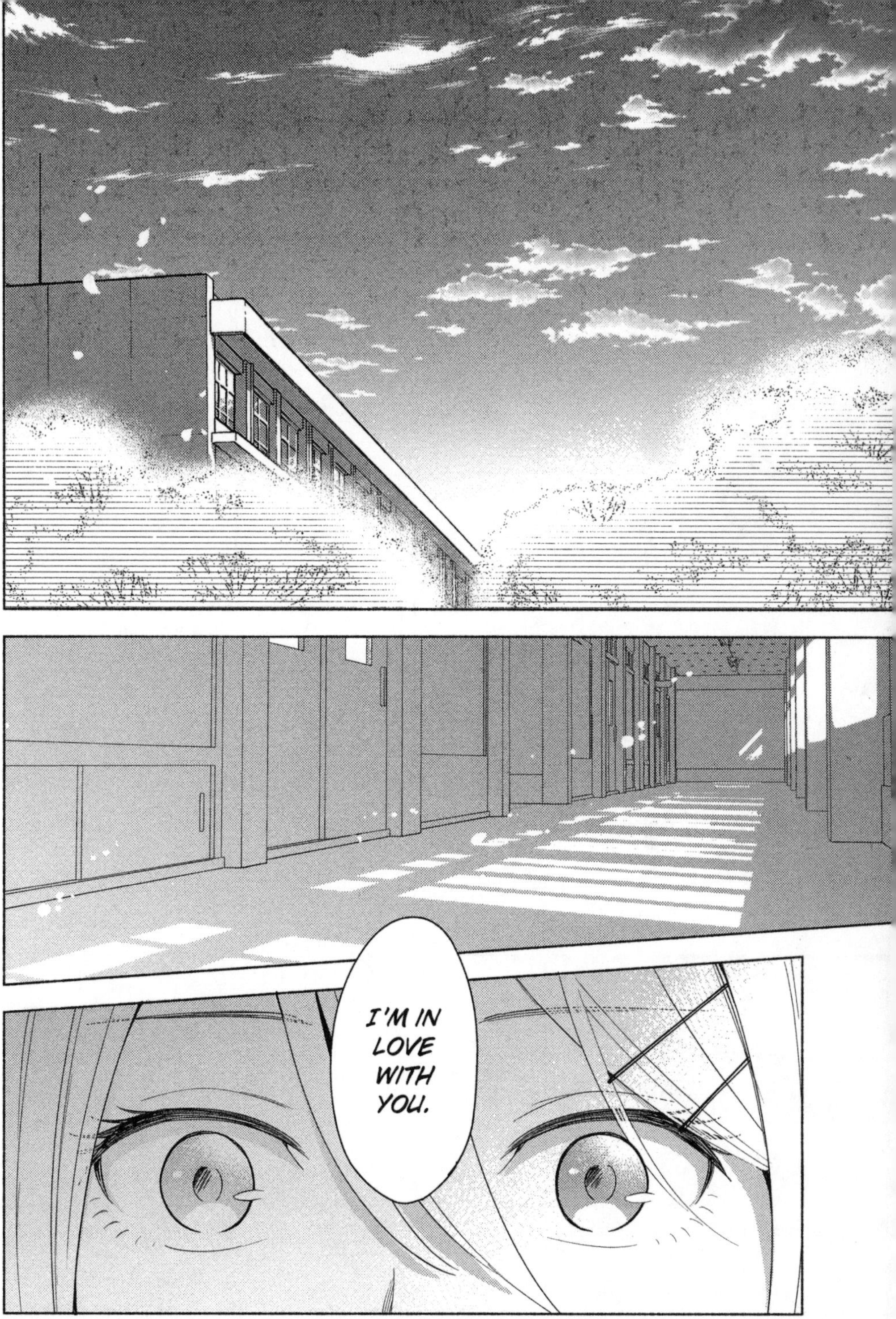
I'M IN LOVE WITH YOU.

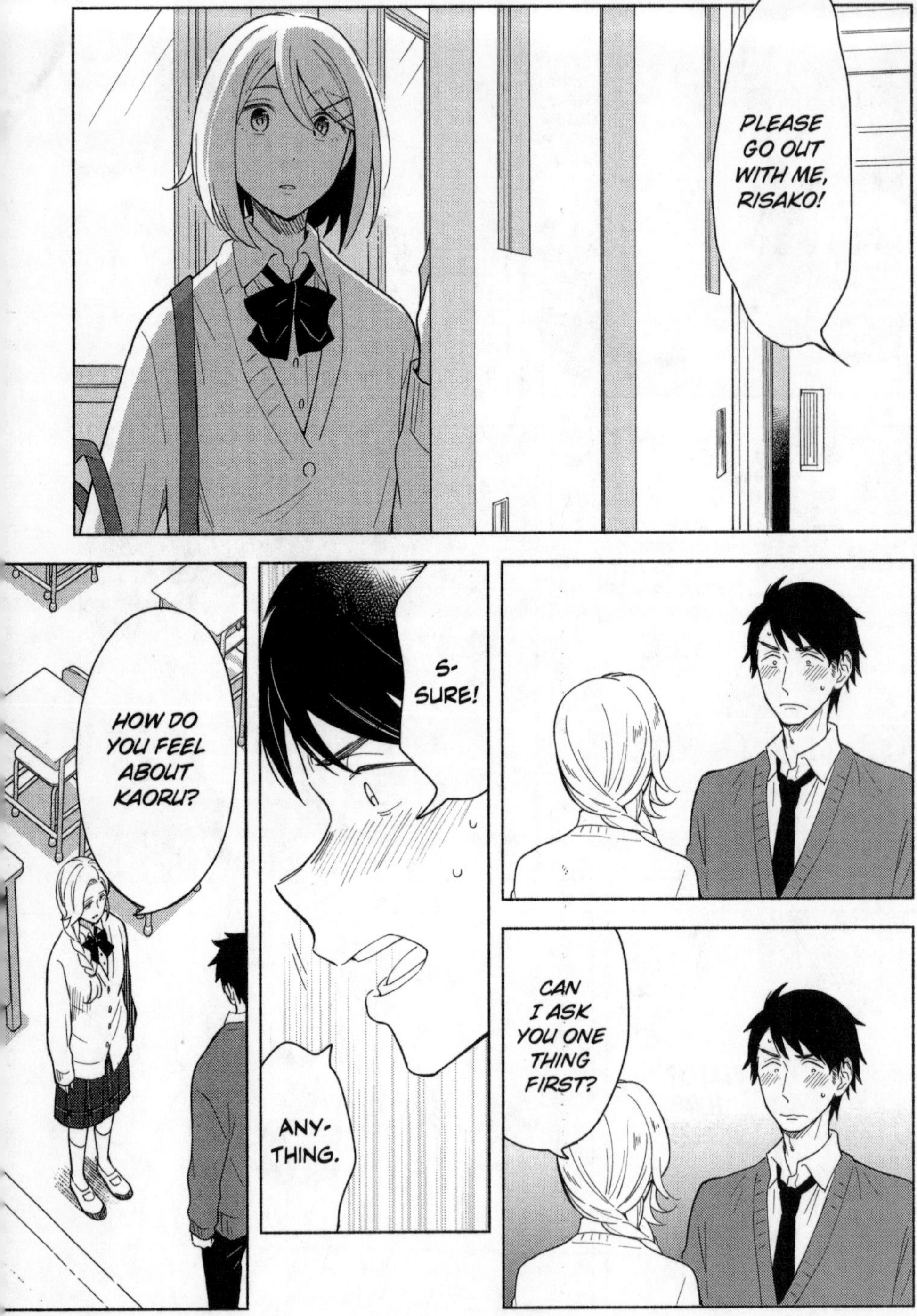
PLEASE GO OUT WITH ME, RISAKO!
CAN I ASK YOU ONE THING FIRST?
S-SURE!
ANY-THING.
HOW DO YOU FEEL ABOUT KAORU?

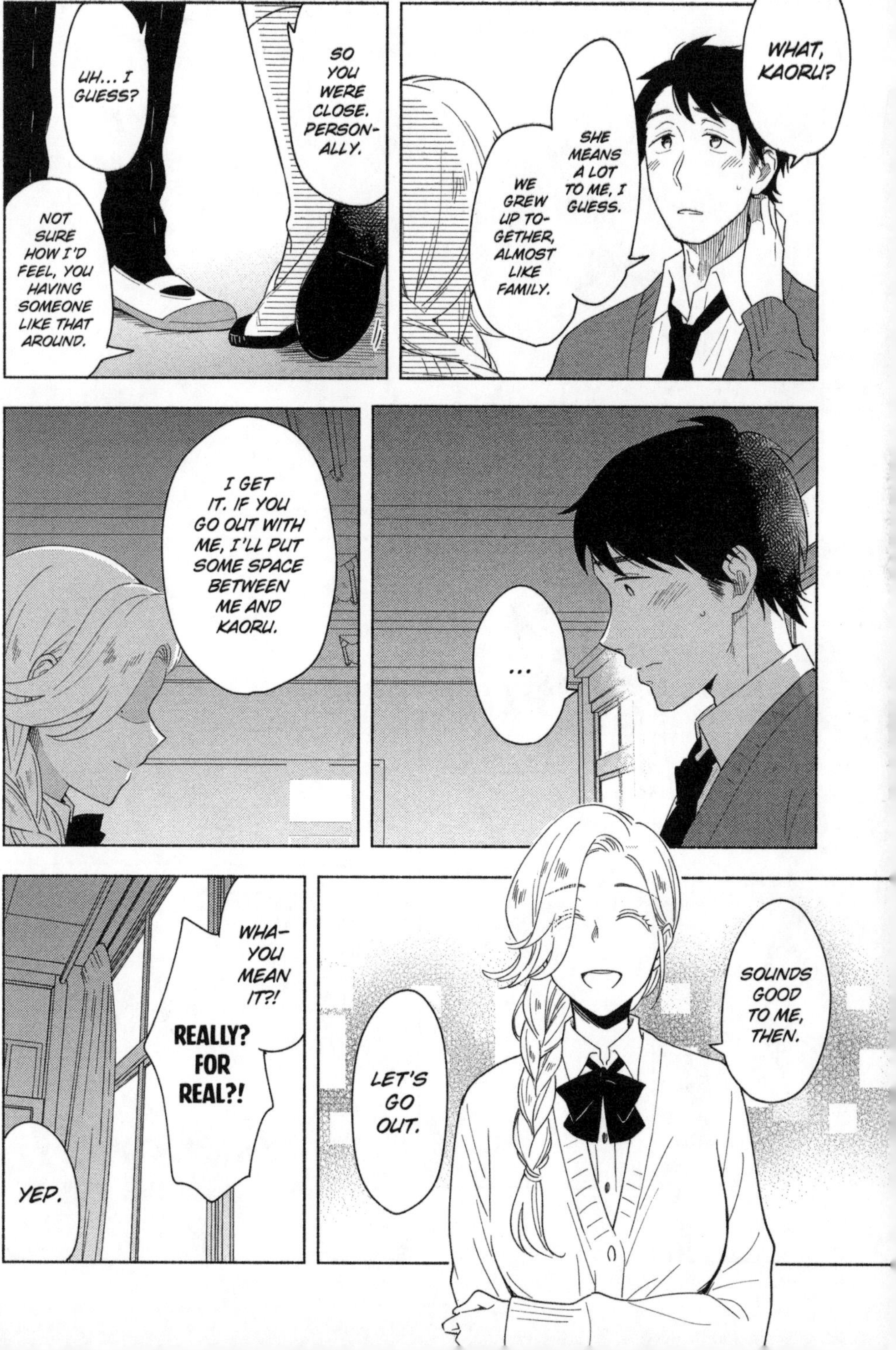
WHAT, KAORU?
SHE MEANS A LOT TO ME, I GUESS.
WE GREW UP TO-GETHER, ALMOST LIKE FAMILY.
SO YOU WERE CLOSE. PERSON-ALLY.
UH... I GUESS?
NOT SURE HOW I'D FEEL, YOU HAVING SOMEONE LIKE THAT AROUND.
...
I GET IT. IF YOU GO OUT WITH ME, I'LL PUT SOME SPACE BETWEEN ME AND KAORU.
SOUNDS GOOD TO ME, THEN.
LET'S GO OUT.
WHA- YOU MEAN IT?!
REALLY? FOR REAL?!
YEP.

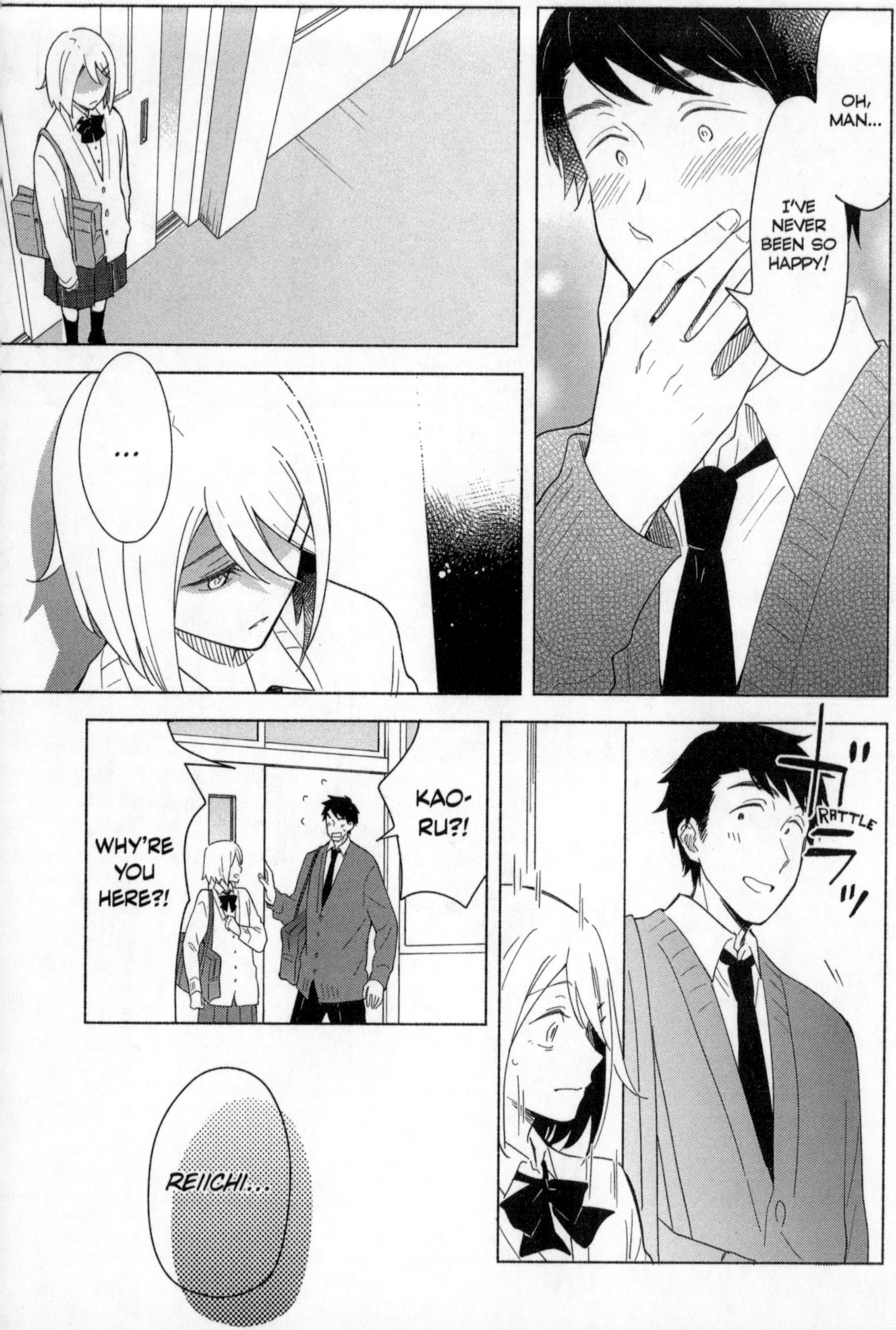
OH, MAN...
I'VE NEVER BEEN SO HAPPY!
...
RATTLE
KAO-RU?!
WHY'RE YOU HERE?!
REIICHI...

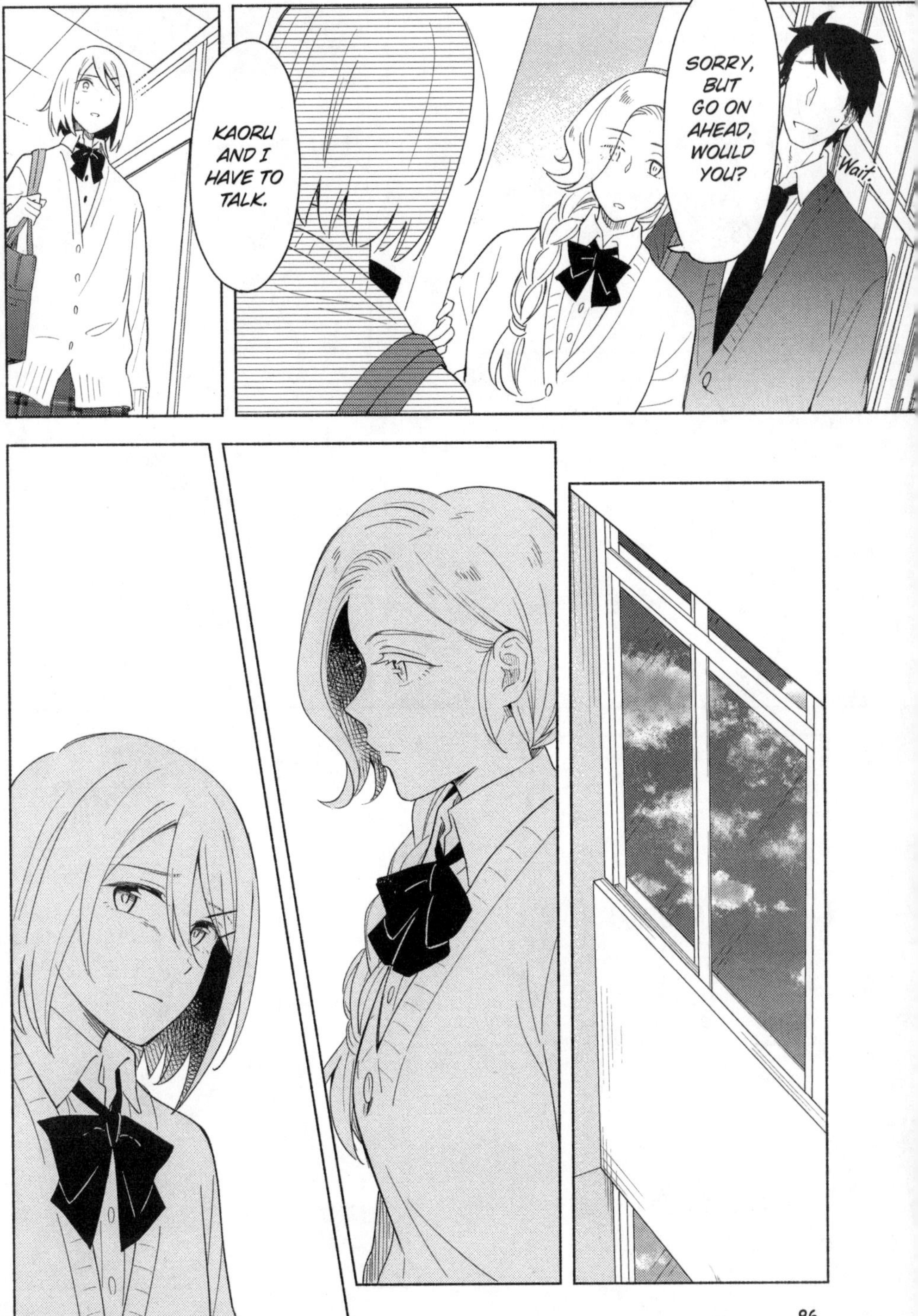
SORRY, BUT GO ON AHEAD, WOULD YOU?
Wait.
KAORU AND I HAVE TO TALK.

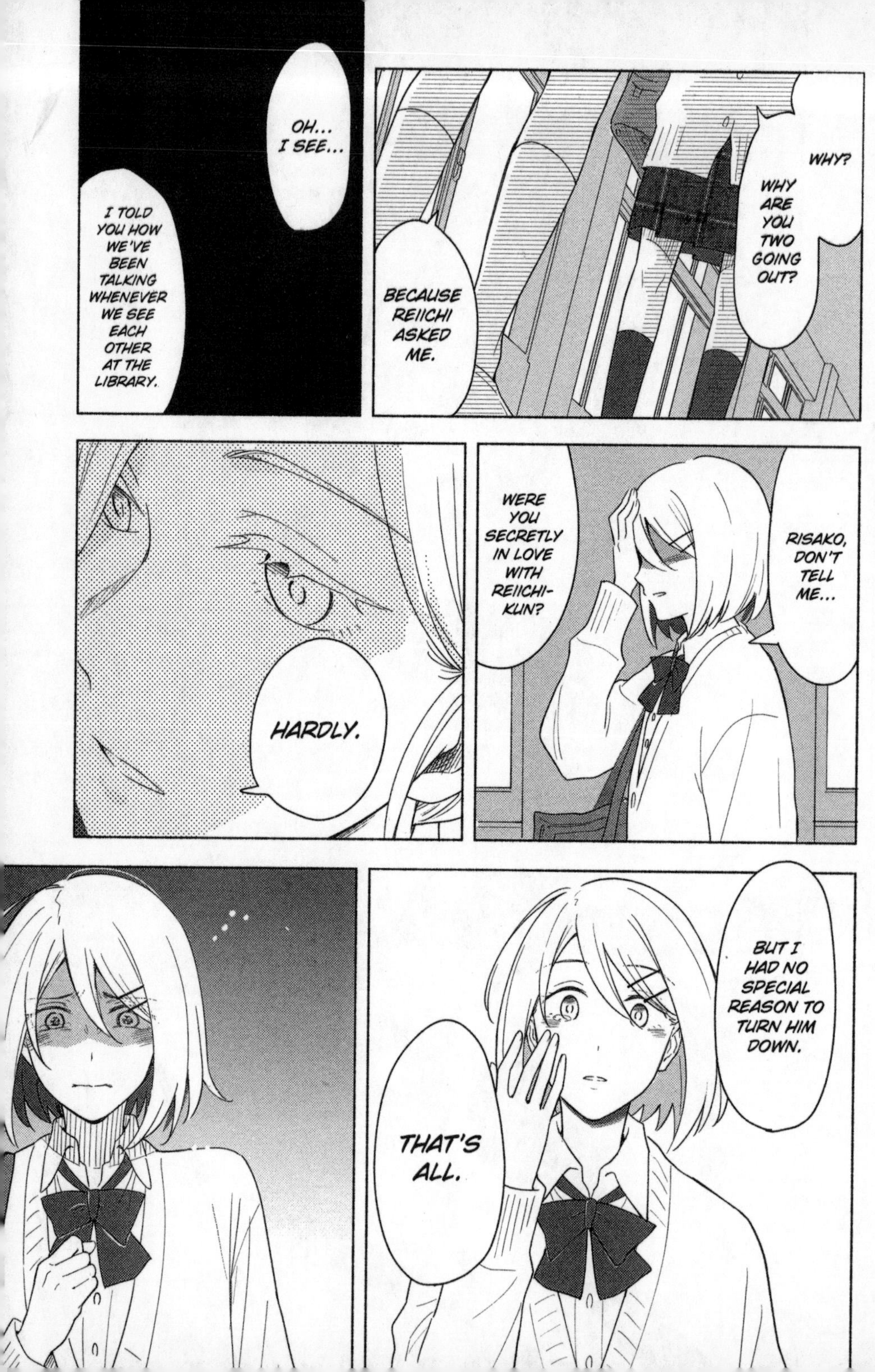
WHY?
WHY ARE YOU TWO GOING OUT?
BECAUSE REIICHI ASKED ME.
OH... I SEE...
I TOLD YOU HOW WE'VE BEEN TALKING WHENEVER WE SEE EACH OTHER AT THE LIBRARY.
RISAKO, DON'T TELL ME...
WERE YOU SECRETLY IN LOVE WITH REIICHI-KUN?
HARDLY.
BUT I HAD NO SPECIAL REASON TO TURN HIM DOWN.
THAT'S ALL.

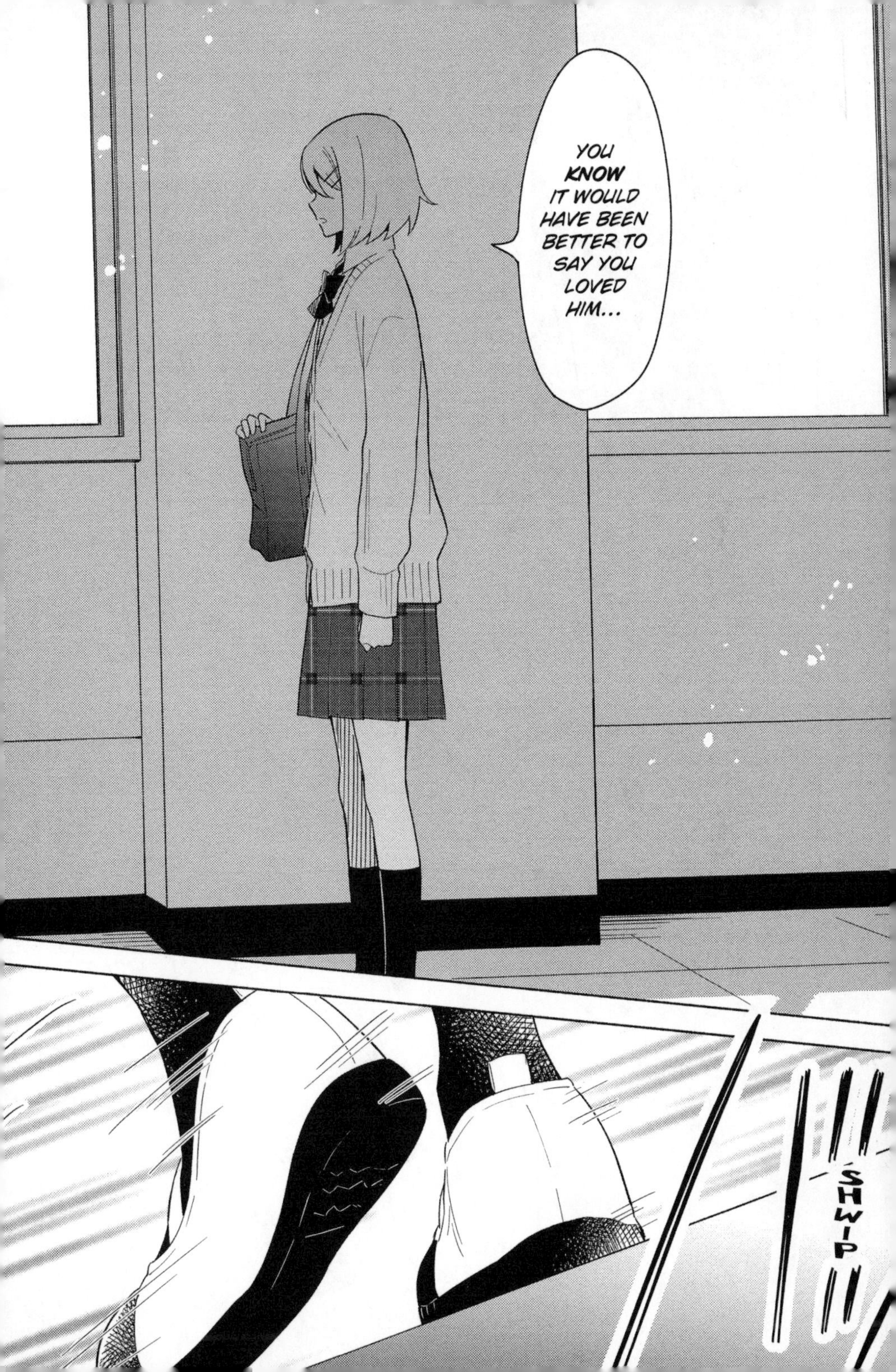
YOU KNOW IT WOULD HAVE BEEN BETTER TO SAY YOU LOVED HIM...
SHWIP

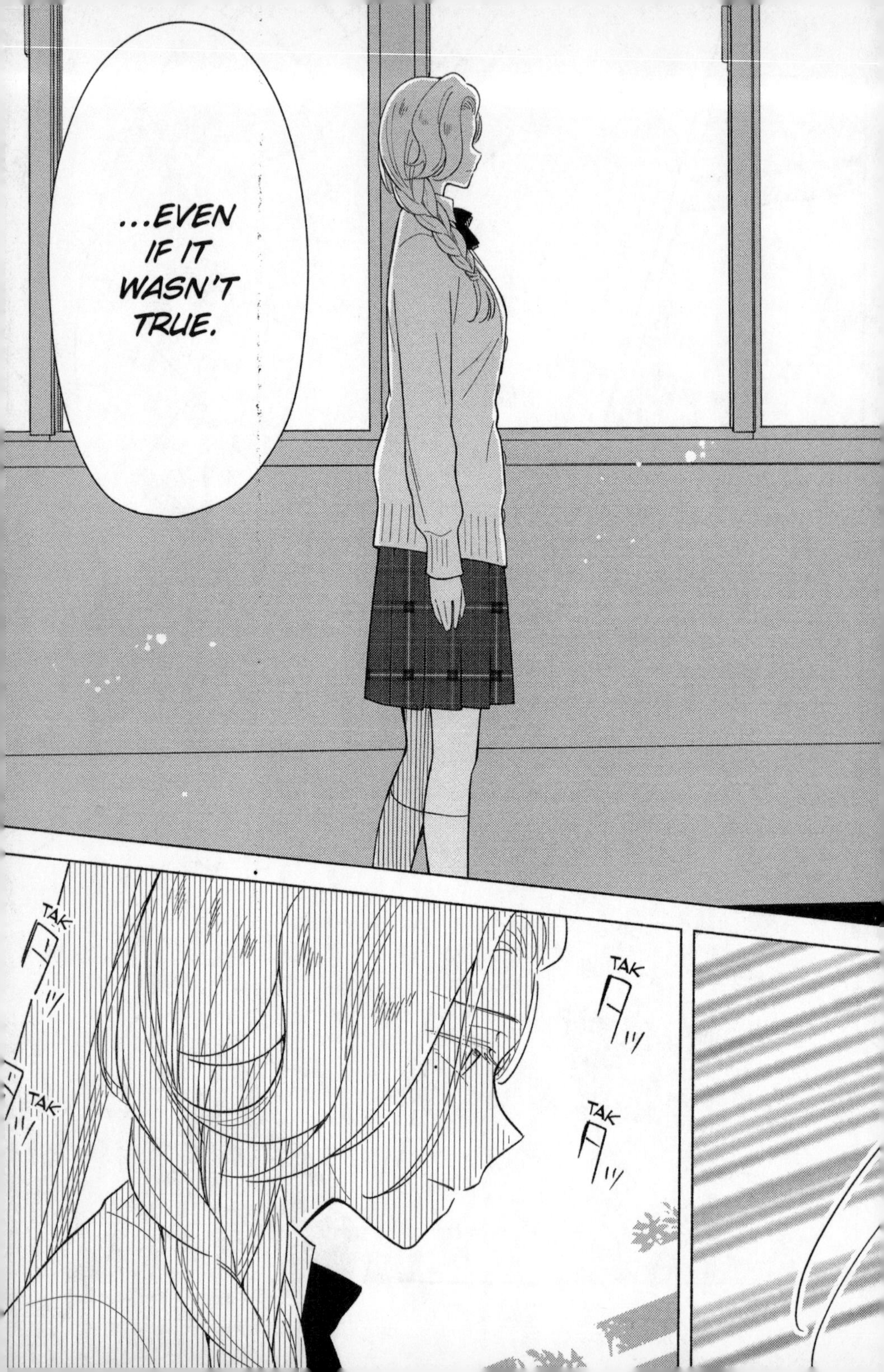
...EVEN IF IT WASN'T TRUE.
TAK
TAK
TAK
TAK

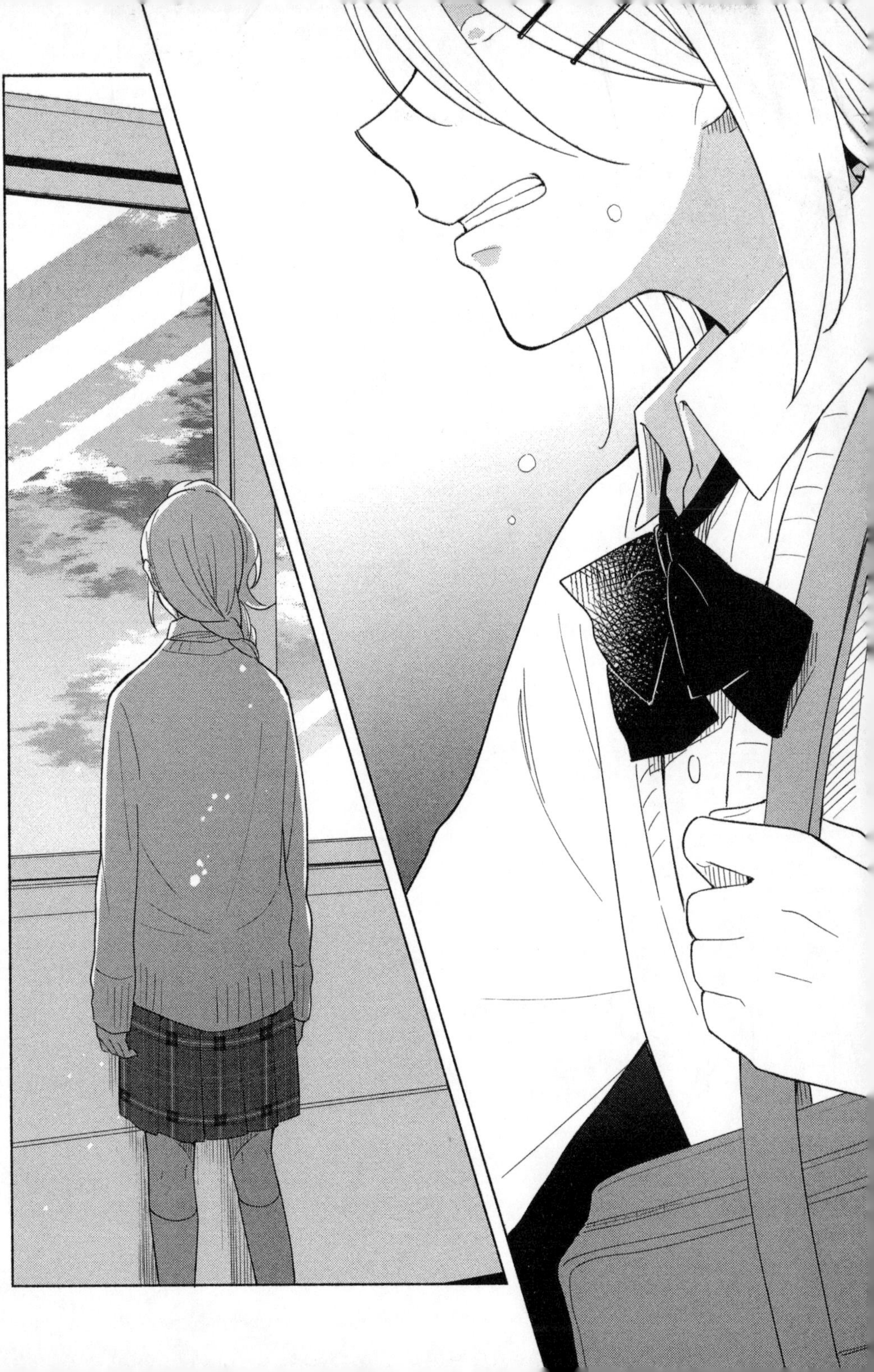

If I Could
Reach You

If I Could
Reach You

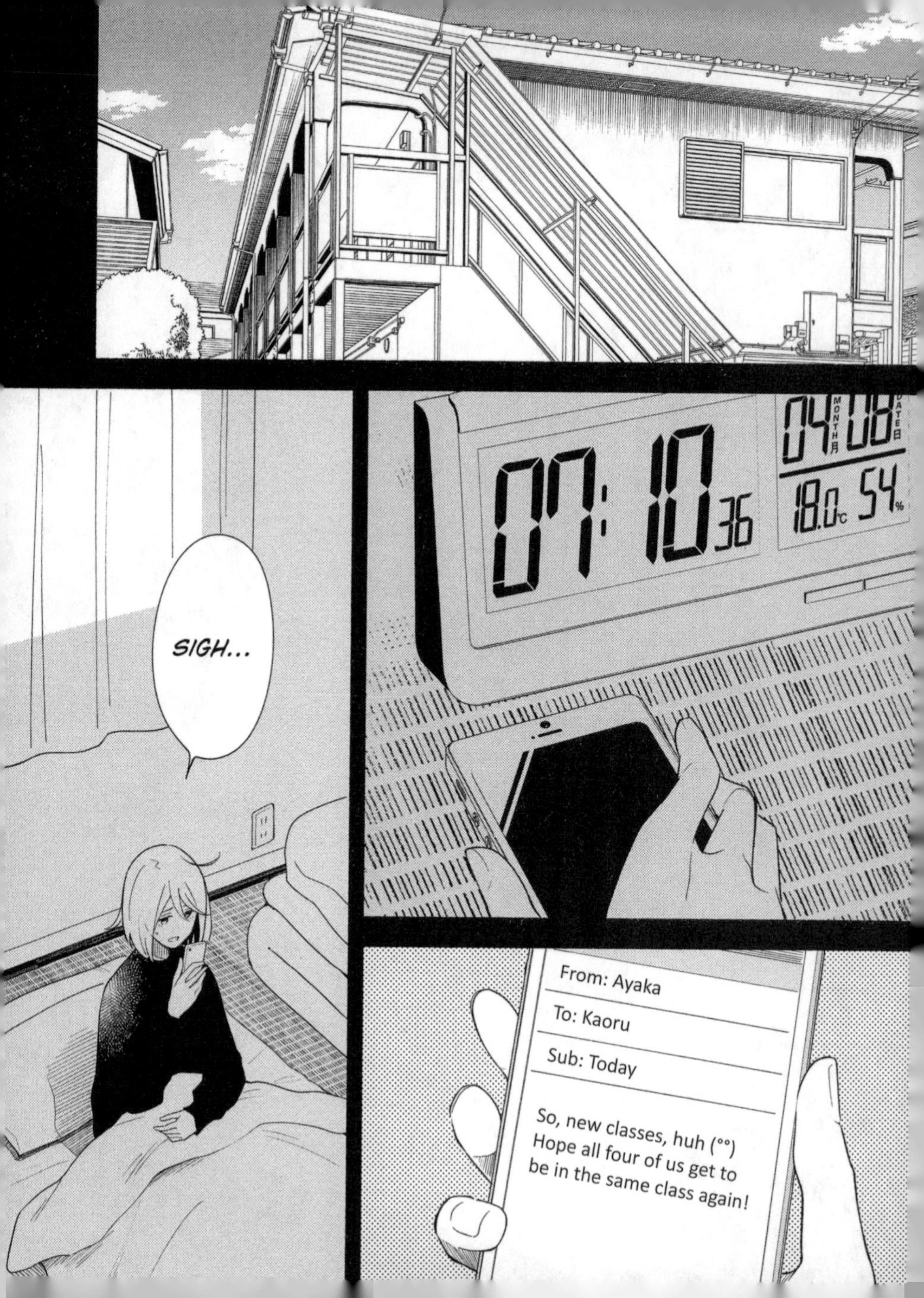
07:10 36
04 08
18.0°C 54%
From: Ayaka
To: Kaoru
Sub: Today
So, new classes, huh (°°) Hope all four of us get to be in the same class again!
SIGH...

Chapter 29

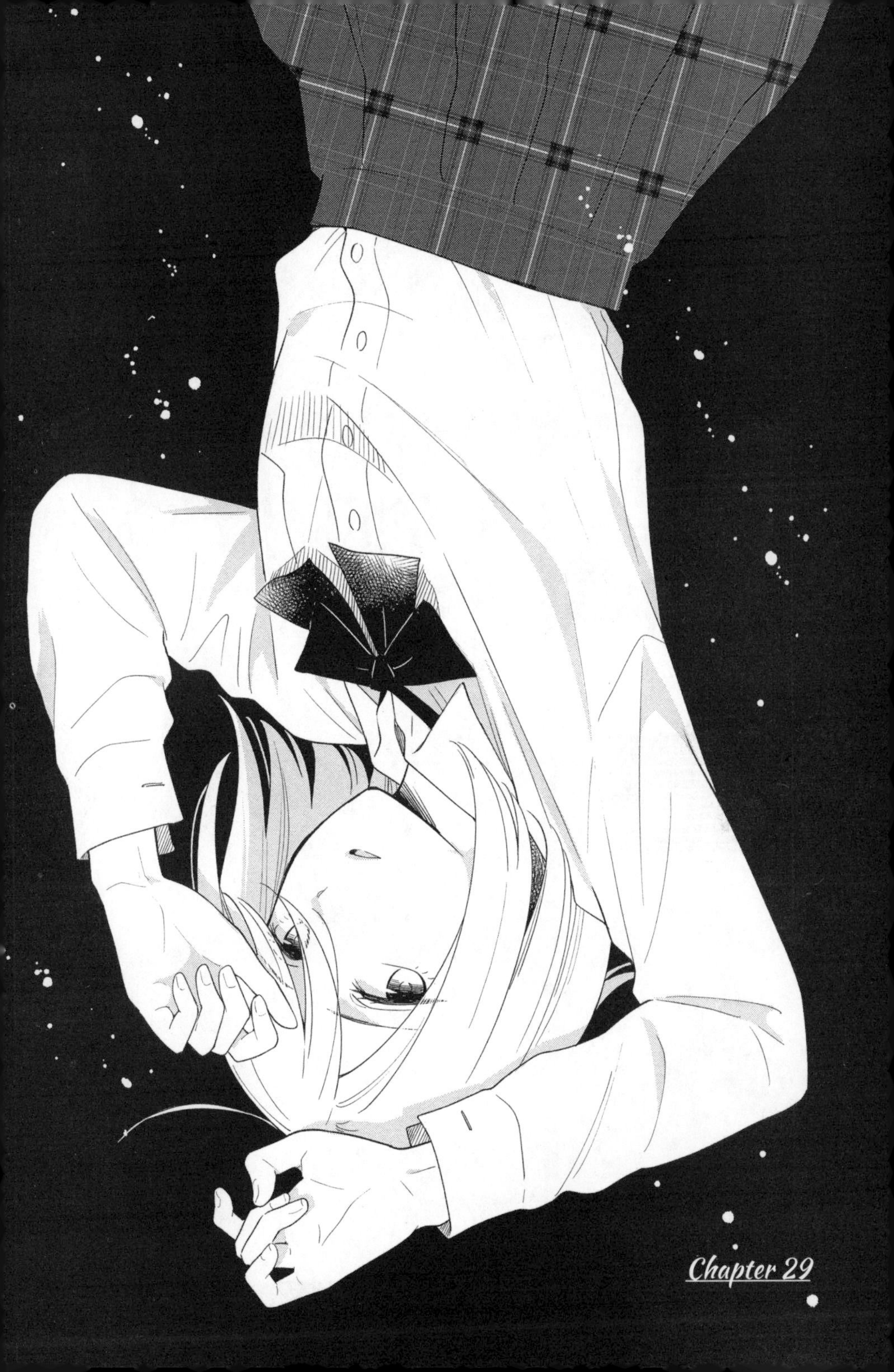

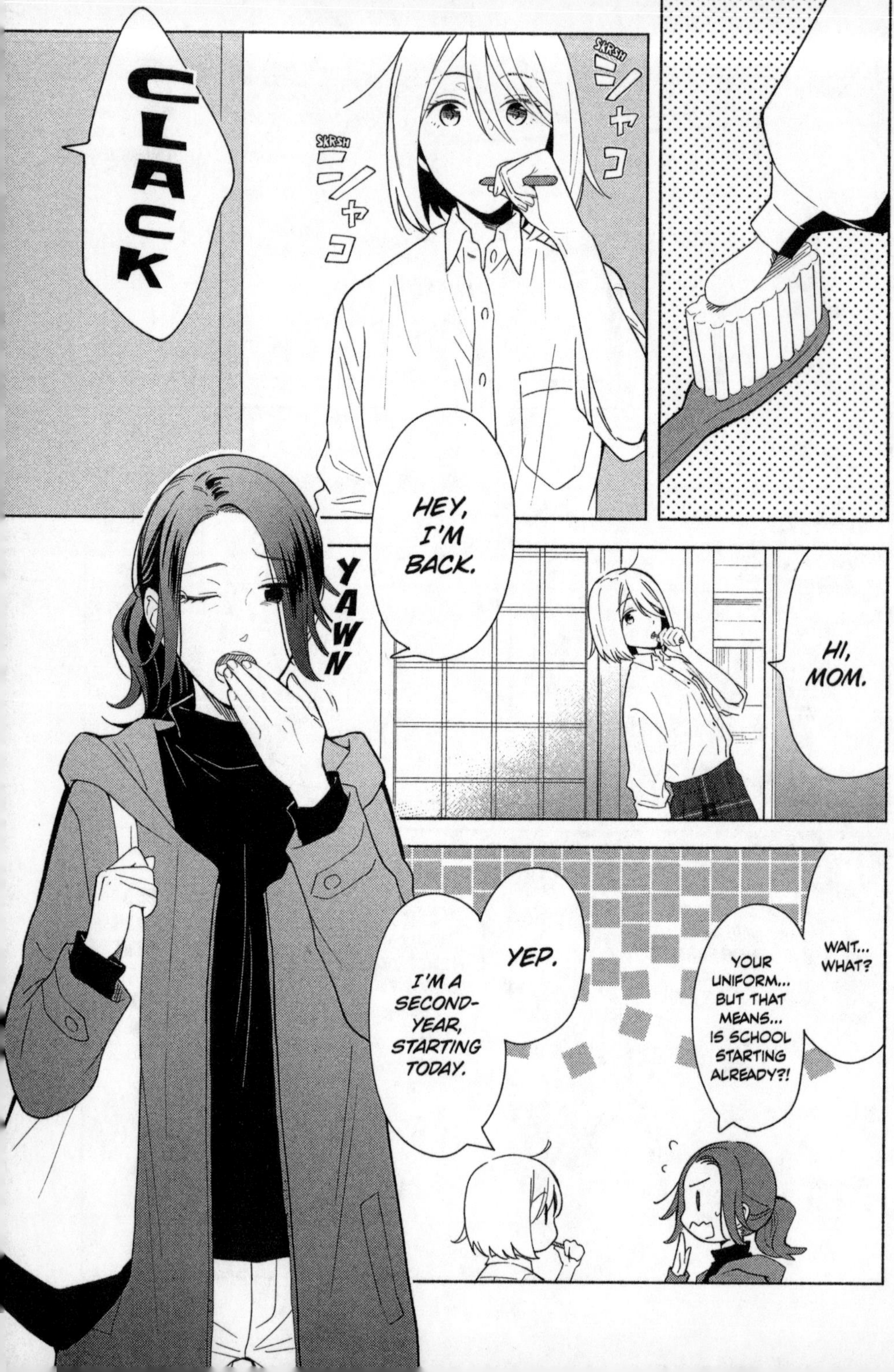
SKRSH
シャコ
SKRSH
シャコ
CLACK
YAWN
HEY, I'M BACK.
HI, MOM.
WAIT... WHAT?
YOUR UNIFORM... BUT THAT MEANS... IS SCHOOL STARTING ALREADY?!
YEP.
I'M A SECOND-YEAR, STARTING TODAY.

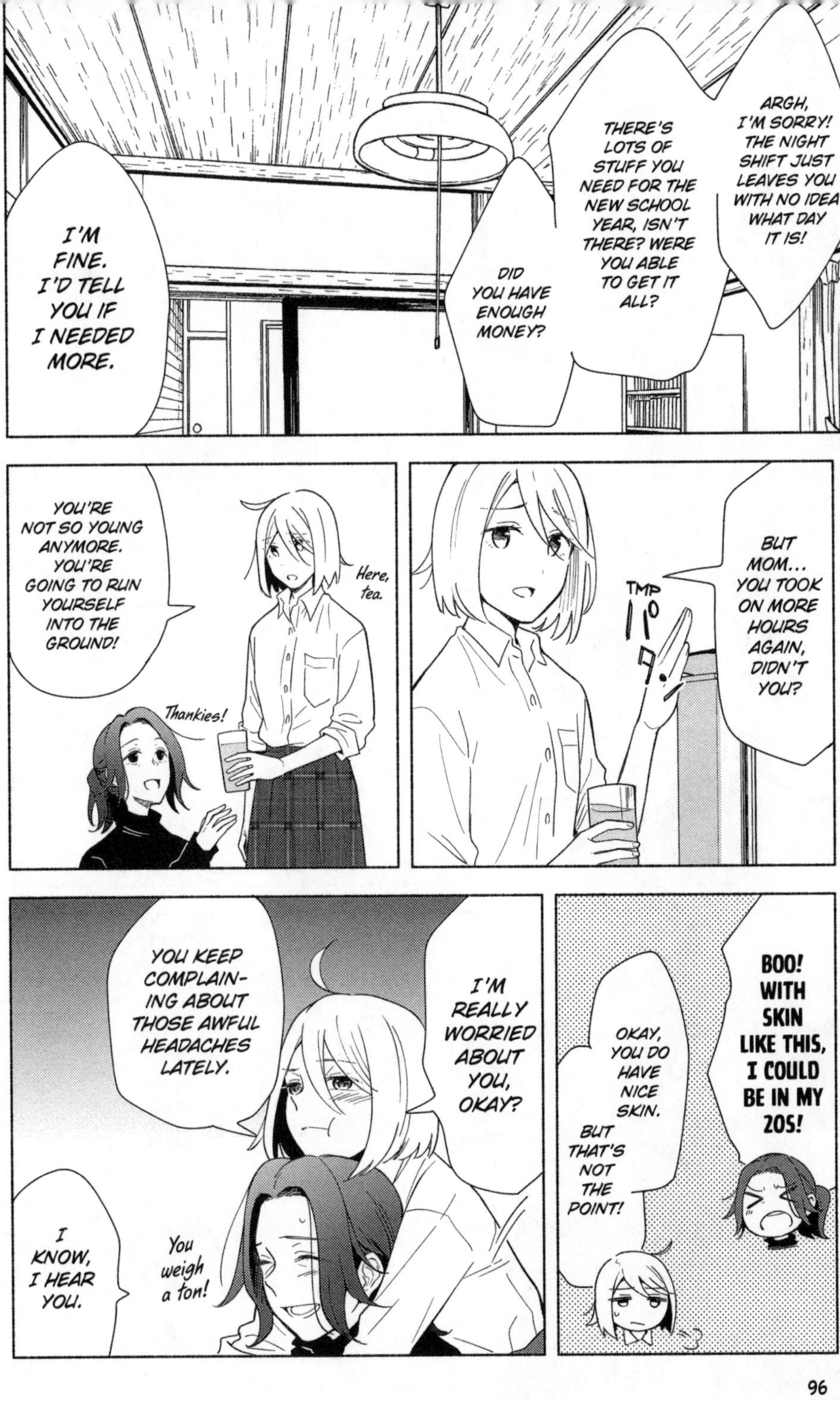
ARGH, I'M SORRY! THE NIGHT SHIFT JUST LEAVES YOU WITH NO IDEA WHAT DAY IT IS!
THERE'S LOTS OF STUFF YOU NEED FOR THE NEW SCHOOL YEAR, ISN'T THERE? WERE YOU ABLE TO GET IT ALL?
DID YOU HAVE ENOUGH MONEY?
I'M FINE. I'D TELL YOU IF I NEEDED MORE.
BUT MOM... YOU TOOK ON MORE HOURS AGAIN, DIDN'T YOU?
TMP
Here, tea.
YOU'RE NOT SO YOUNG ANYMORE. YOU'RE GOING TO RUN YOURSELF INTO THE GROUND!
Thankies!
BOO! WITH SKIN LIKE THIS, I COULD BE IN MY 20S!
OKAY, YOU DO HAVE NICE SKIN.
BUT THAT'S NOT THE POINT!
I'M REALLY WORRIED ABOUT YOU, OKAY?
YOU KEEP COMPLAIN-ING ABOUT THOSE AWFUL HEADACHES LATELY.
You weigh a ton!
I KNOW, I HEAR YOU.

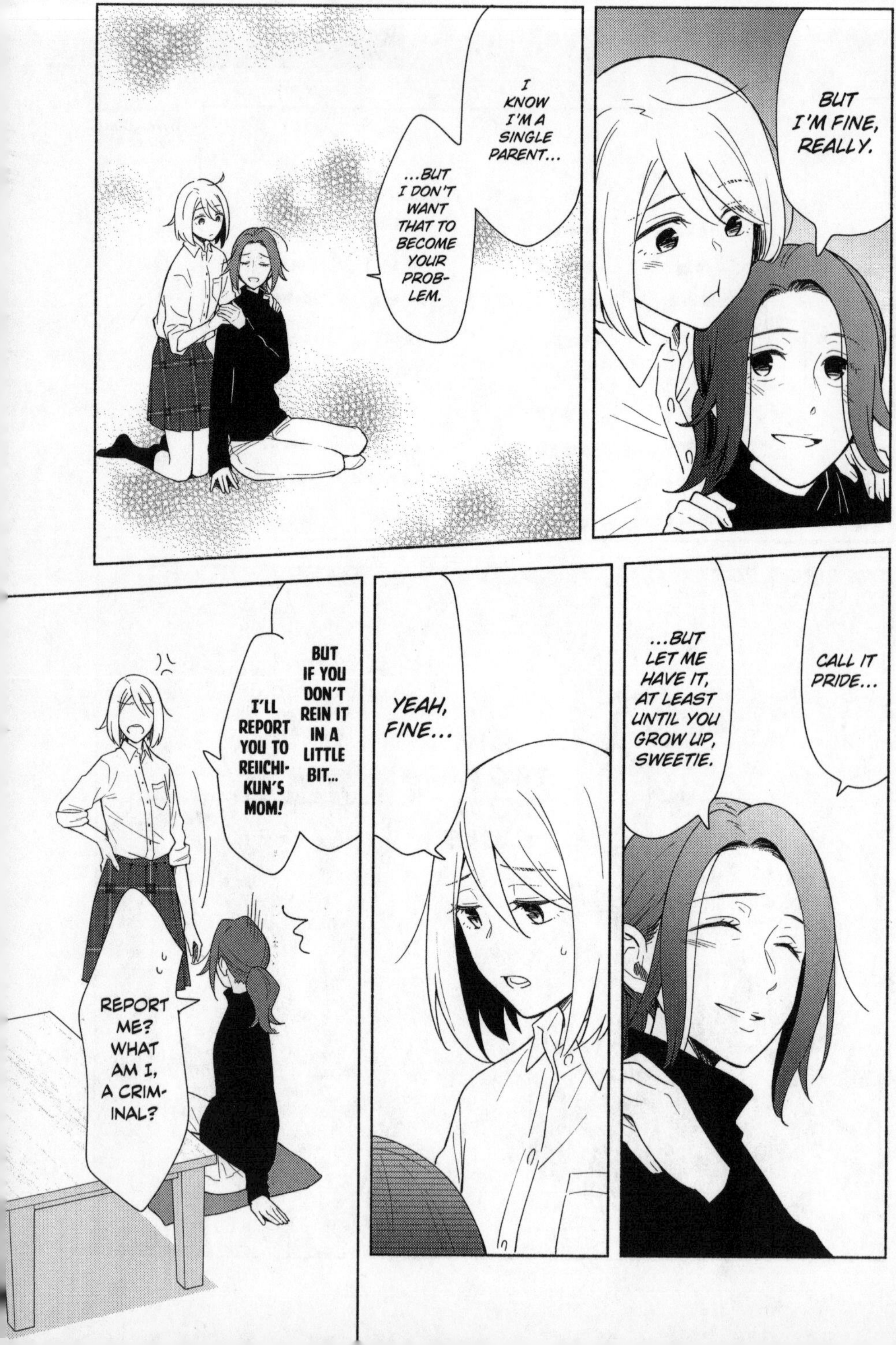
BUT I'M FINE, REALLY.
I KNOW I'M A SINGLE PARENT...
...BUT I DON'T WANT THAT TO BECOME YOUR PROB-LEM.
CALL IT PRIDE...
...BUT LET ME HAVE IT, AT LEAST UNTIL YOU GROW UP, SWEETIE.
YEAH, FINE...
BUT IF YOU DON'T REIN IT IN A LITTLE BIT...
I'LL REPORT YOU TO REIICHI-KUN'S MOM!
REPORT ME? WHAT AM I, A CRIM-INAL?

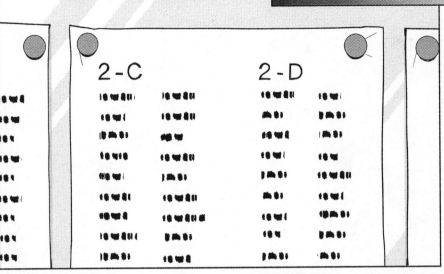

2 - C   2 - D

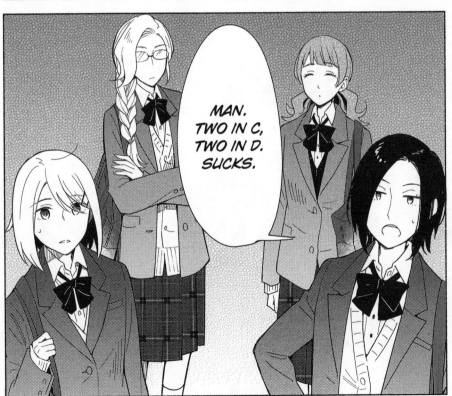

MAN.
TWO IN C,
TWO IN D.
SUCKS.

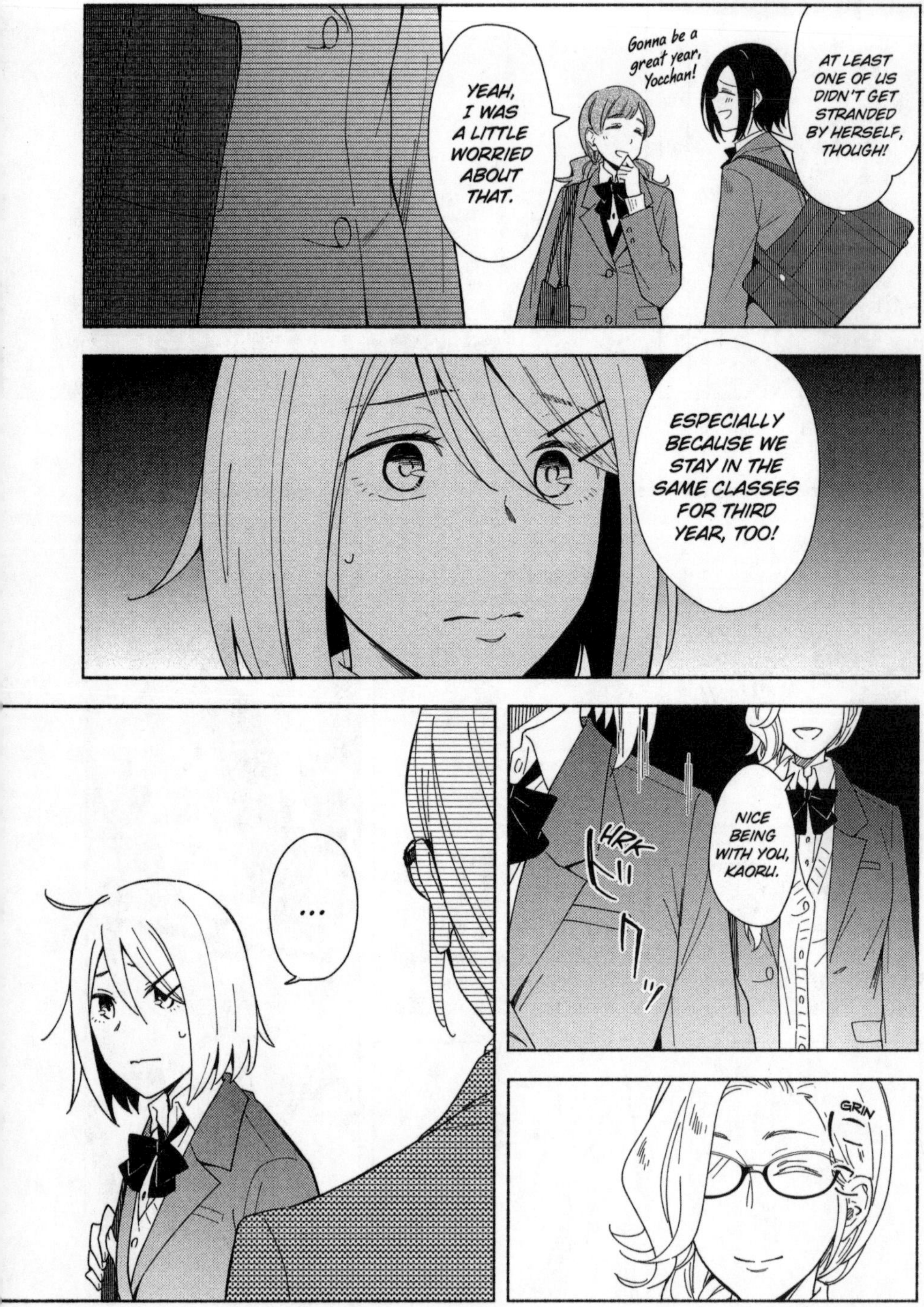
AT LEAST ONE OF US DIDN'T GET STRANDED BY HERSELF, THOUGH!
Gonna be a great year, Yocchan!
YEAH, I WAS A LITTLE WORRIED ABOUT THAT.
ESPECIALLY BECAUSE WE STAY IN THE SAME CLASSES FOR THIRD YEAR, TOO!
NICE BEING WITH YOU, KAORU.
HRK
GRIN
...

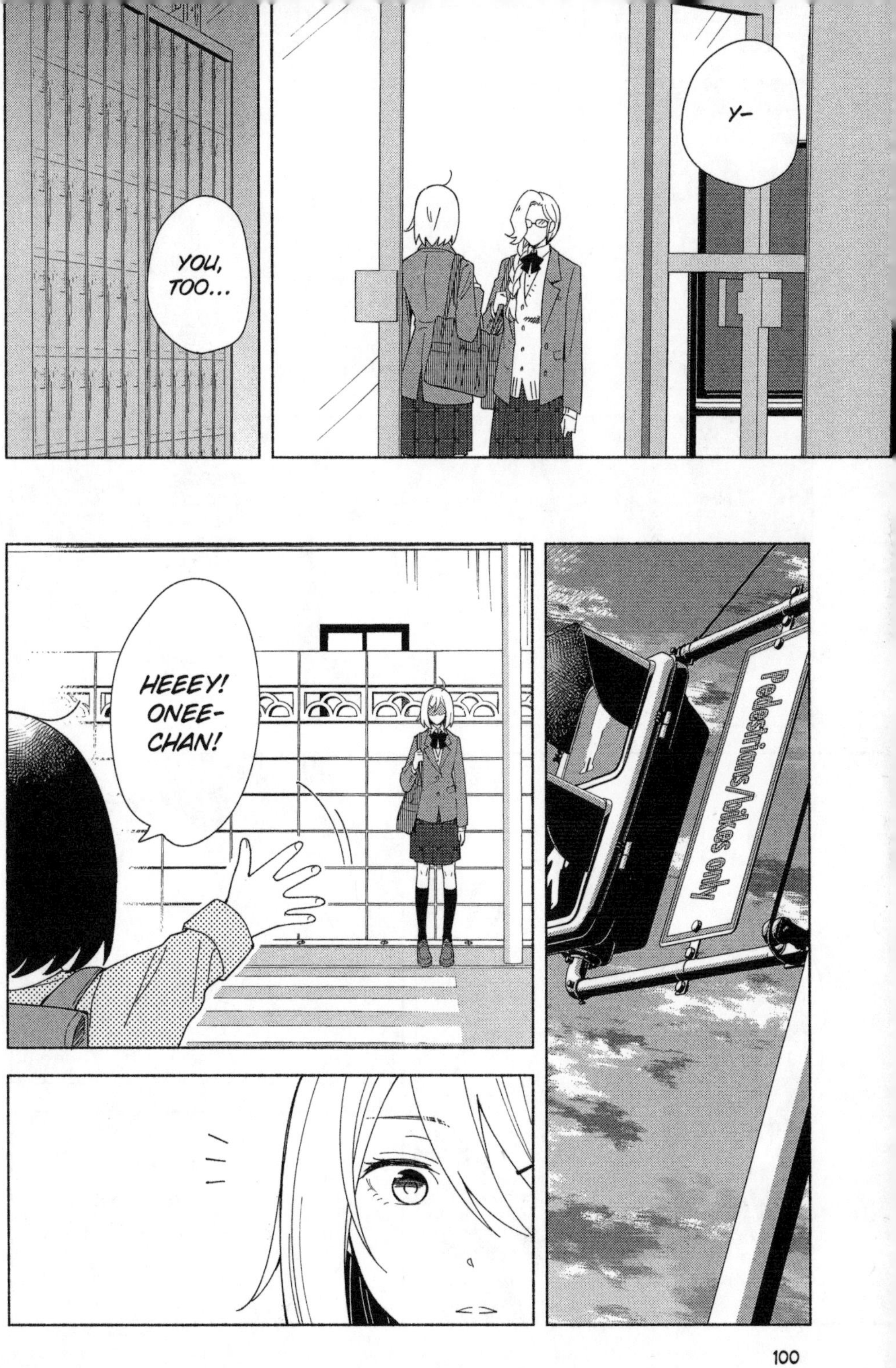
Y-
YOU, TOO...
Pedestrians/bikes only
HEEEY! ONEE-CHAN!

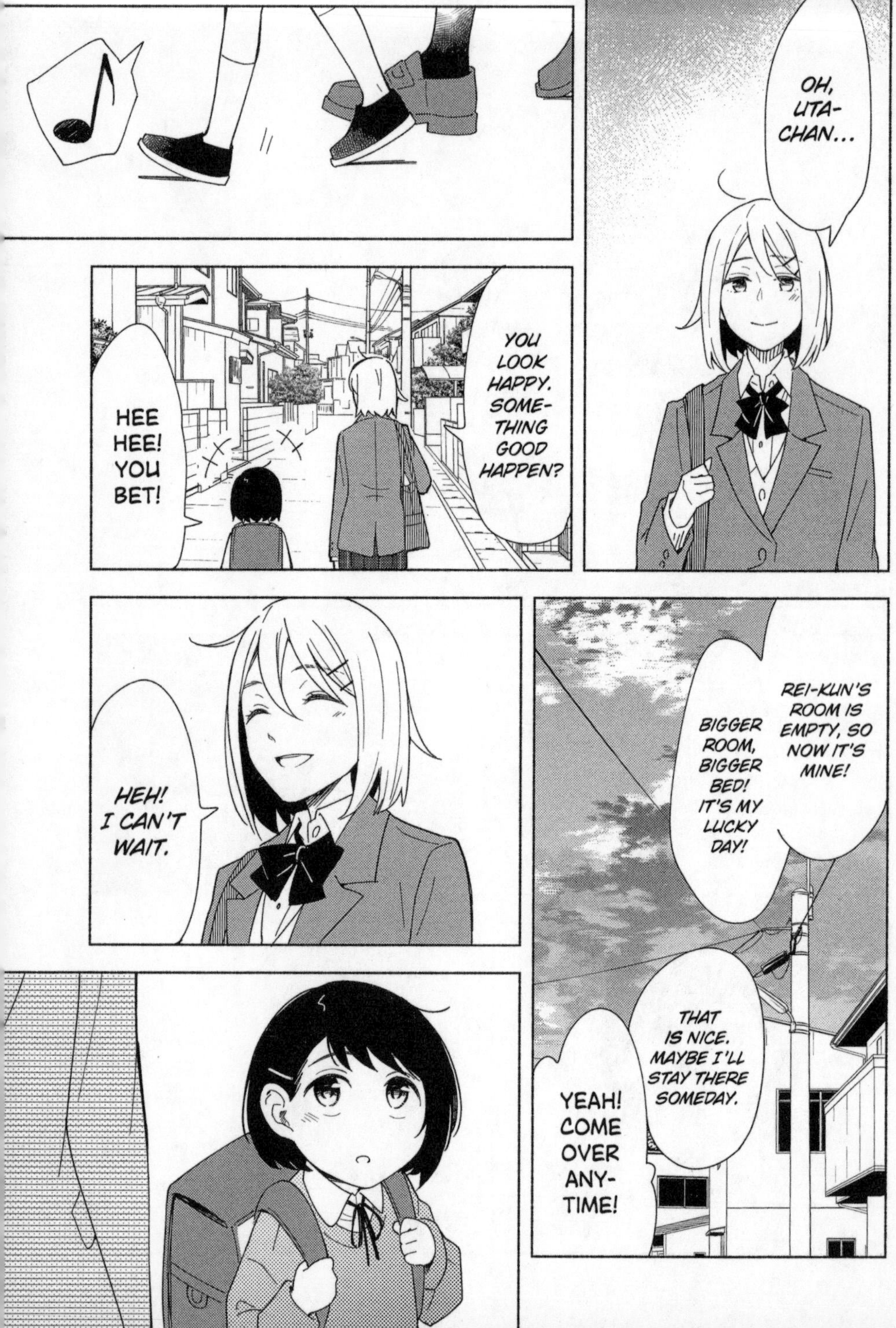
OH, UTA-CHAN...
YOU LOOK HAPPY. SOMETHING GOOD HAPPEN?
HEE HEE! YOU BET!
REI-KUN'S ROOM IS EMPTY, SO NOW IT'S MINE!
BIGGER ROOM, BIGGER BED! IT'S MY LUCKY DAY!
THAT IS NICE. MAYBE I'LL STAY THERE SOMEDAY.
YEAH! COME OVER ANY-TIME!
HEH! I CAN'T WAIT.

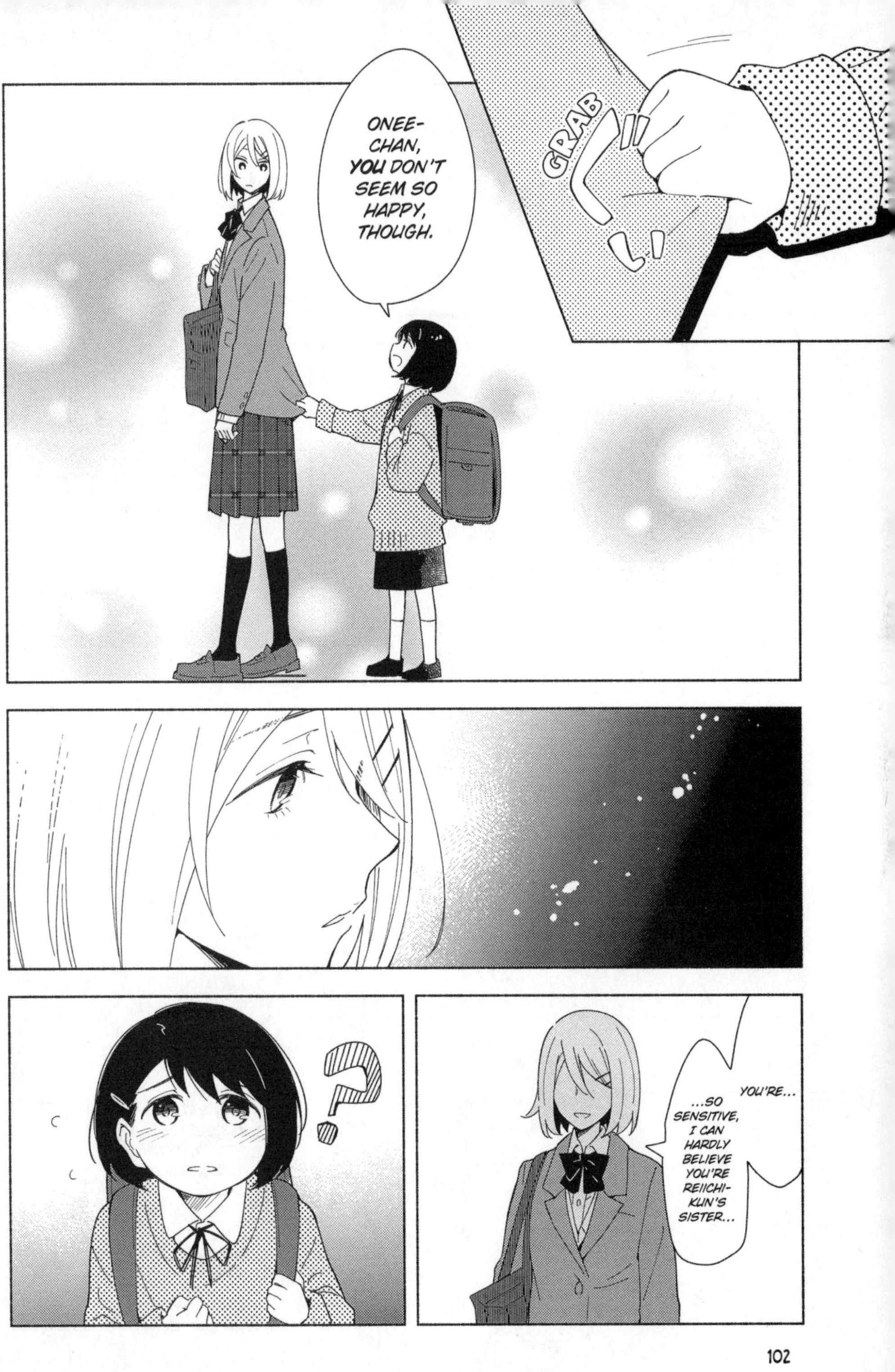
GRAB
ONEE-CHAN, YOU DON'T SEEM SO HAPPY, THOUGH.
YOU'RE...
...SO SENSITIVE, I CAN HARDLY BELIEVE YOU'RE REIICHI-KUN'S SISTER...
?

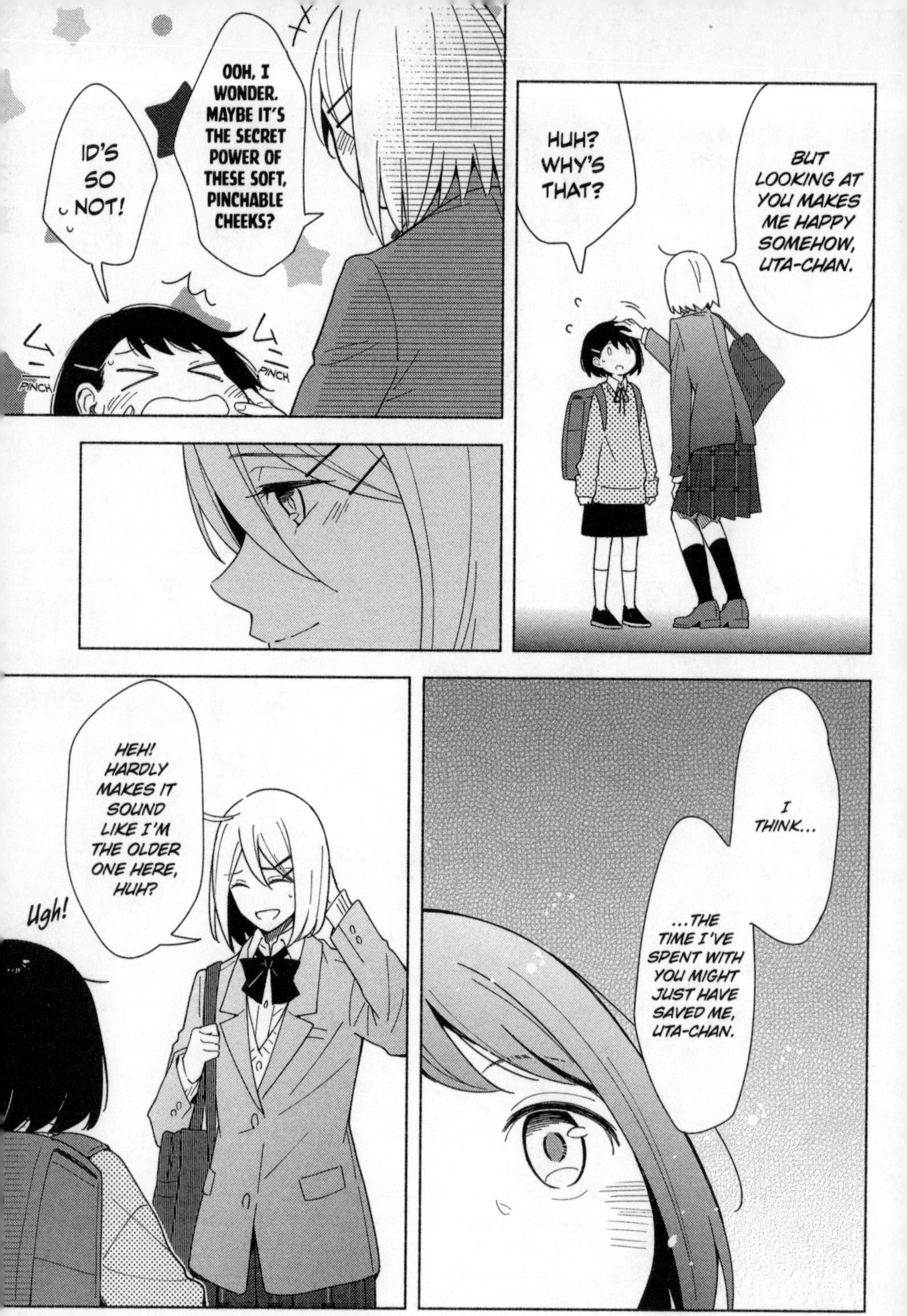
BUT LOOKING AT YOU MAKES ME HAPPY SOMEHOW, UTA-CHAN.
HUH? WHY'S THAT?
OOH, I WONDER. MAYBE IT'S THE SECRET POWER OF THESE SOFT, PINCHABLE CHEEKS?
ID'S SO NOT!
PINCH
PINCH
I THINK...
...THE TIME I'VE SPENT WITH YOU MIGHT JUST HAVE SAVED ME, UTA-CHAN.
HEH! HARDLY MAKES IT SOUND LIKE I'M THE OLDER ONE HERE, HUH?
Ugh!

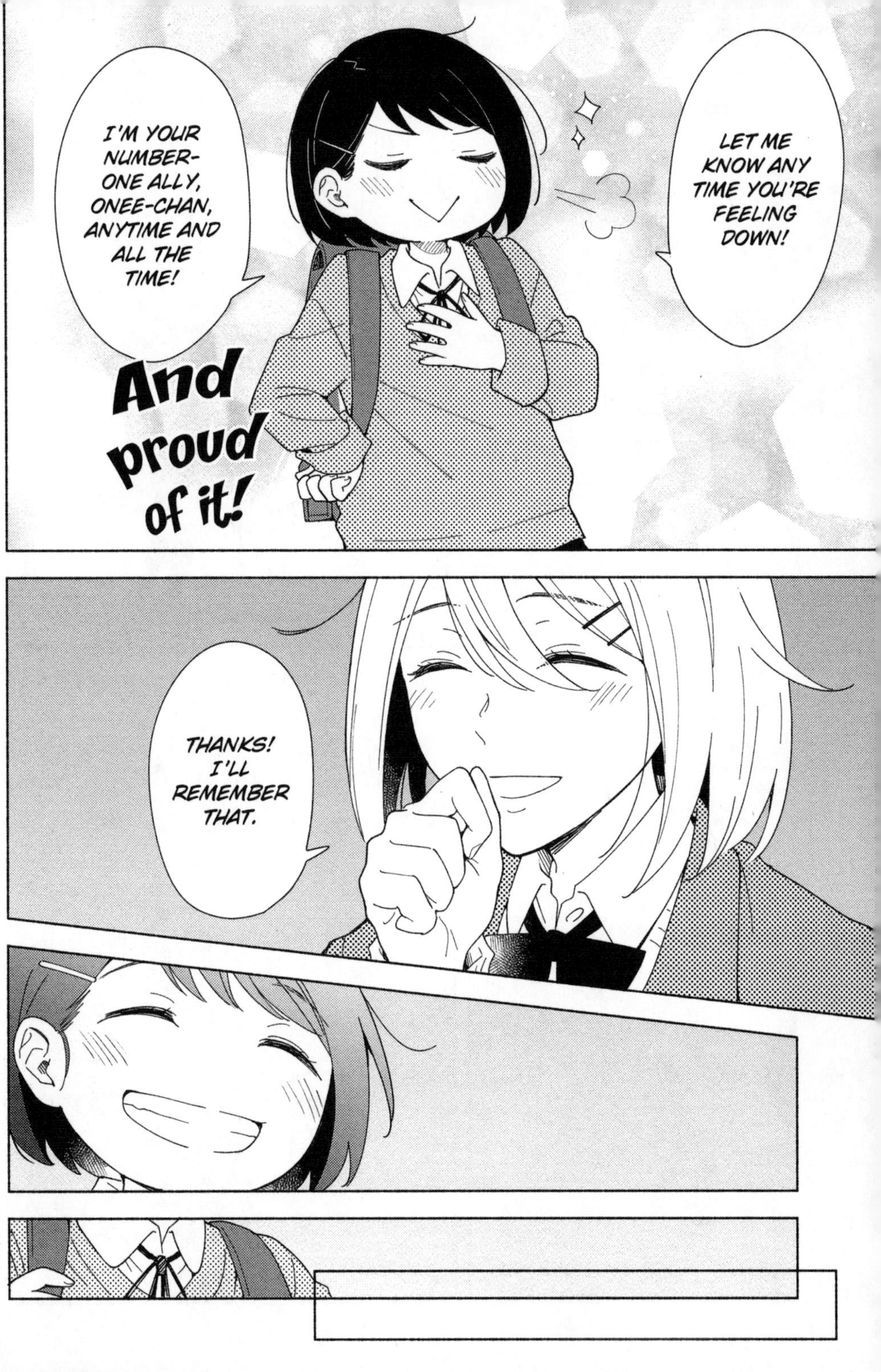
LET ME KNOW ANY TIME YOU'RE FEELING DOWN!
I'M YOUR NUMBER-ONE ALLY, ONEE-CHAN, ANYTIME AND ALL THE TIME!
And proud of it!
THANKS! I'LL REMEMBER THAT.

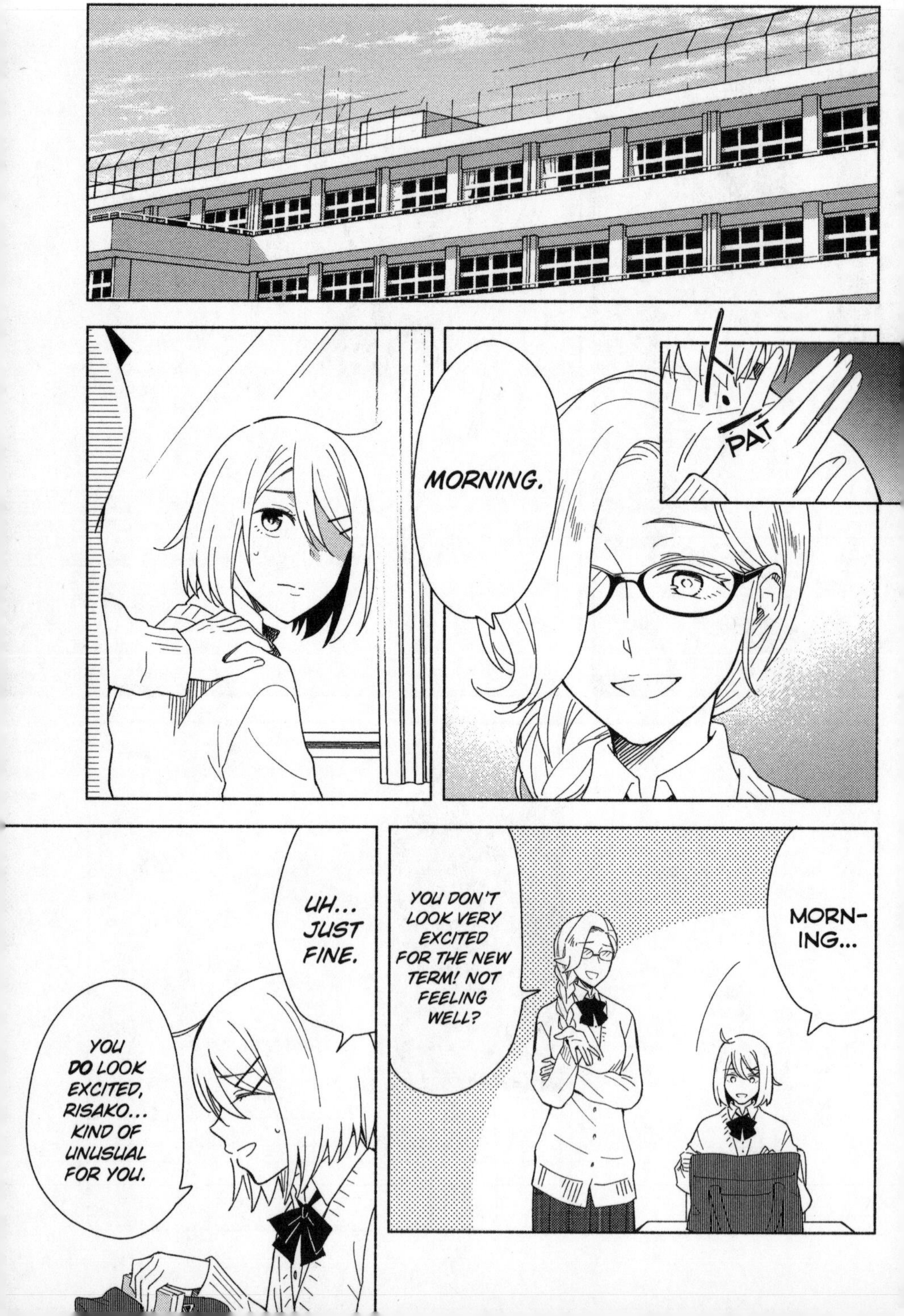
PAT
MORNING.
MORN-ING...
YOU DON'T LOOK VERY EXCITED FOR THE NEW TERM! NOT FEELING WELL?
UH... JUST FINE.
YOU DO LOOK EXCITED, RISAKO... KIND OF UNUSUAL FOR YOU.

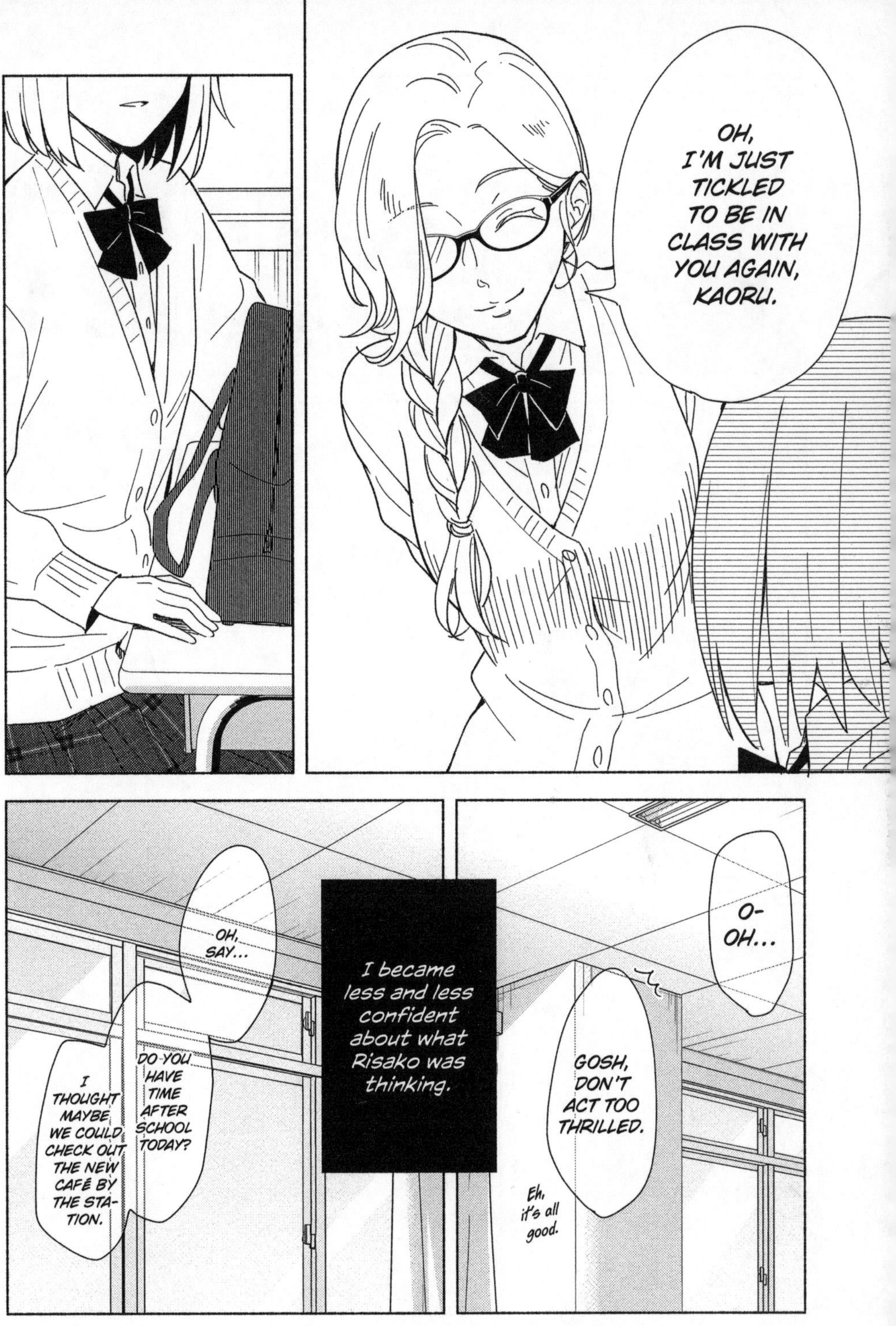
OH, I'M JUST TICKLED TO BE IN CLASS WITH YOU AGAIN, KAORU.
O-OH...
GOSH, DON'T ACT TOO THRILLED.
Eh, it's all good.
I became less and less confident about what Risako was thinking.
OH, SAY...
DO YOU HAVE TIME AFTER SCHOOL TODAY?
I THOUGHT MAYBE WE COULD CHECK OUT THE NEW CAFÉ BY THE STATION.

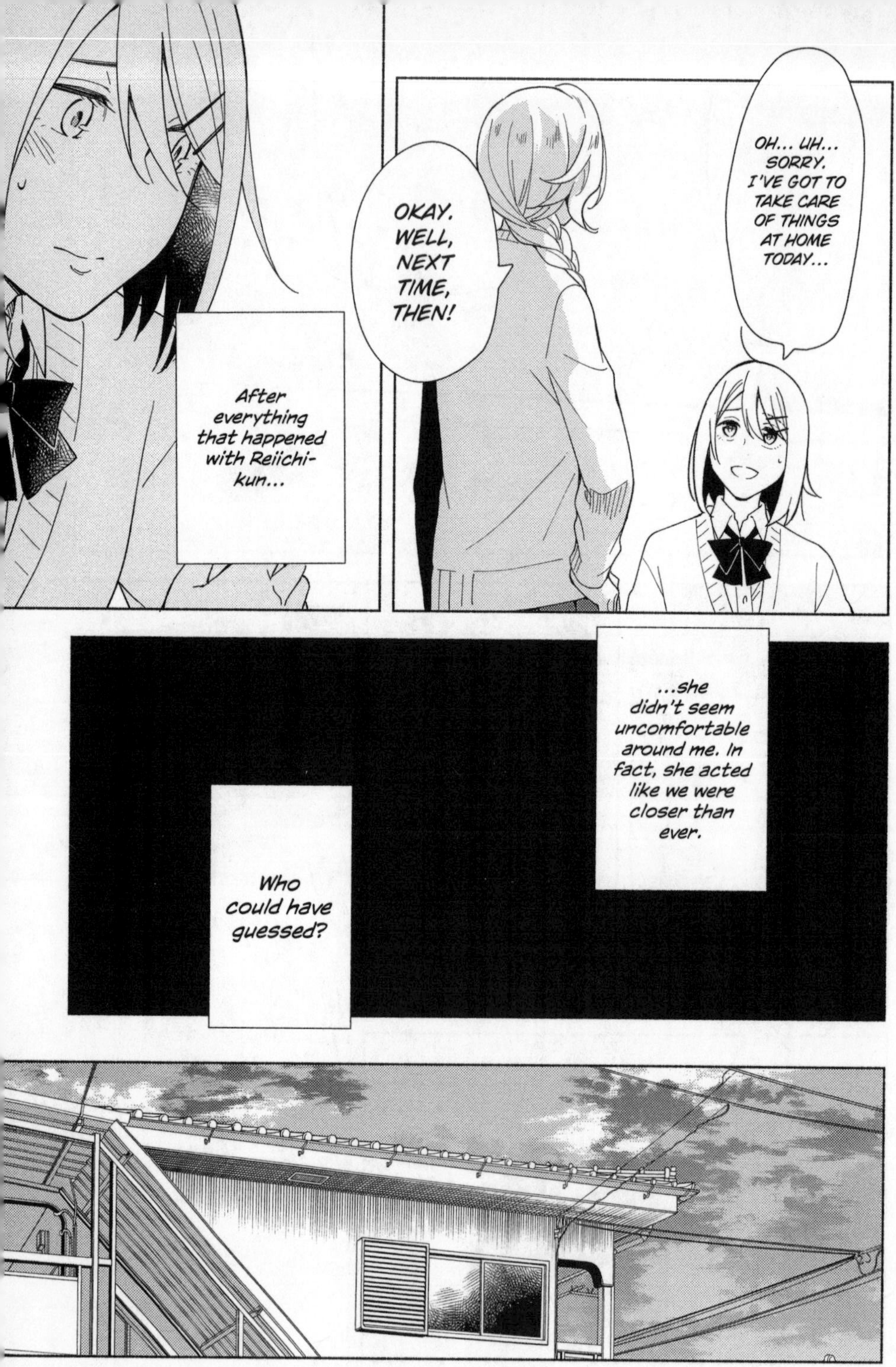
OH... UH... SORRY. I'VE GOT TO TAKE CARE OF THINGS AT HOME TODAY...
OKAY. WELL, NEXT TIME, THEN!
After everything that happened with Reiichi-kun...
...she didn't seem uncomfortable around me. In fact, she acted like we were closer than ever.
Who could have guessed?

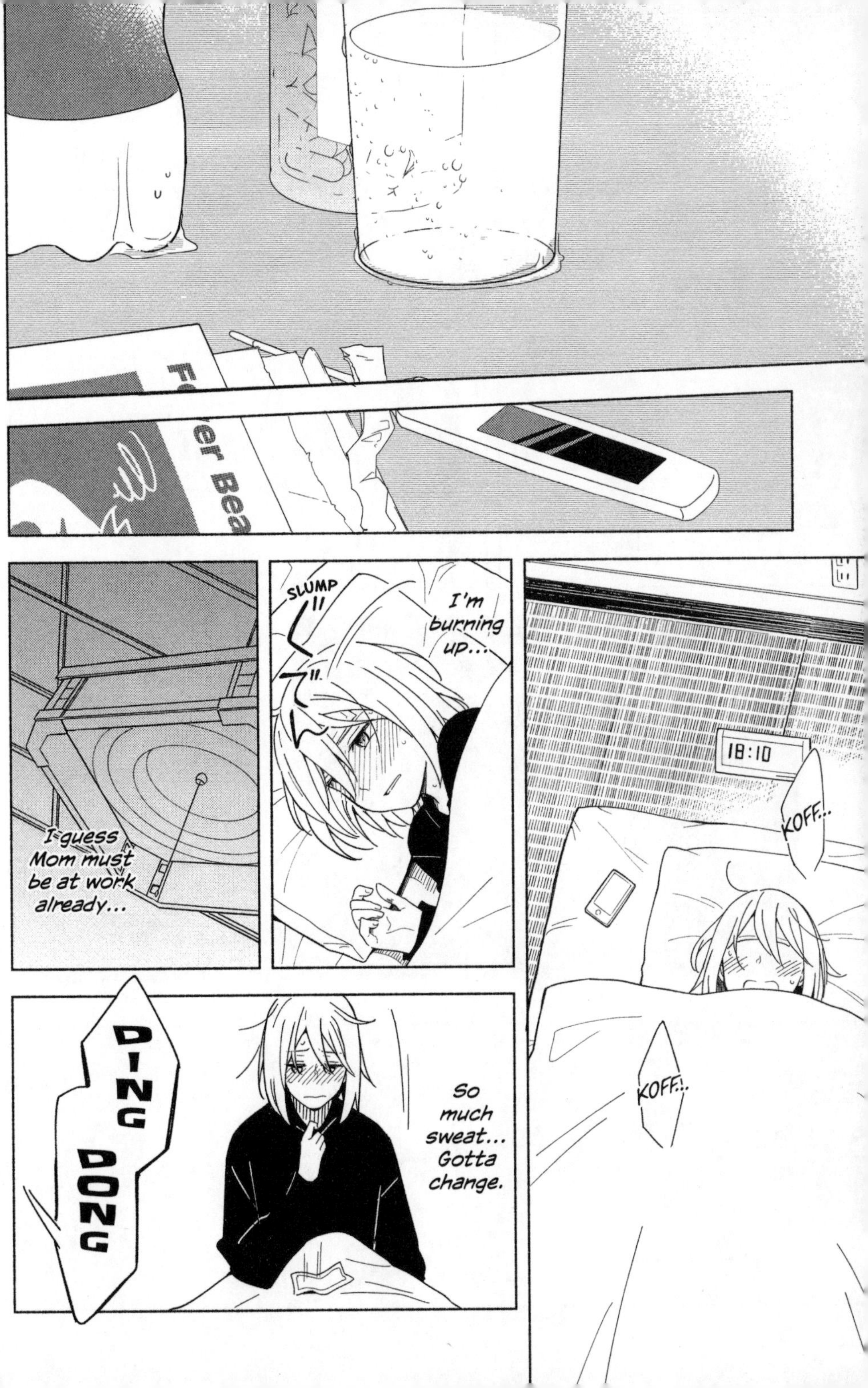
18:10
KOFF...
KOFF...
SLUMP
I'm burning up...
I guess Mom must be at work already...
So much sweat... Gotta change.
DING DONG

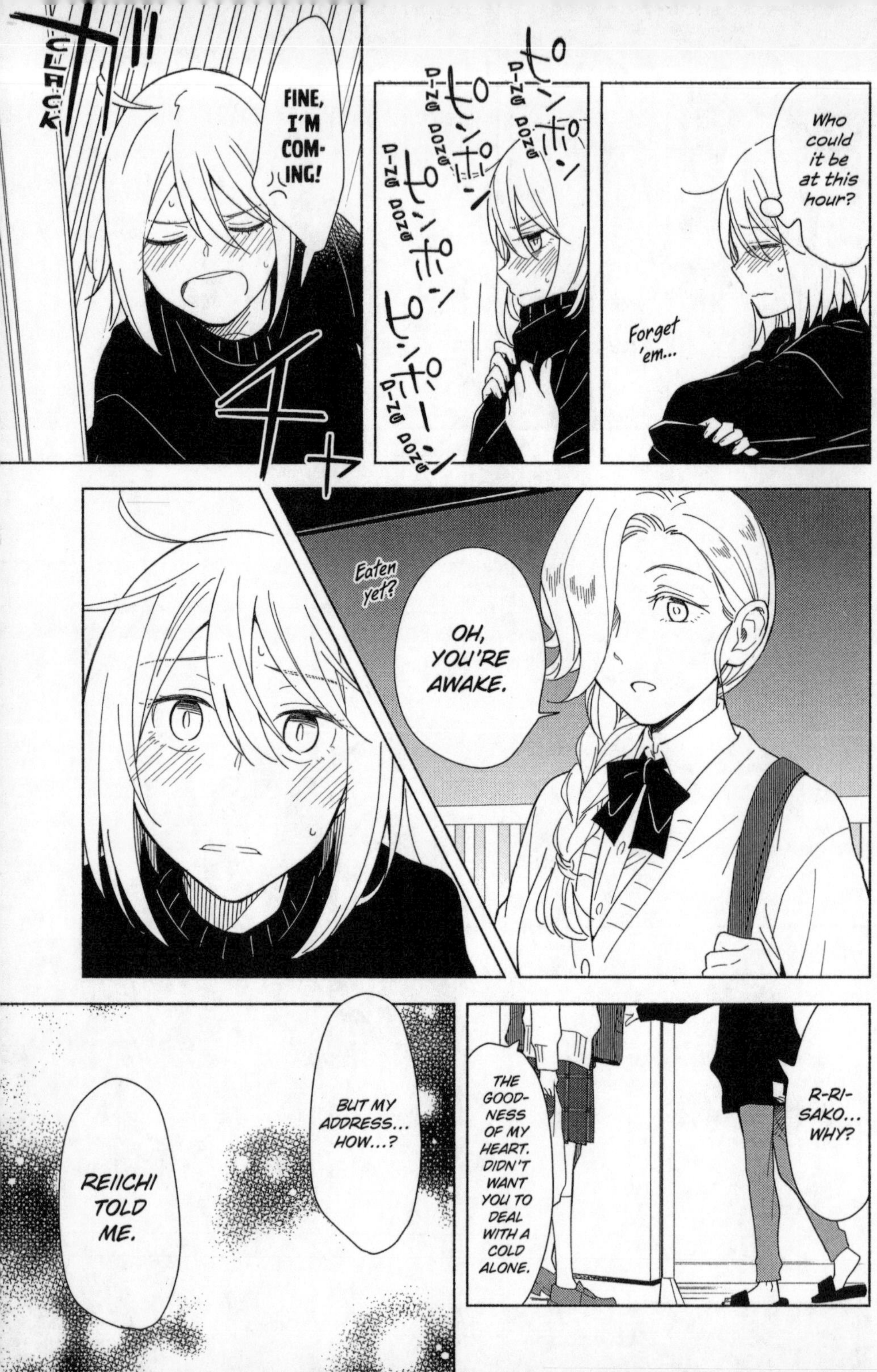
Who could it be at this hour?
Forget 'em...
DING DONG
DING DONG
DING DONG
DING DONG
FINE, I'M COMING!
CLACK
Eaten yet?
OH, YOU'RE AWAKE.
R-RI-SAKO... WHY?
THE GOODNESS OF MY HEART. DIDN'T WANT YOU TO DEAL WITH A COLD ALONE.
BUT MY ADDRESS... HOW...?
REIICHI TOLD ME.

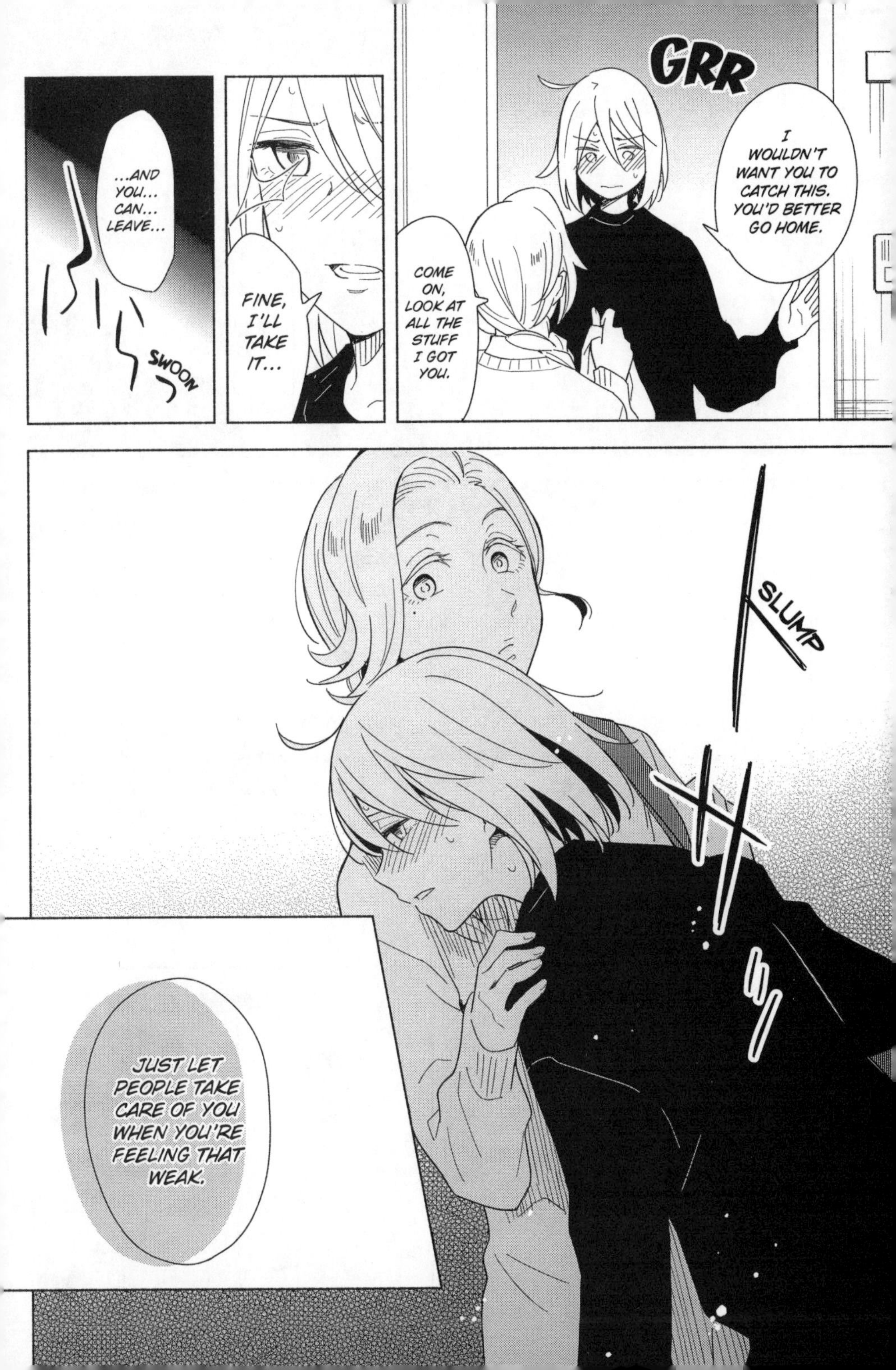
GRR
I WOULDN'T WANT YOU TO CATCH THIS. YOU'D BETTER GO HOME.
COME ON, LOOK AT ALL THE STUFF I GOT YOU.
FINE, I'LL TAKE IT...
...AND YOU... CAN... LEAVE...
SWOON
SLUMP
JUST LET PEOPLE TAKE CARE OF YOU WHEN YOU'RE FEELING THAT WEAK.

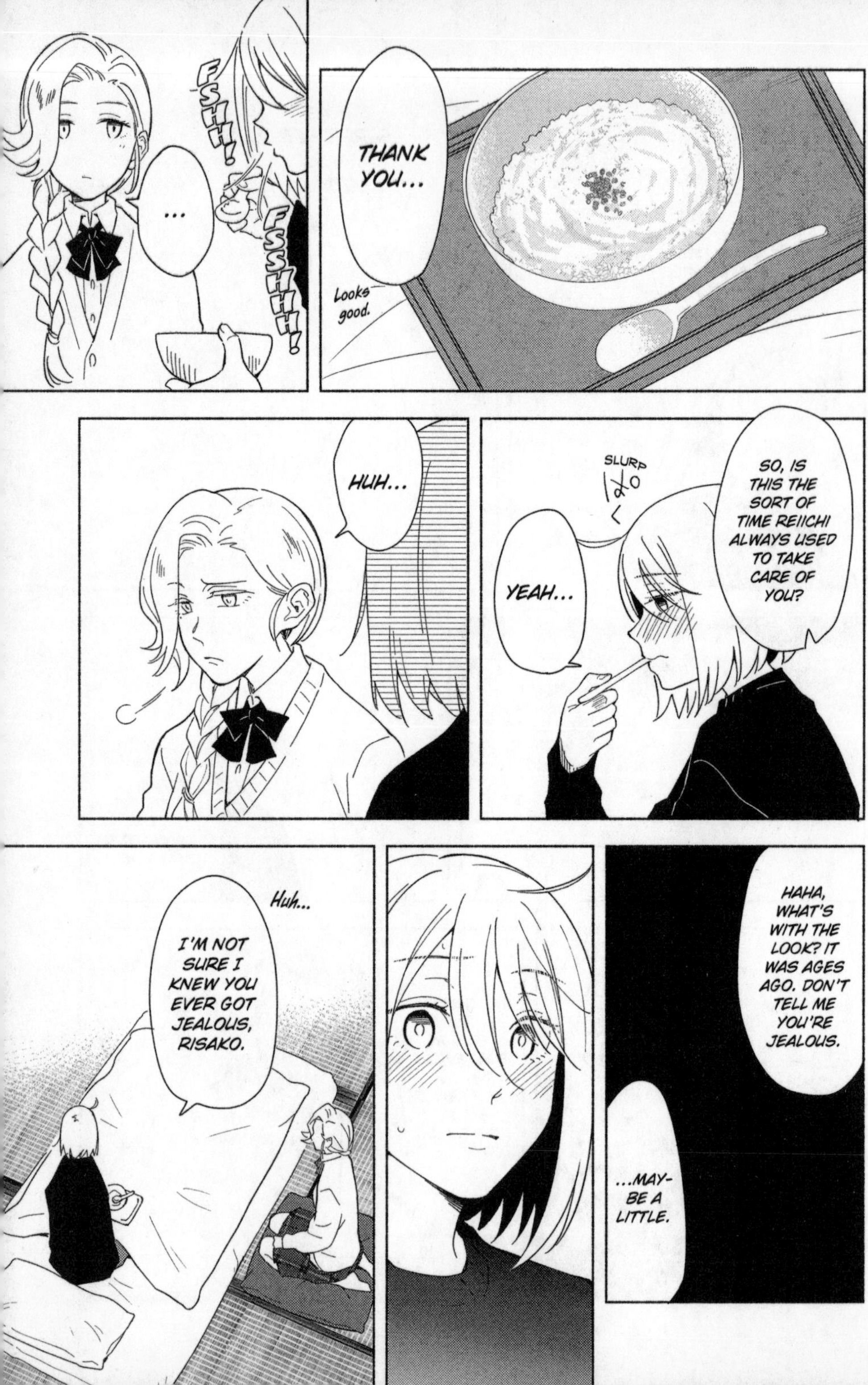
THANK YOU...
Looks good.
FSHH!
FSSHHH!
...
SO, IS THIS THE SORT OF TIME REIICHI ALWAYS USED TO TAKE CARE OF YOU?
SLURP
YEAH...
HUH...
HAHA, WHAT'S WITH THE LOOK? IT WAS AGES AGO. DON'T TELL ME YOU'RE JEALOUS.
...MAY-BE A LITTLE.
Huh...
I'M NOT SURE I KNEW YOU EVER GOT JEALOUS, RISAKO.

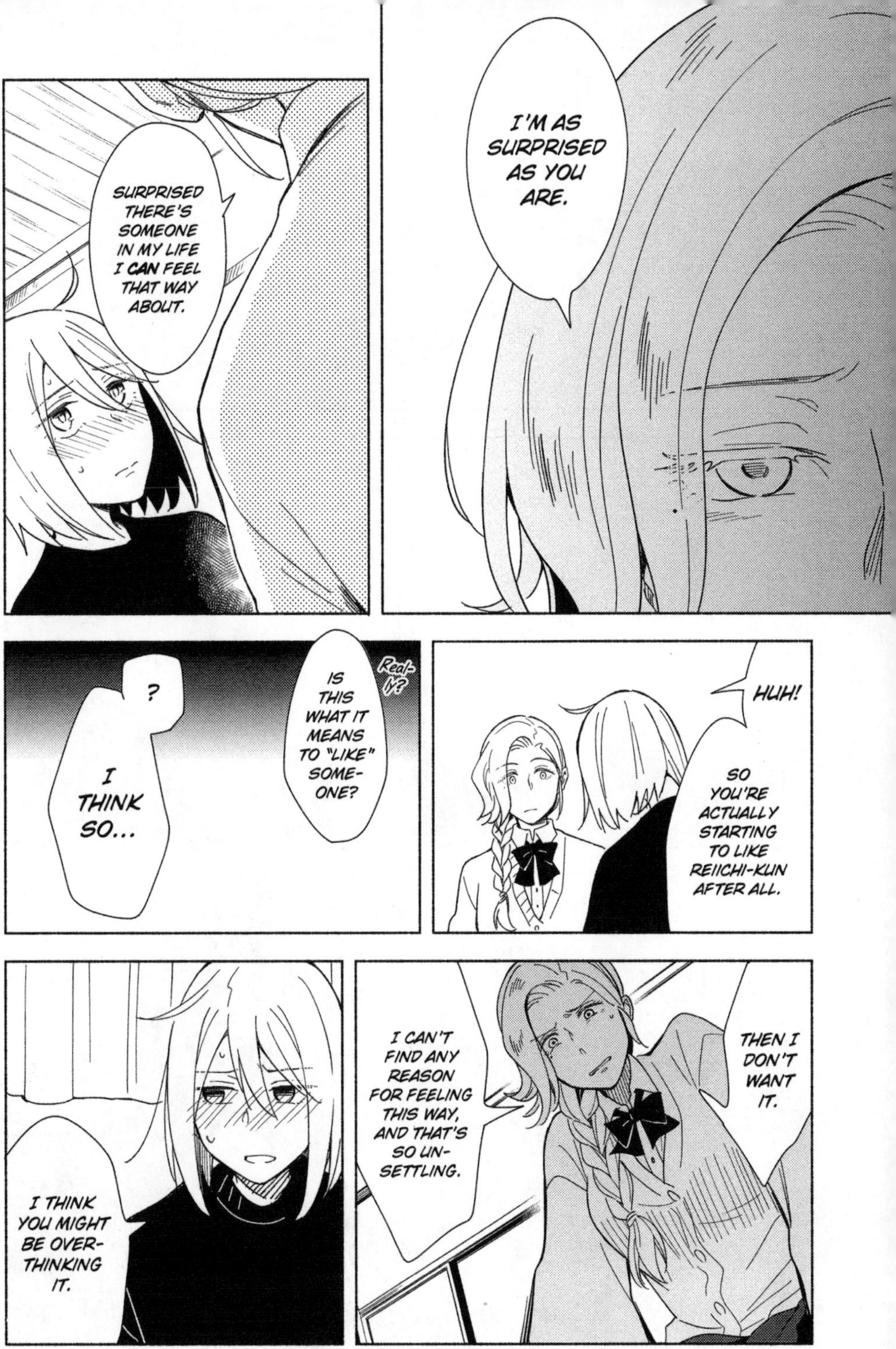
I'M AS SURPRISED AS YOU ARE.
SURPRISED THERE'S SOMEONE IN MY LIFE I CAN FEEL THAT WAY ABOUT.
HUH!
SO YOU'RE ACTUALLY STARTING TO LIKE REIICHI-KUN AFTER ALL.
Real-ly?
IS THIS WHAT IT MEANS TO "LIKE" SOME-ONE?
?
I THINK SO...
THEN I DON'T WANT IT.
I CAN'T FIND ANY REASON FOR FEELING THIS WAY, AND THAT'S SO UN-SETTLING.
I THINK YOU MIGHT BE OVER-THINKING IT.

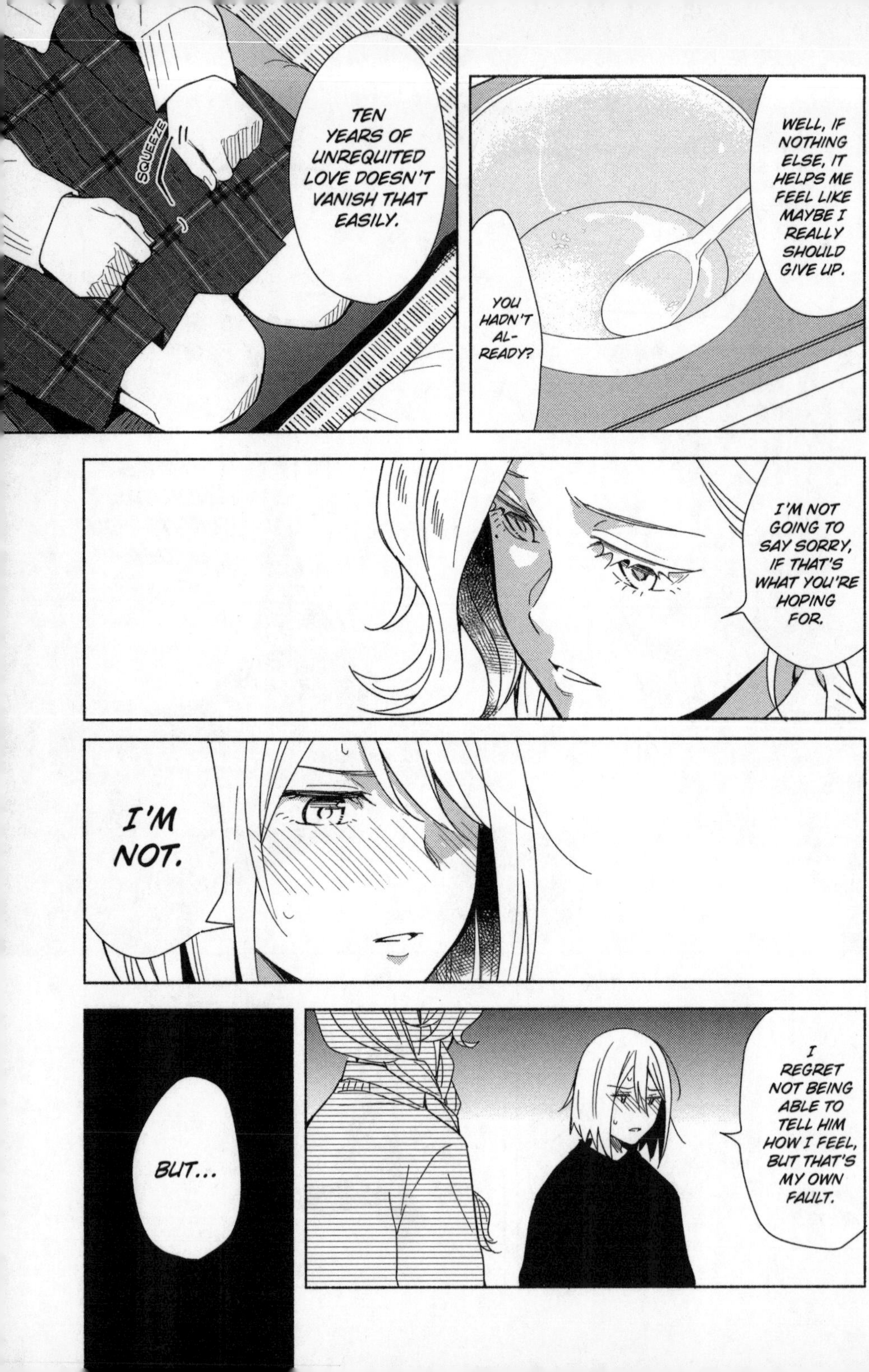
WELL, IF NOTHING ELSE, IT HELPS ME FEEL LIKE MAYBE I REALLY SHOULD GIVE UP.
YOU HADN'T AL-READY?
TEN YEARS OF UNREQUITED LOVE DOESN'T VANISH THAT EASILY.
SQUEEZE
I'M NOT GOING TO SAY SORRY, IF THAT'S WHAT YOU'RE HOPING FOR.
I'M NOT.
I REGRET NOT BEING ABLE TO TELL HIM HOW I FEEL, BUT THAT'S MY OWN FAULT.
BUT...

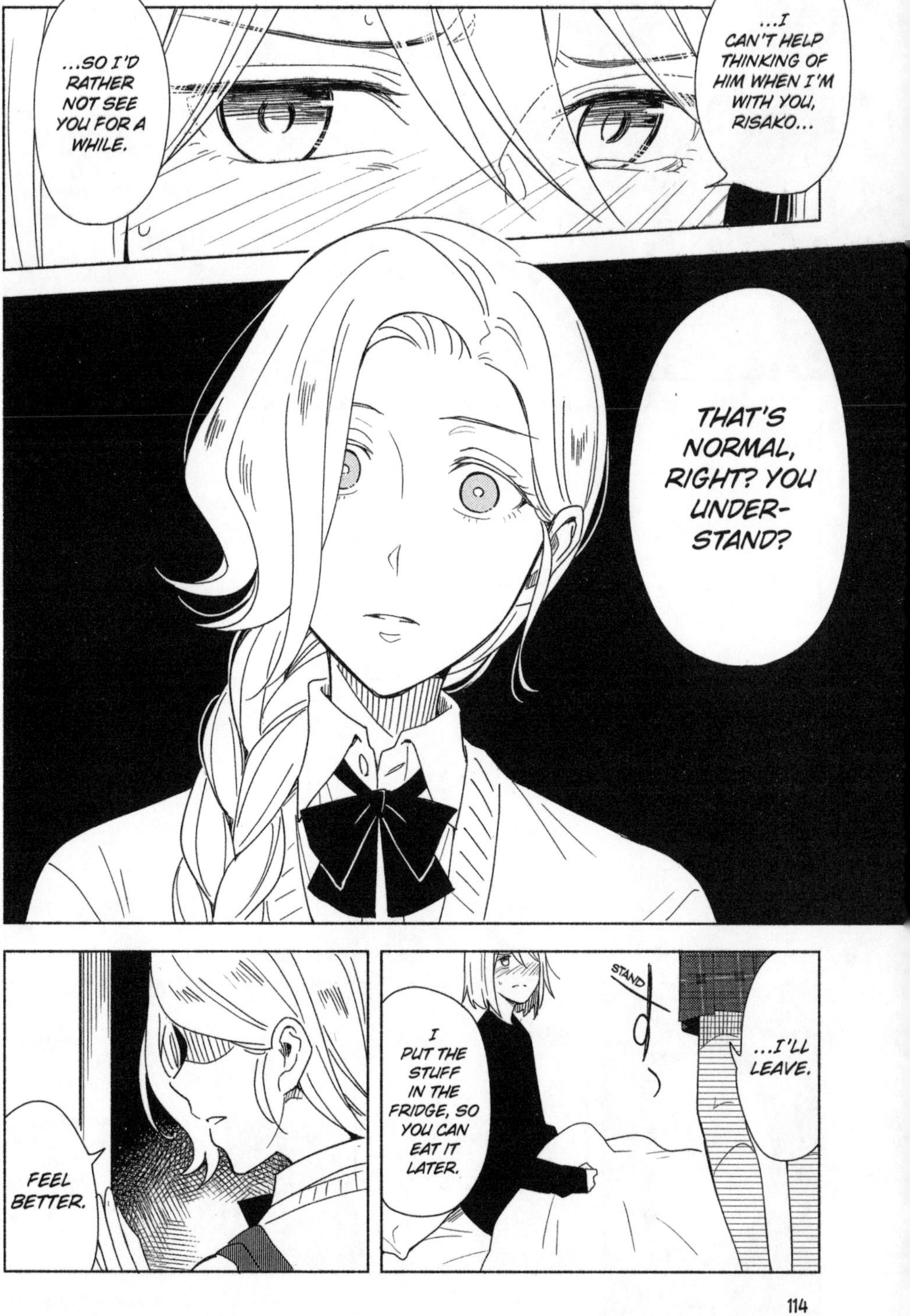
...I CAN'T HELP THINKING OF HIM WHEN I'M WITH YOU, RISAKO...
...SO I'D RATHER NOT SEE YOU FOR A WHILE.
THAT'S NORMAL, RIGHT? YOU UNDER-STAND?
STAND
...I'LL LEAVE.
I PUT THE STUFF IN THE FRIDGE, SO YOU CAN EAT IT LATER.
FEEL BETTER.

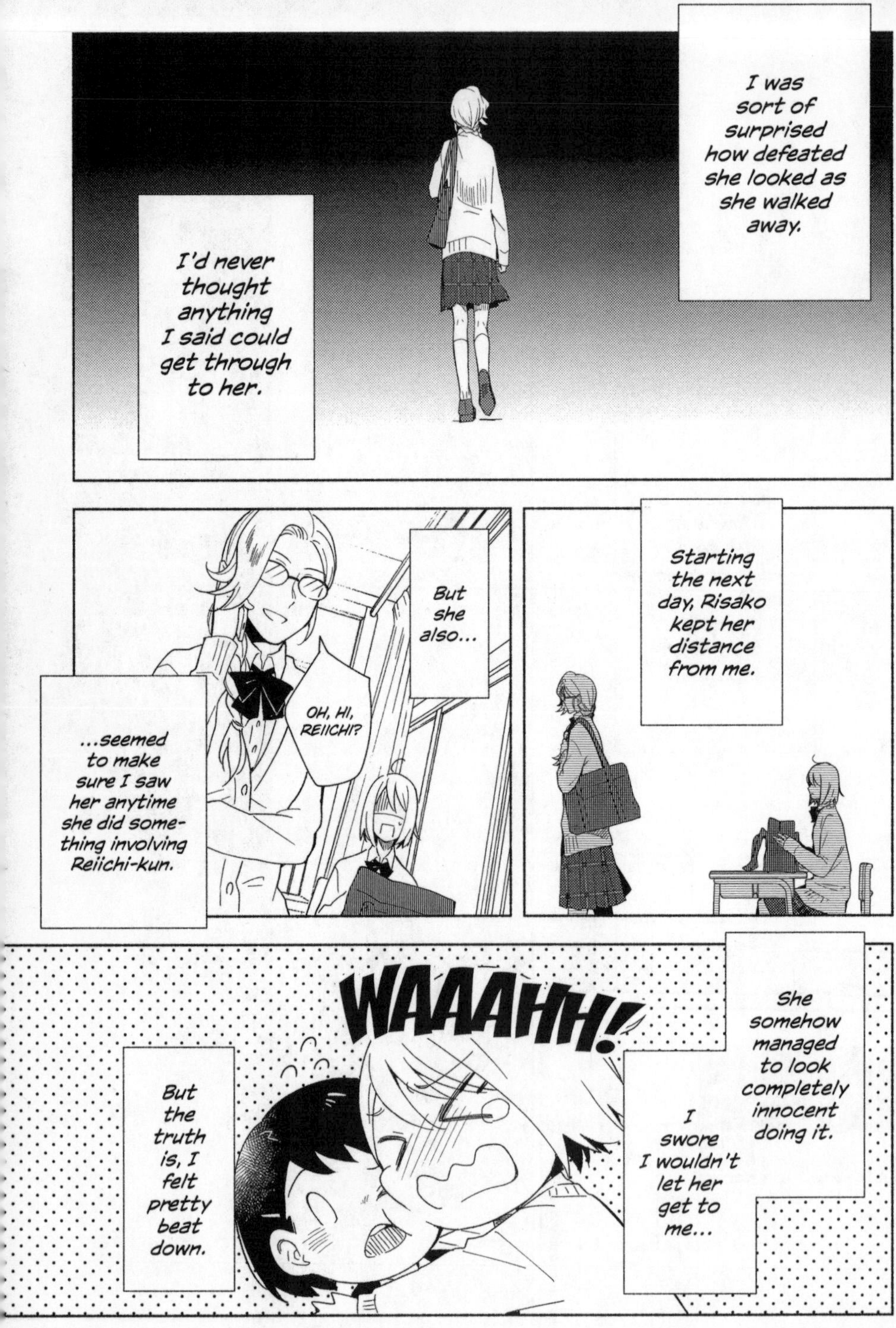
I was sort of surprised how defeated she looked as she walked away.
I'd never thought anything I said could get through to her.
Starting the next day, Risako kept her distance from me.
But she also...
OH, HI, REIICHI?
...seemed to make sure I saw her anytime she did something involving Reiichi-kun.
She somehow managed to look completely innocent doing it.
WAAAHH!
I swore I wouldn't let her get to me...
But the truth is, I felt pretty beat down.

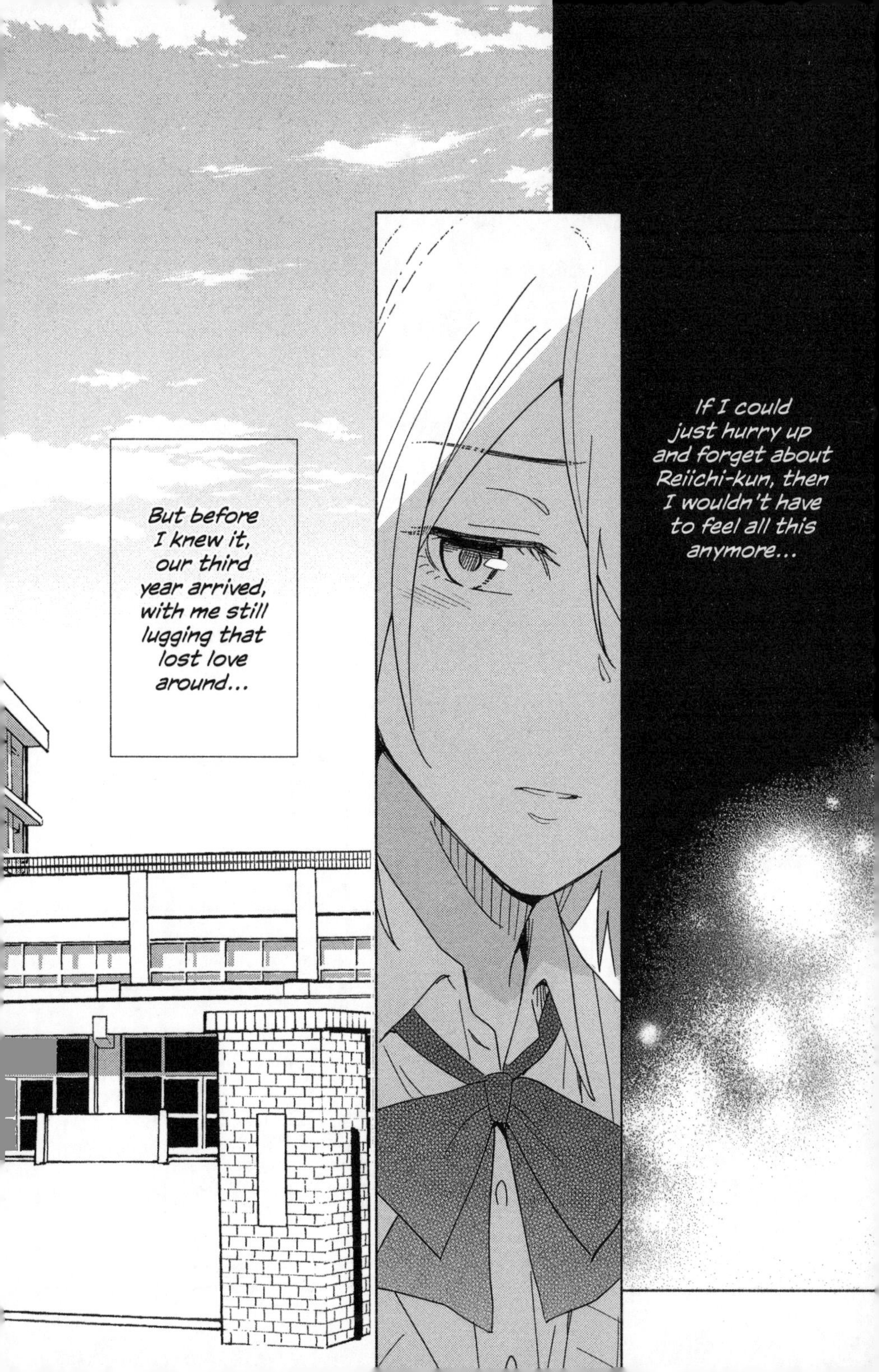
If I could just hurry up and forget about Reiichi-kun, then I wouldn't have to feel all this anymore...
But before I knew it, our third year arrived, with me still lugging that lost love around...

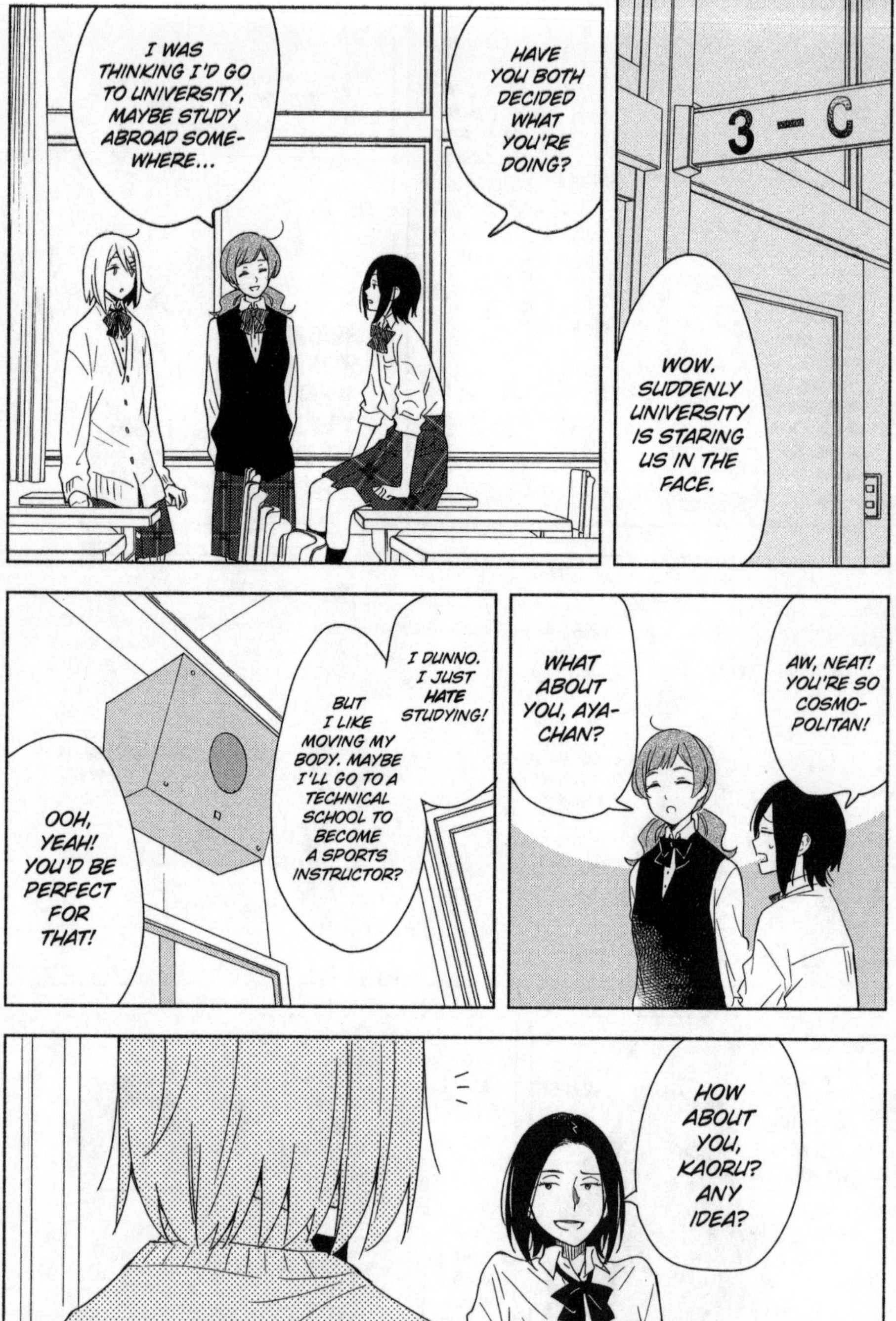
3 – C
WOW. SUDDENLY UNIVERSITY IS STARING US IN THE FACE.
HAVE YOU BOTH DECIDED WHAT YOU'RE DOING?
I WAS THINKING I'D GO TO UNIVERSITY, MAYBE STUDY ABROAD SOME-WHERE...
AW, NEAT! YOU'RE SO COSMO-POLITAN!
WHAT ABOUT YOU, AYA-CHAN?
I DUNNO. I JUST HATE STUDYING!
BUT I LIKE MOVING MY BODY. MAYBE I'LL GO TO A TECHNICAL SCHOOL TO BECOME A SPORTS INSTRUCTOR?
OOH, YEAH! YOU'D BE PERFECT FOR THAT!
HOW ABOUT YOU, KAORU? ANY IDEA?

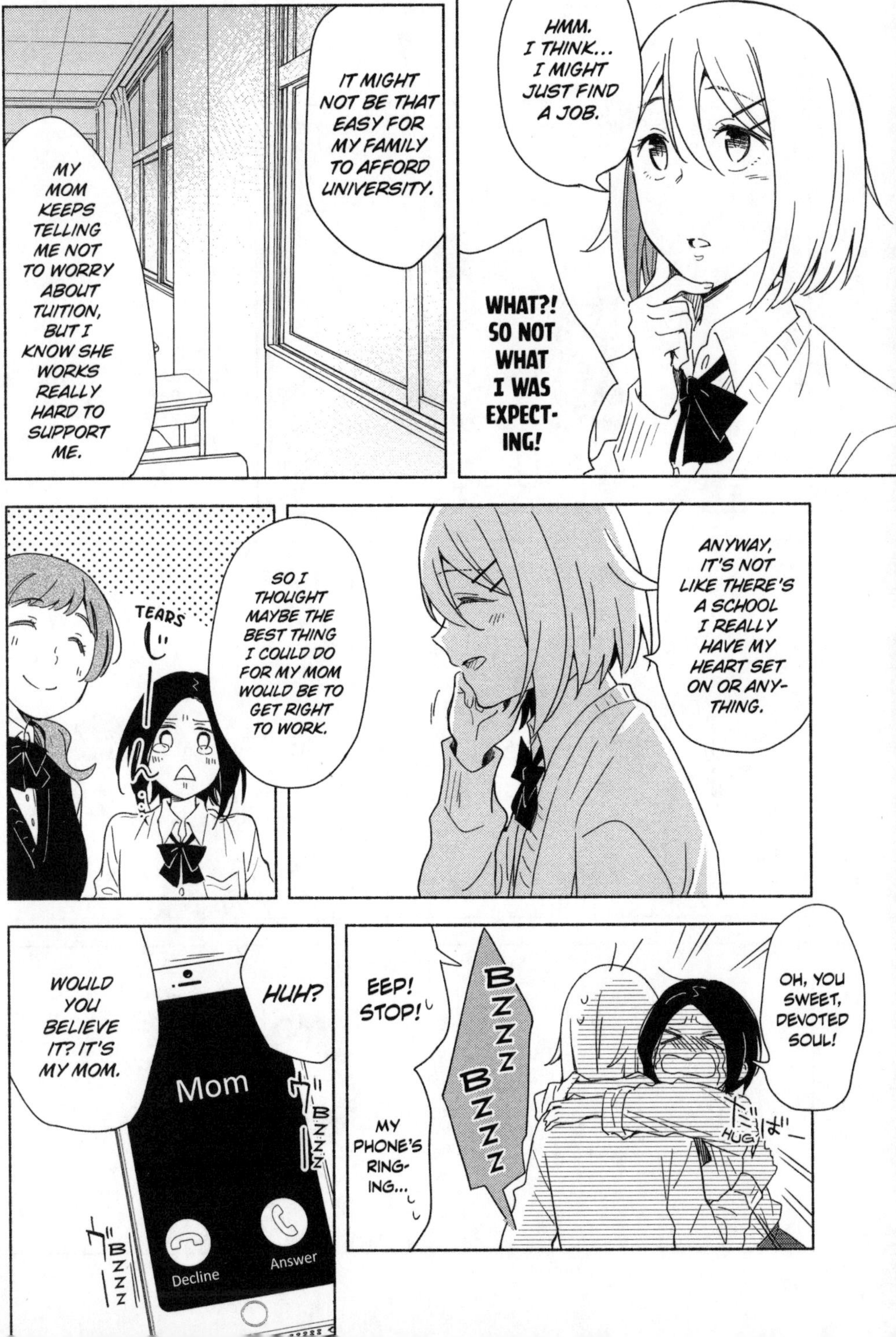
HMM. I THINK... I MIGHT JUST FIND A JOB.
WHAT?! SO NOT WHAT I WAS EXPECTING!
IT MIGHT NOT BE THAT EASY FOR MY FAMILY TO AFFORD UNIVERSITY.
MY MOM KEEPS TELLING ME NOT TO WORRY ABOUT TUITION, BUT I KNOW SHE WORKS REALLY HARD TO SUPPORT ME.
ANYWAY, IT'S NOT LIKE THERE'S A SCHOOL I REALLY HAVE MY HEART SET ON OR ANYTHING.
SO I THOUGHT MAYBE THE BEST THING I COULD DO FOR MY MOM WOULD BE TO GET RIGHT TO WORK.
TEARS
OH, YOU SWEET, DEVOTED SOUL!
HUG
BZZZ BZZZ
EEP! STOP!
MY PHONE'S RINGING...
HUH?
WOULD YOU BELIEVE IT? IT'S MY MOM.
Mom
BZZZ
Decline
Answer
BZZZ

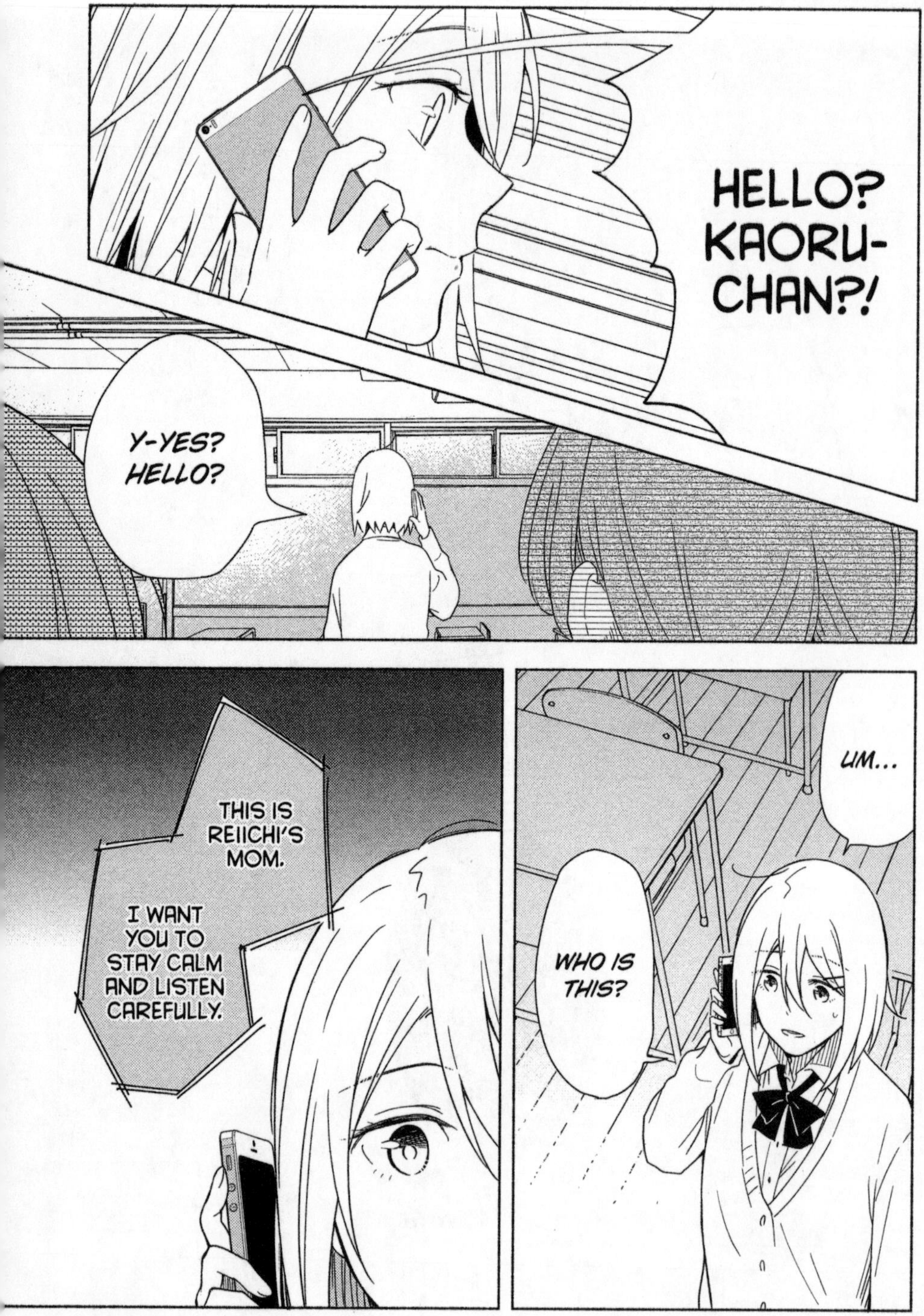
HELLO? KAORU-CHAN?!
Y-YES? HELLO?
UM...
WHO IS THIS?
THIS IS REIICHI'S MOM.
I WANT YOU TO STAY CALM AND LISTEN CAREFULLY.

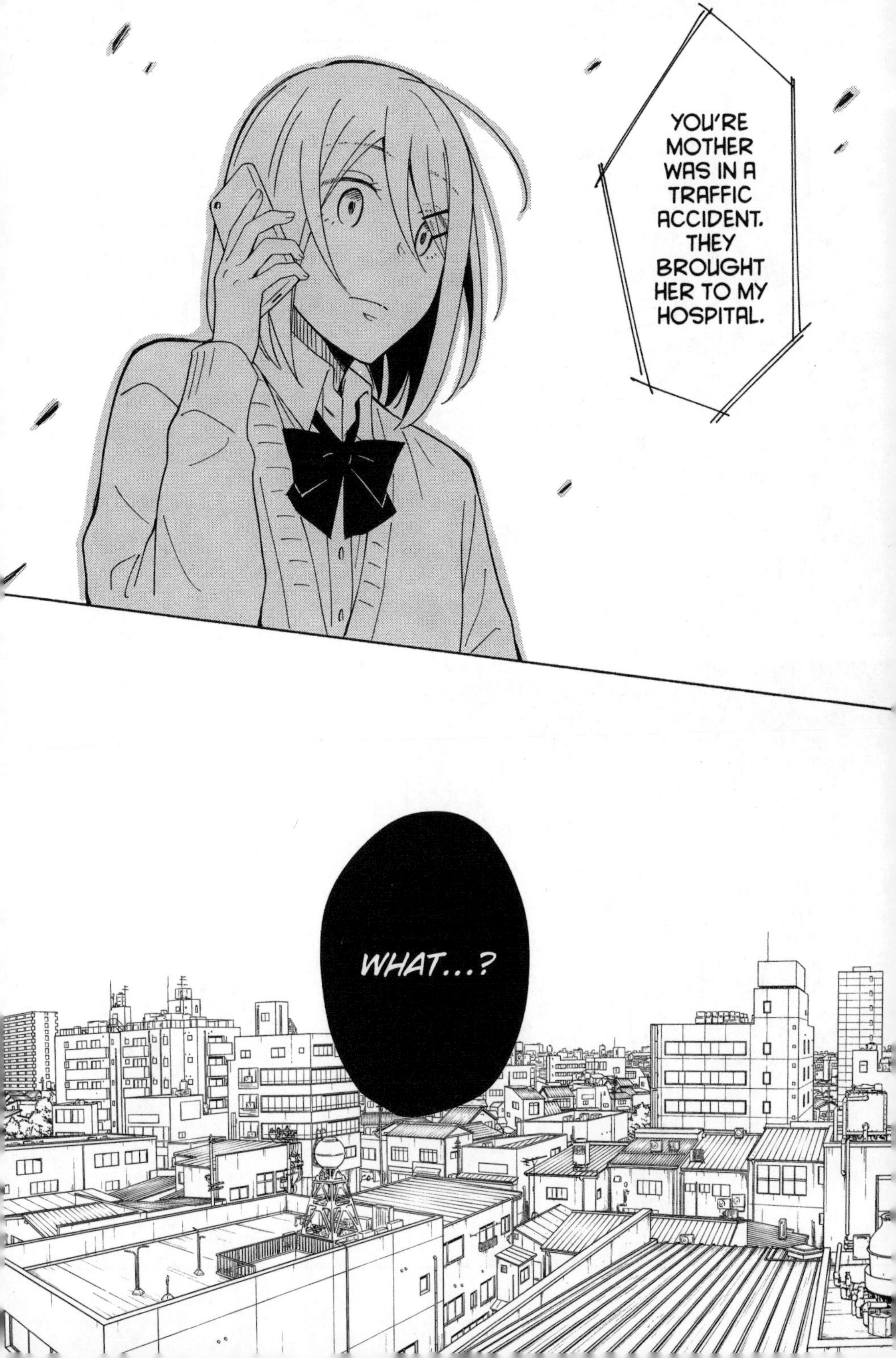
YOU'RE MOTHER WAS IN A TRAFFIC ACCIDENT. THEY BROUGHT HER TO MY HOSPITAL.
WHAT...?

If I Could
Reach You

If I Could
Reach You

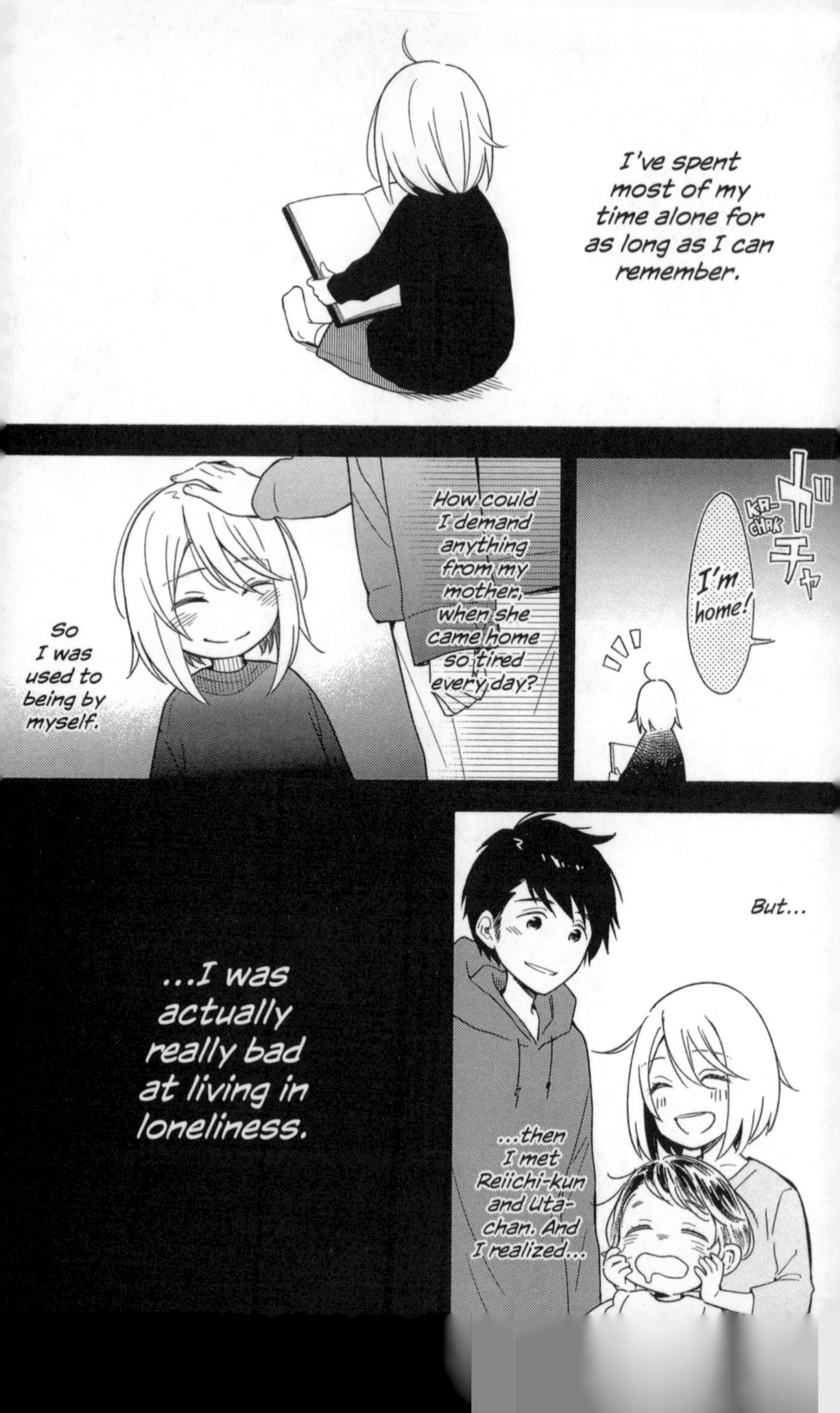
I've spent most of my time alone for as long as I can remember.
ガチャ
KA-CHAK
I'm home!
How could I demand anything from my mother, when she came home so tired every day?
So I was used to being by myself.
But...
...then I met Reiichi-kun and Uta-chan. And I realized...
...I was actually really bad at living in loneliness.

Chapter 30

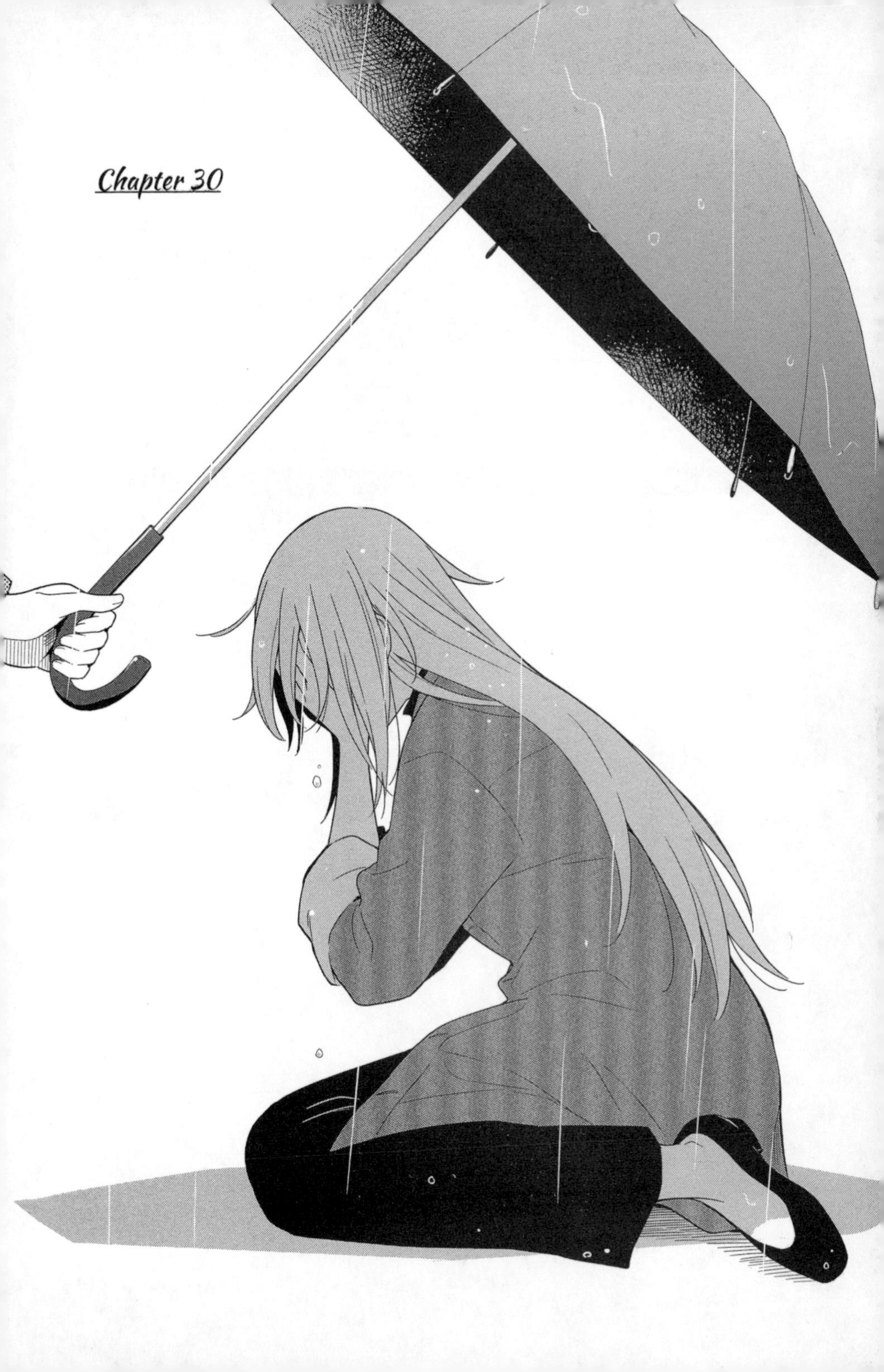

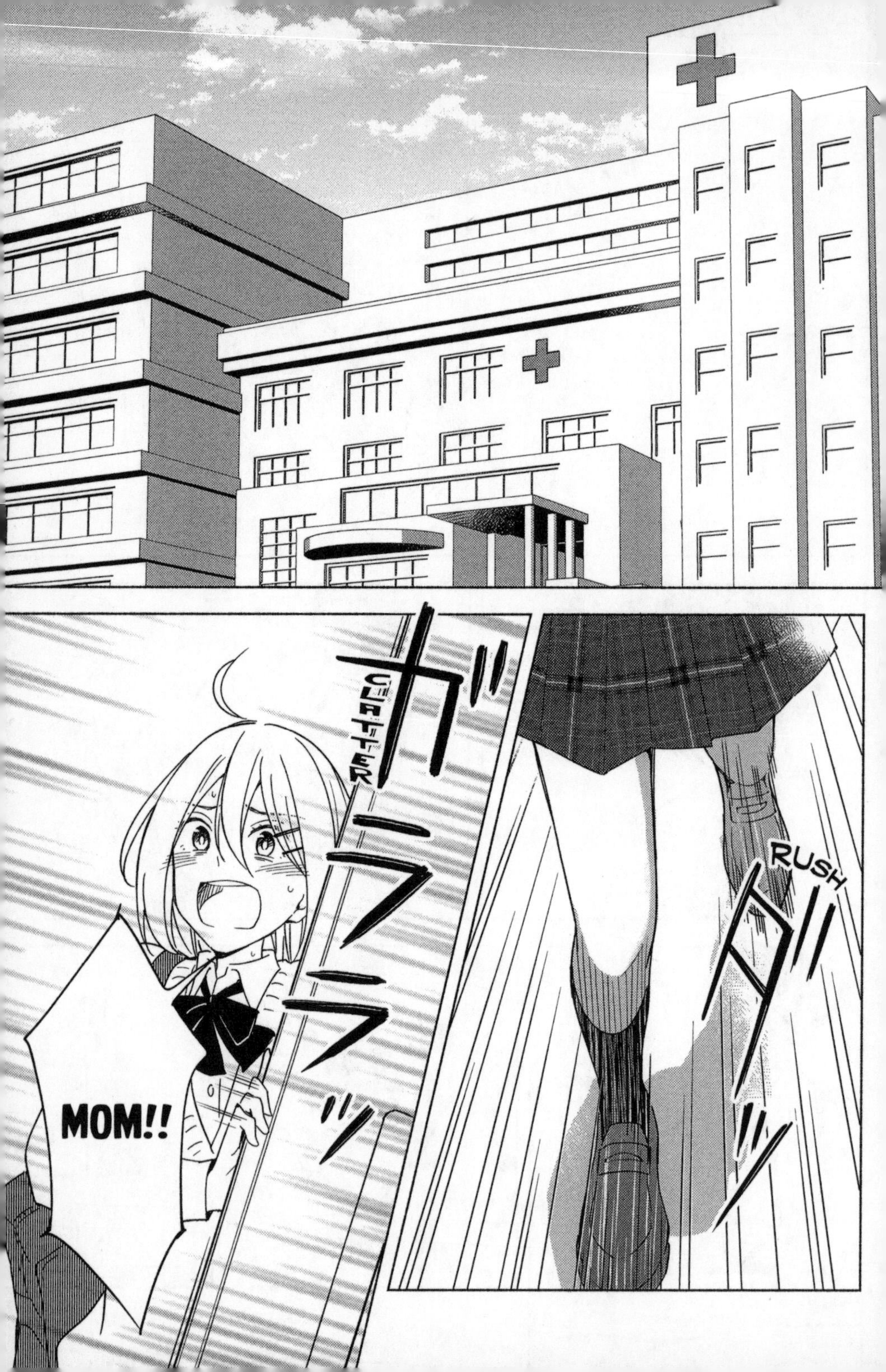
RUSH
CLATTER
MOM!!

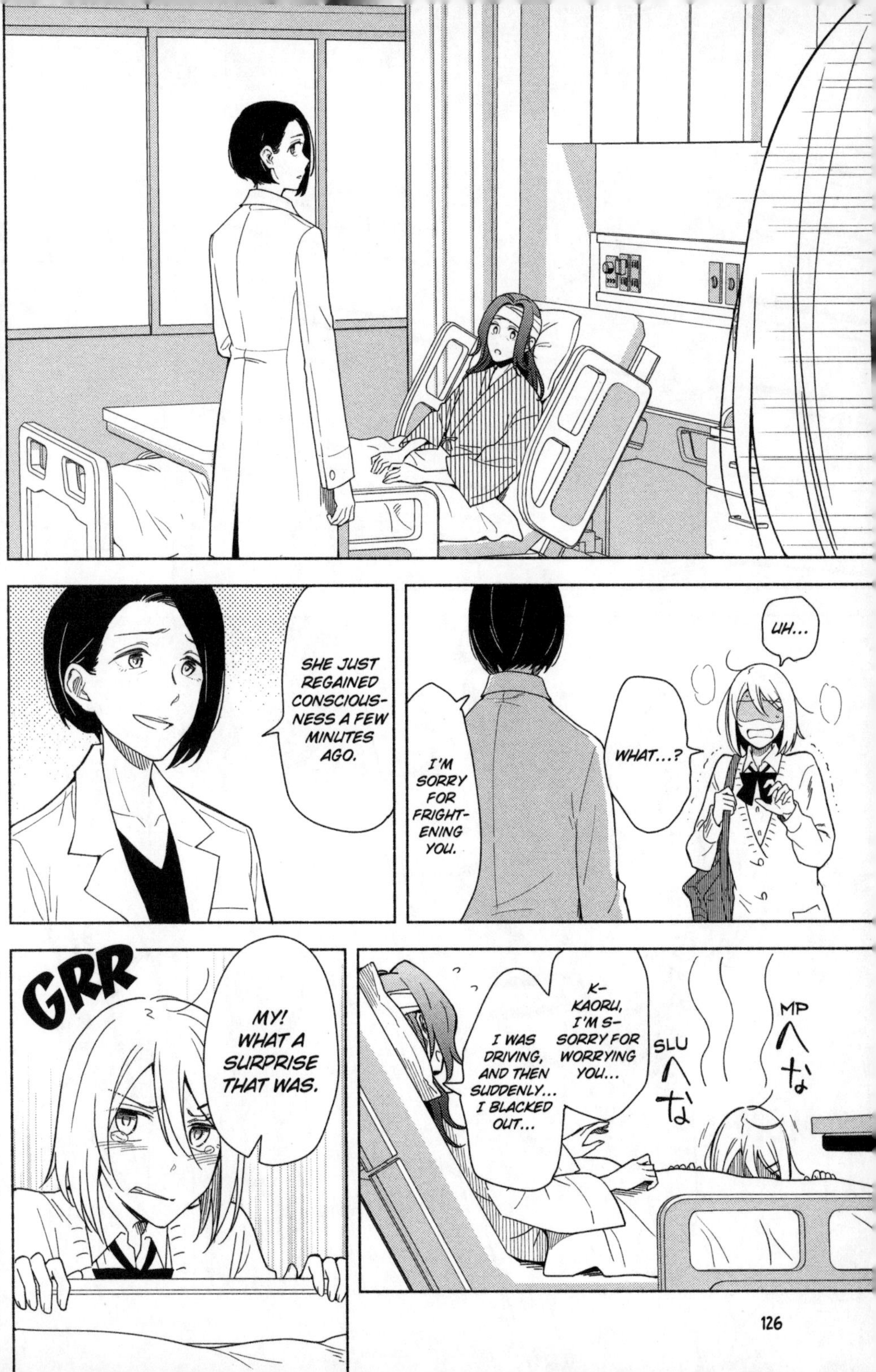
UH...
WHAT...?
I'M SORRY FOR FRIGHT-ENING YOU.
SHE JUST REGAINED CONSCIOUS-NESS A FEW MINUTES AGO.
K-KAORU, I'M S-SORRY FOR WORRYING YOU...
I WAS DRIVING, AND THEN SUDDENLY... I BLACKED OUT...
MP へな
SLU へな
GRR
MY! WHAT A SURPRISE THAT WAS.

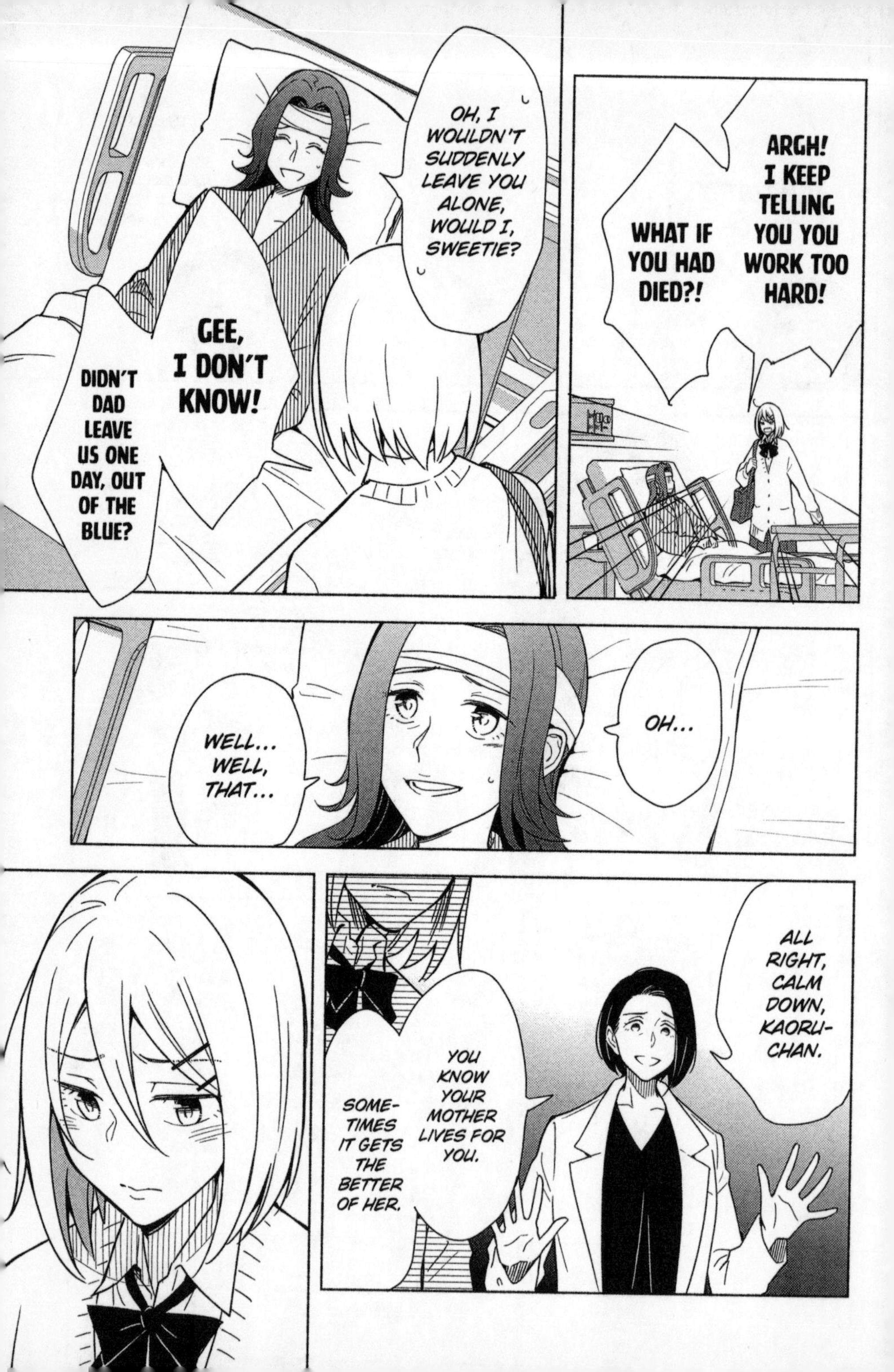
ARGH! I KEEP TELLING YOU YOU WORK TOO HARD!
WHAT IF YOU HAD DIED?!
OH, I WOULDN'T SUDDENLY LEAVE YOU ALONE, WOULD I, SWEETIE?
GEE, I DON'T KNOW!
DIDN'T DAD LEAVE US ONE DAY, OUT OF THE BLUE?
OH...
WELL... WELL, THAT...
ALL RIGHT, CALM DOWN, KAORU-CHAN.
YOU KNOW YOUR MOTHER LIVES FOR YOU.
SOME-TIMES IT GETS THE BETTER OF HER.

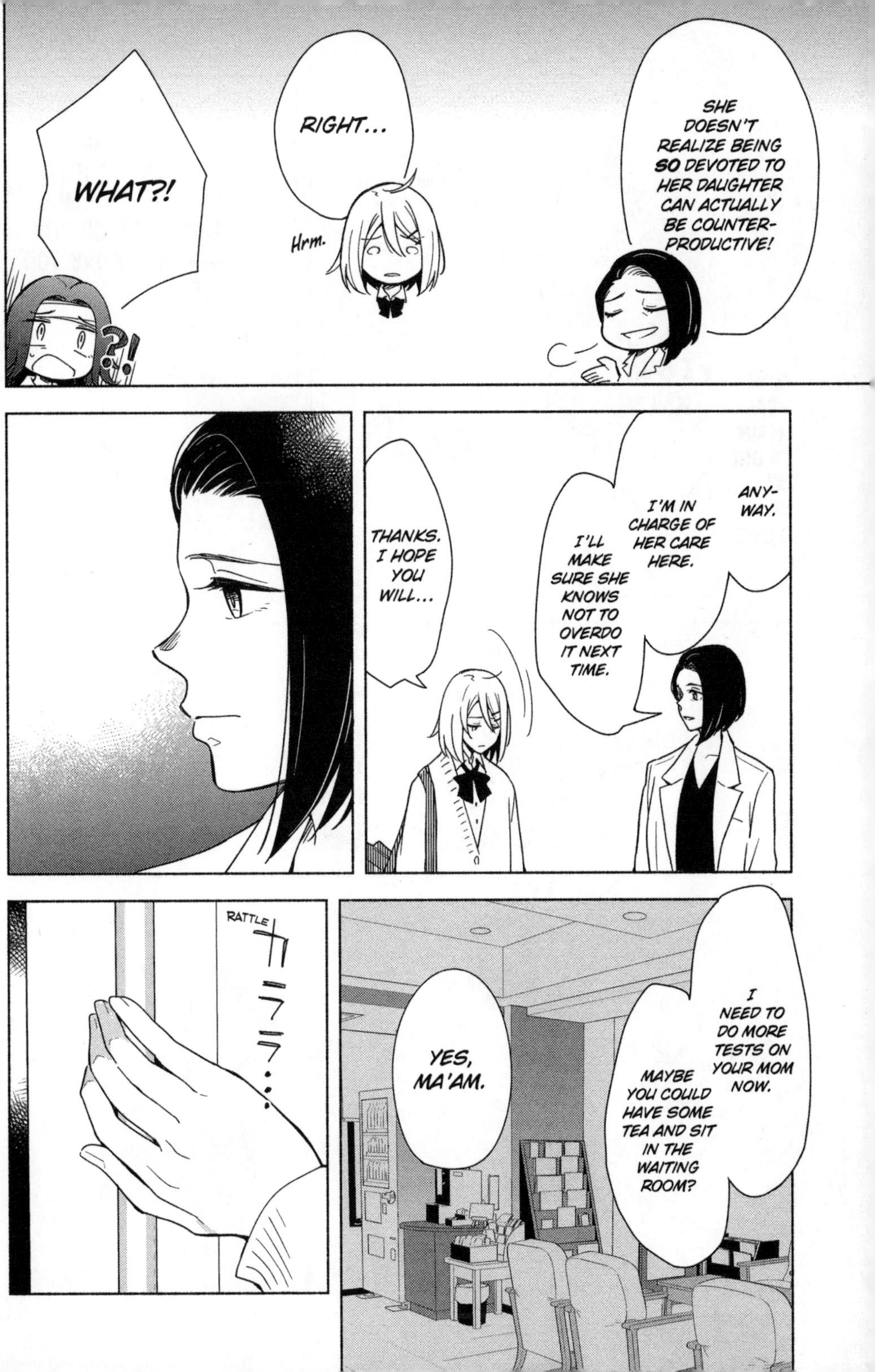
SHE DOESN'T REALIZE BEING SO DEVOTED TO HER DAUGHTER CAN ACTUALLY BE COUNTER-PRODUCTIVE!
RIGHT...
Hrm.
WHAT?!
ANY-WAY.
I'M IN CHARGE OF HER CARE HERE.
I'LL MAKE SURE SHE KNOWS NOT TO OVERDO IT NEXT TIME.
THANKS. I HOPE YOU WILL...
I NEED TO DO MORE TESTS ON YOUR MOM NOW.
MAYBE YOU COULD HAVE SOME TEA AND SIT IN THE WAITING ROOM?
YES, MA'AM.
RATTLE
カラララ...

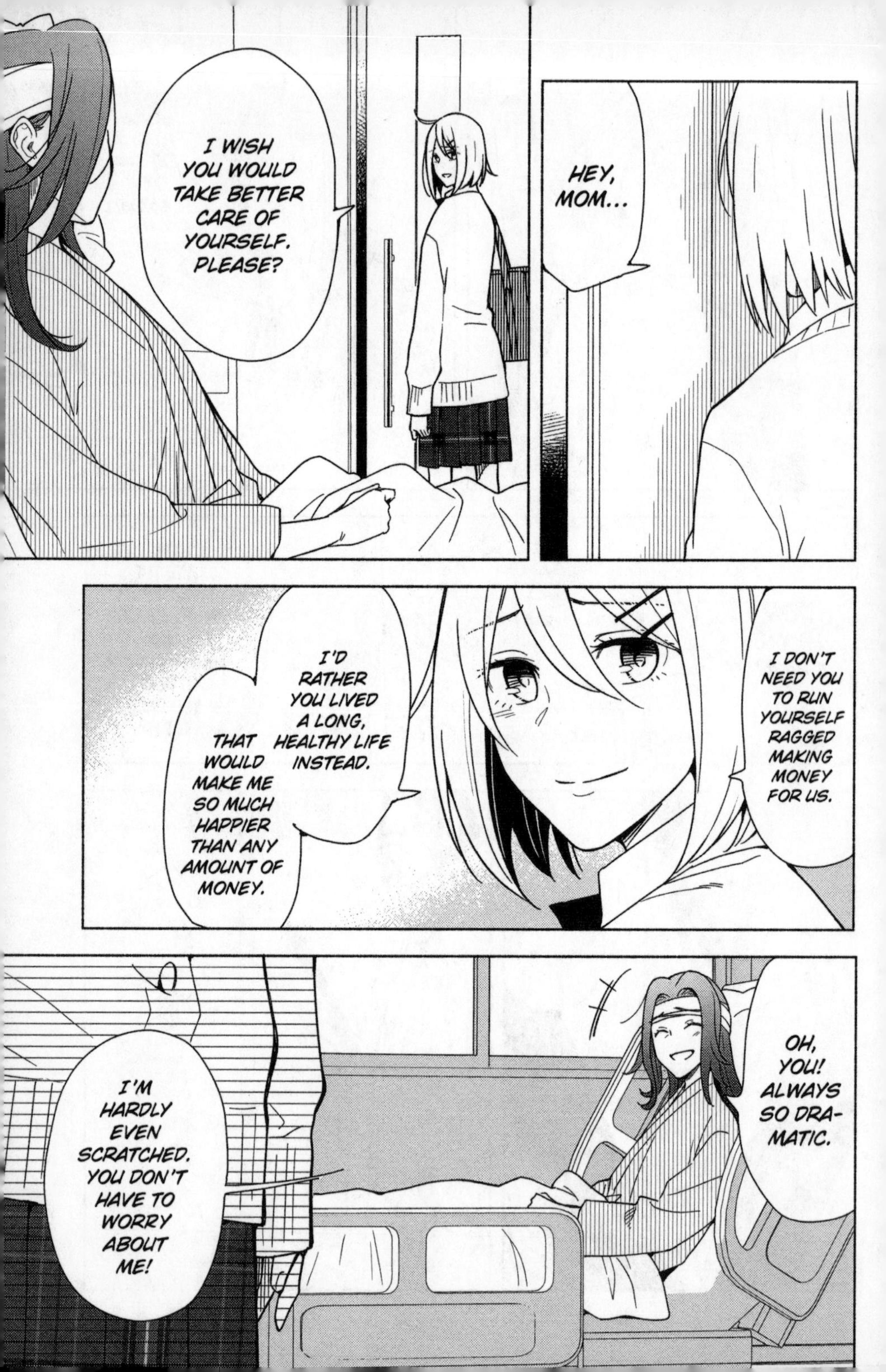
HEY, MOM...
I WISH YOU WOULD TAKE BETTER CARE OF YOURSELF. PLEASE?
I DON'T NEED YOU TO RUN YOURSELF RAGGED MAKING MONEY FOR US.
I'D RATHER YOU LIVED A LONG, HEALTHY LIFE INSTEAD.
THAT WOULD MAKE ME SO MUCH HAPPIER THAN ANY AMOUNT OF MONEY.
OH, YOU! ALWAYS SO DRA-MATIC.
I'M HARDLY EVEN SCRATCHED. YOU DON'T HAVE TO WORRY ABOUT ME!

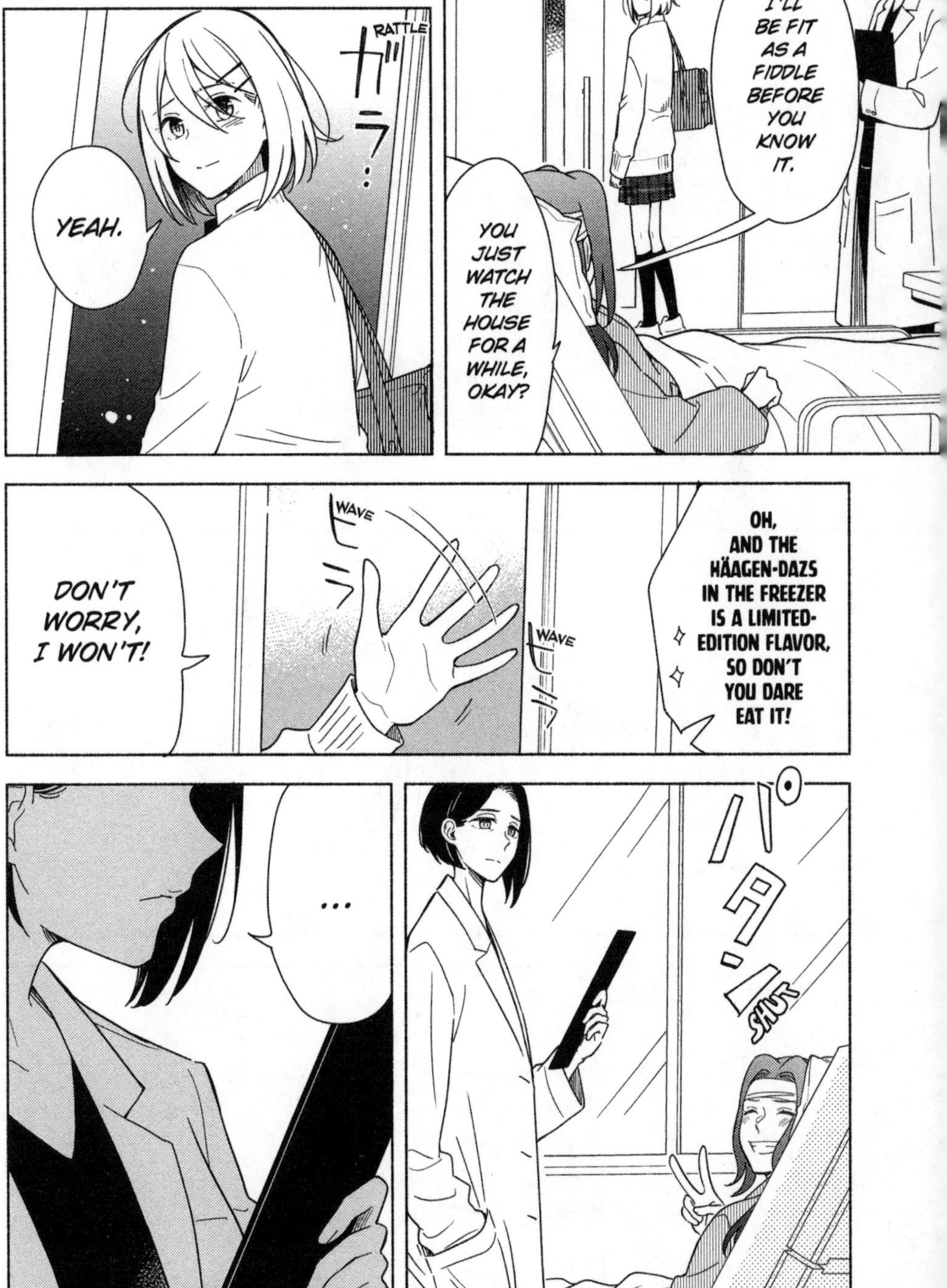
I'LL BE FIT AS A FIDDLE BEFORE YOU KNOW IT.
YOU JUST WATCH THE HOUSE FOR A WHILE, OKAY?
RATTLE
YEAH.
OH, AND THE HÄAGEN-DAZS IN THE FREEZER IS A LIMITED-EDITION FLAVOR, SO DON'T YOU DARE EAT IT!
WAVE
WAVE
DON'T WORRY, I WON'T!
SHUT
...

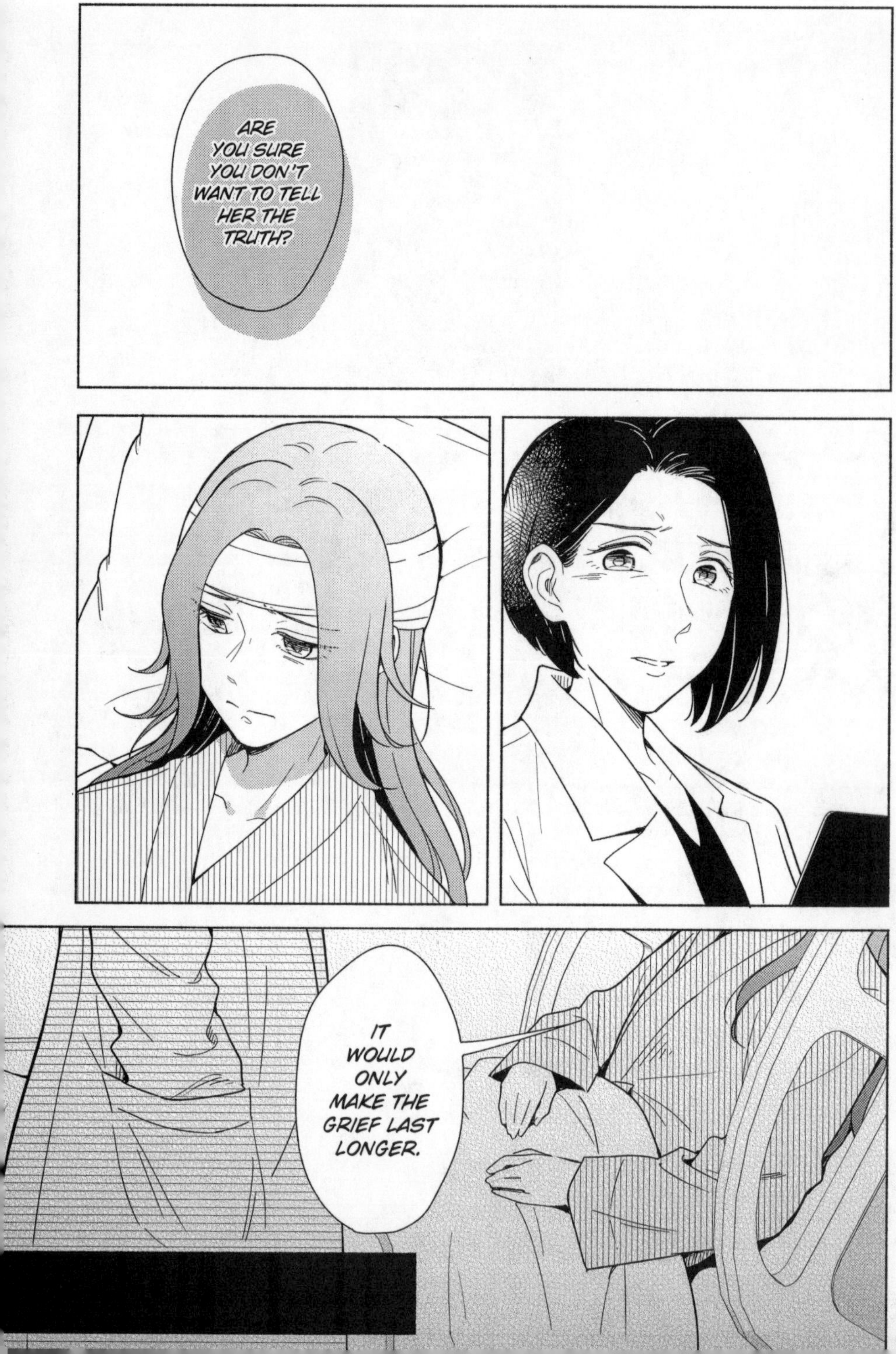
ARE YOU SURE YOU DON'T WANT TO TELL HER THE TRUTH?
IT WOULD ONLY MAKE THE GRIEF LAST LONGER.

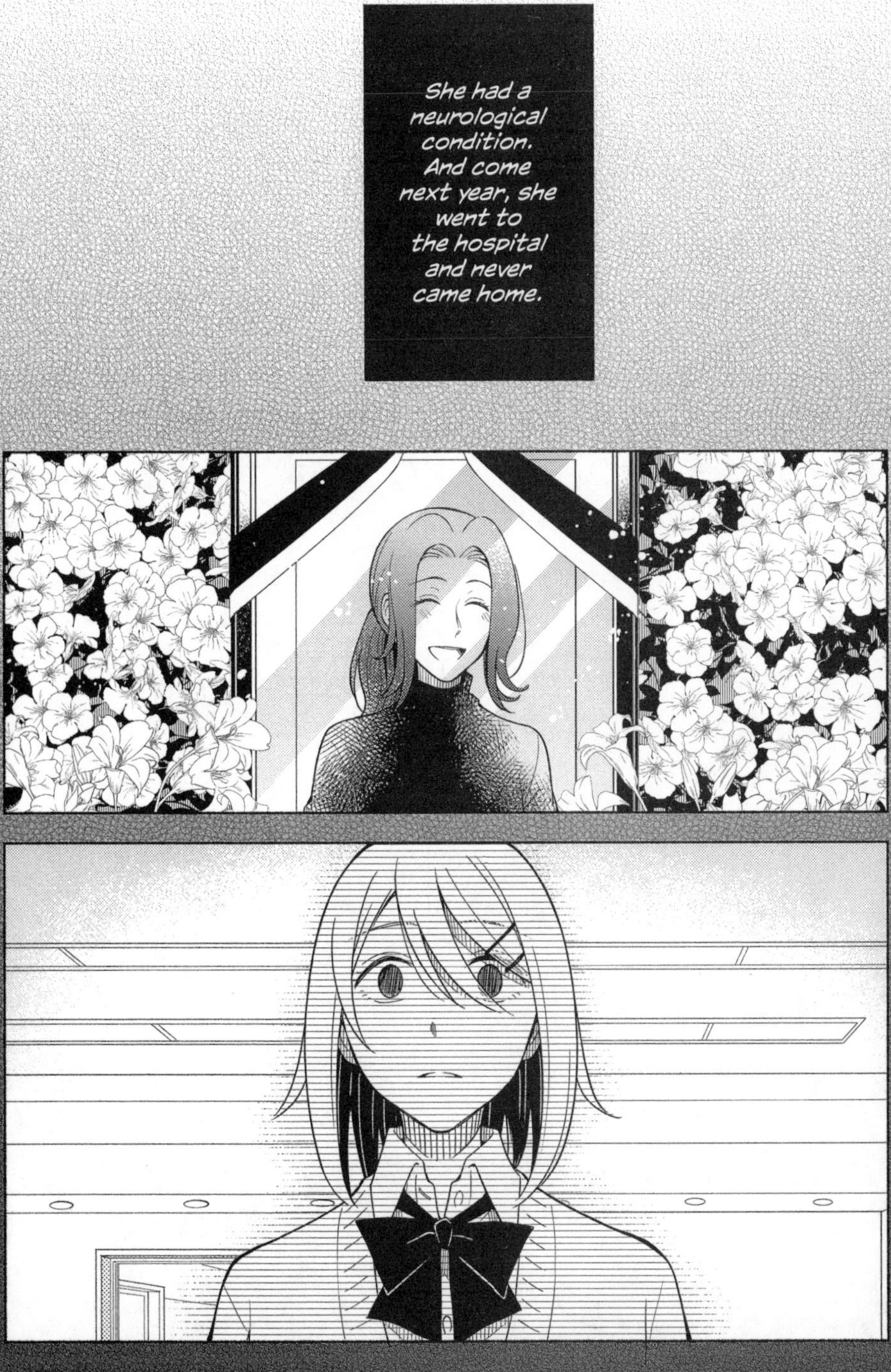
She had a neurological condition. And come next year, she went to the hospital and never came home.

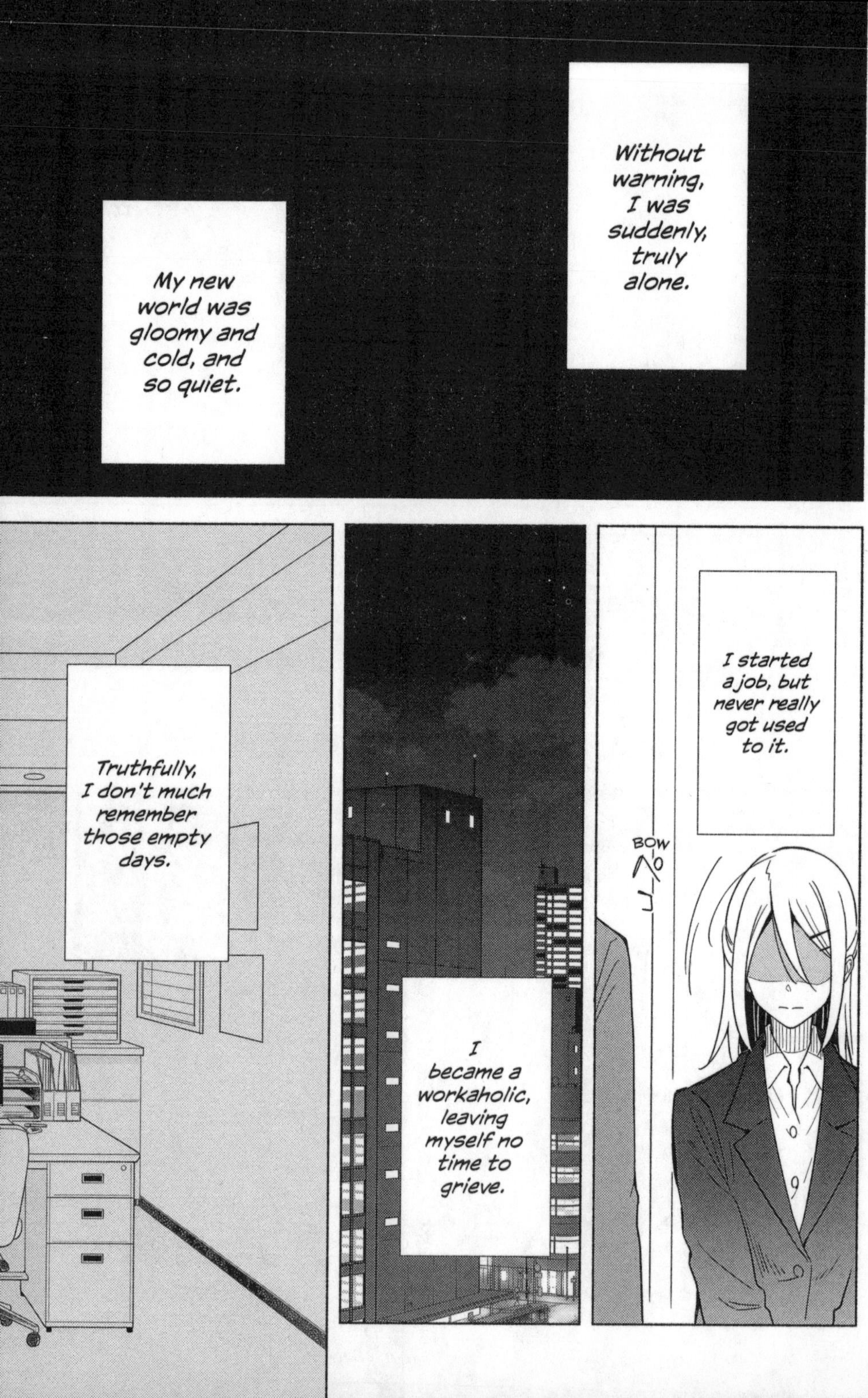
Without warning, I was suddenly, truly alone.
My new world was gloomy and cold, and so quiet.
I started a job, but never really got used to it.
BOW
I became a workaholic, leaving myself no time to grieve.
Truthfully, I don't much remember those empty days.

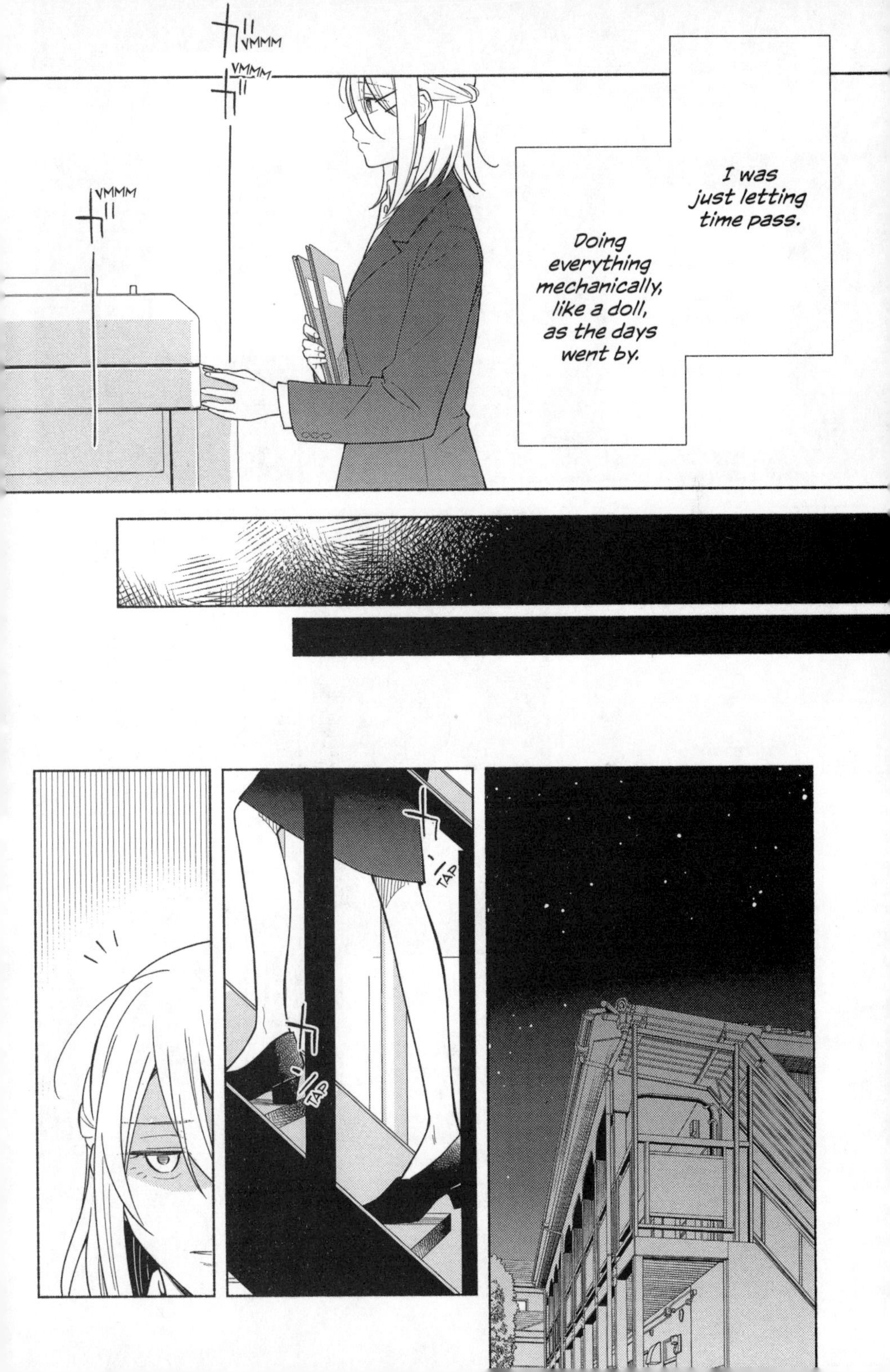
I was just letting time pass.
Doing everything mechanically, like a doll, as the days went by.
VMMM
VMMM
VMMM
TAP
TAP

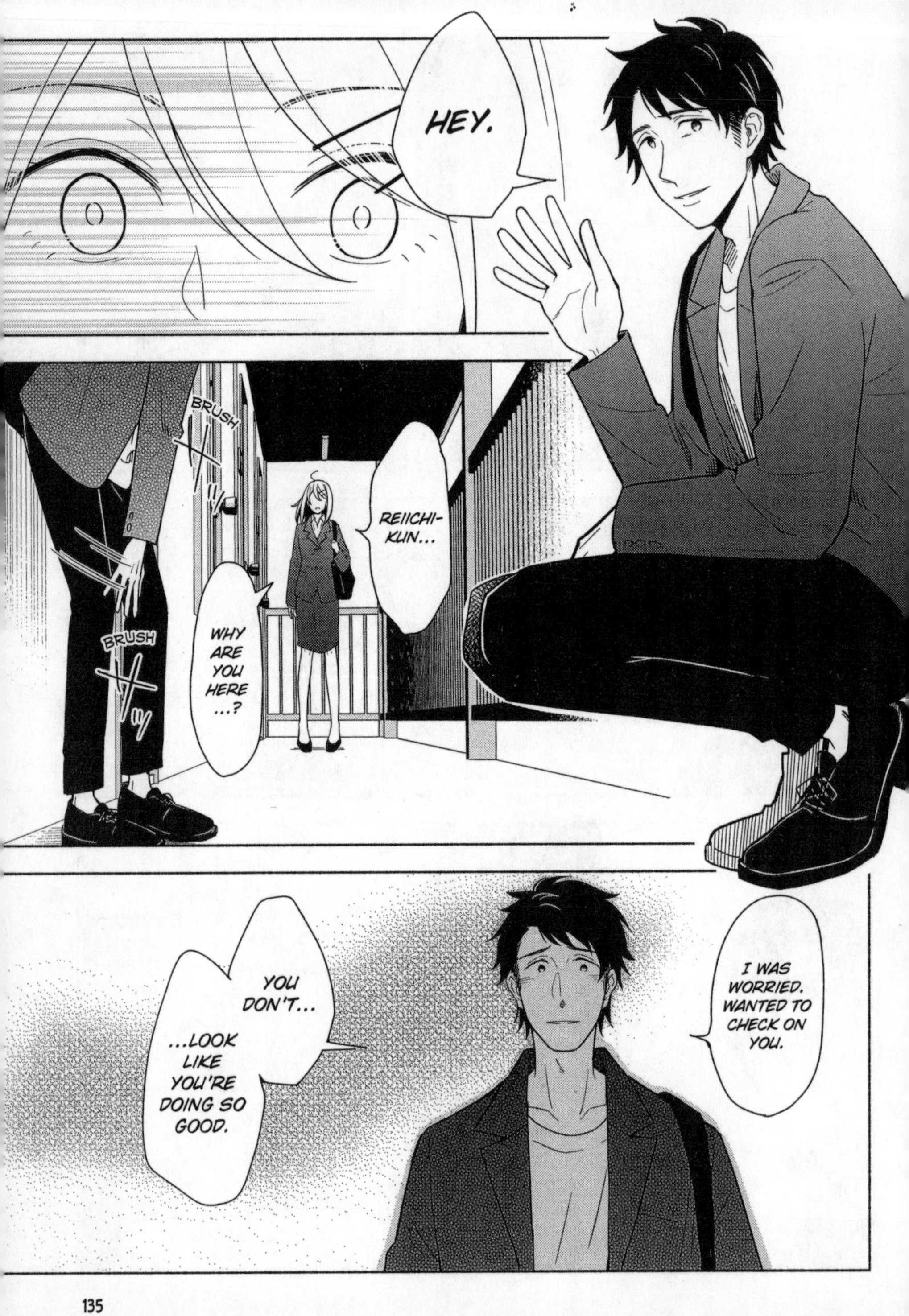
HEY.
REIICHI-KUN...
BRUSH
BRUSH
WHY ARE YOU HERE ...?
I WAS WORRIED. WANTED TO CHECK ON YOU.
YOU DON'T...
...LOOK LIKE YOU'RE DOING SO GOOD.

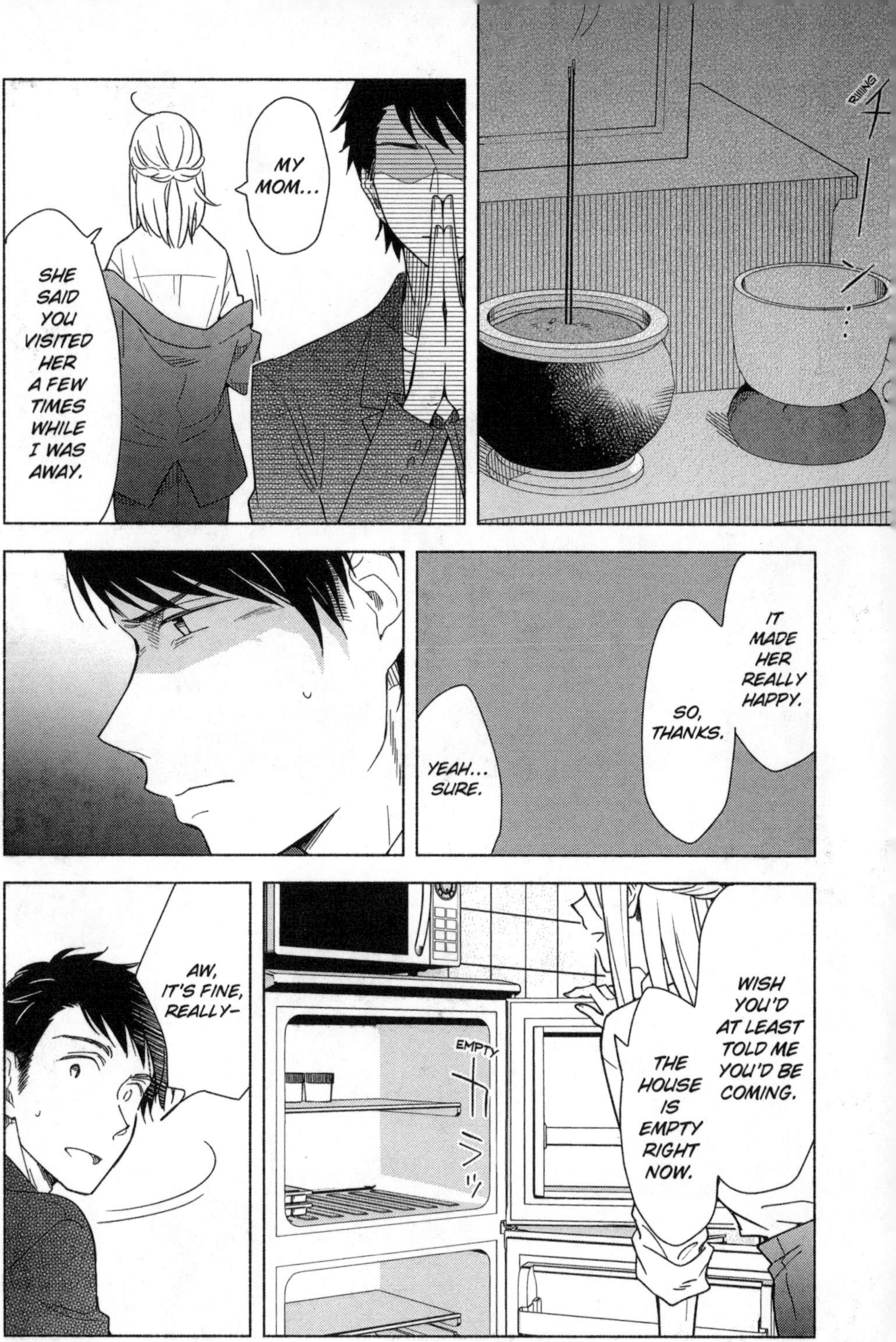
RIIING
MY MOM...
SHE SAID YOU VISITED HER A FEW TIMES WHILE I WAS AWAY.
IT MADE HER REALLY HAPPY.
SO, THANKS.
YEAH... SURE.
WISH YOU'D AT LEAST TOLD ME YOU'D BE COMING.
THE HOUSE IS EMPTY RIGHT NOW.
EMPTY
AW, IT'S FINE, REALLY-

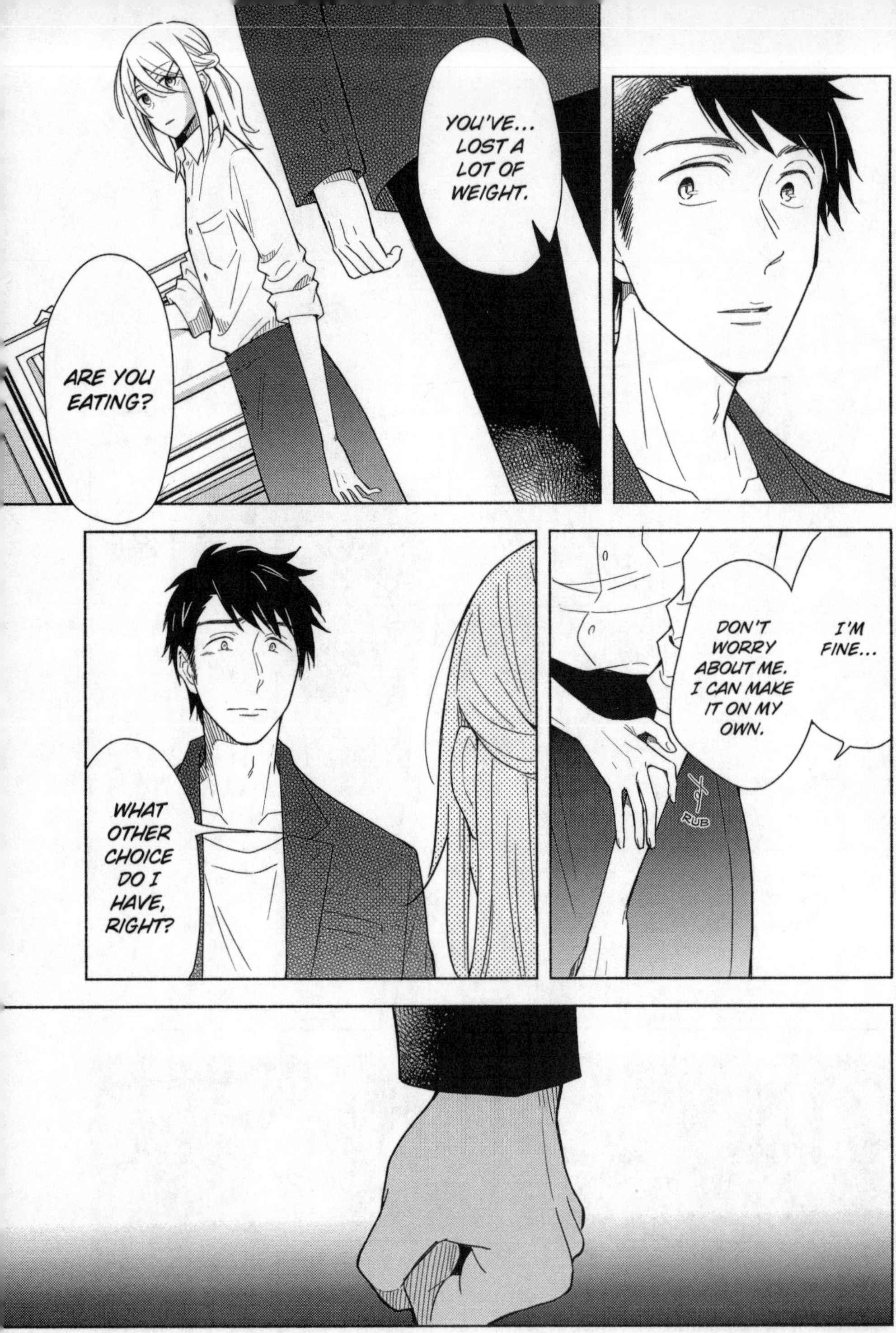
YOU'VE... LOST A LOT OF WEIGHT.
ARE YOU EATING?
I'M FINE...
DON'T WORRY ABOUT ME. I CAN MAKE IT ON MY OWN.
RUB
WHAT OTHER CHOICE DO I HAVE, RIGHT?

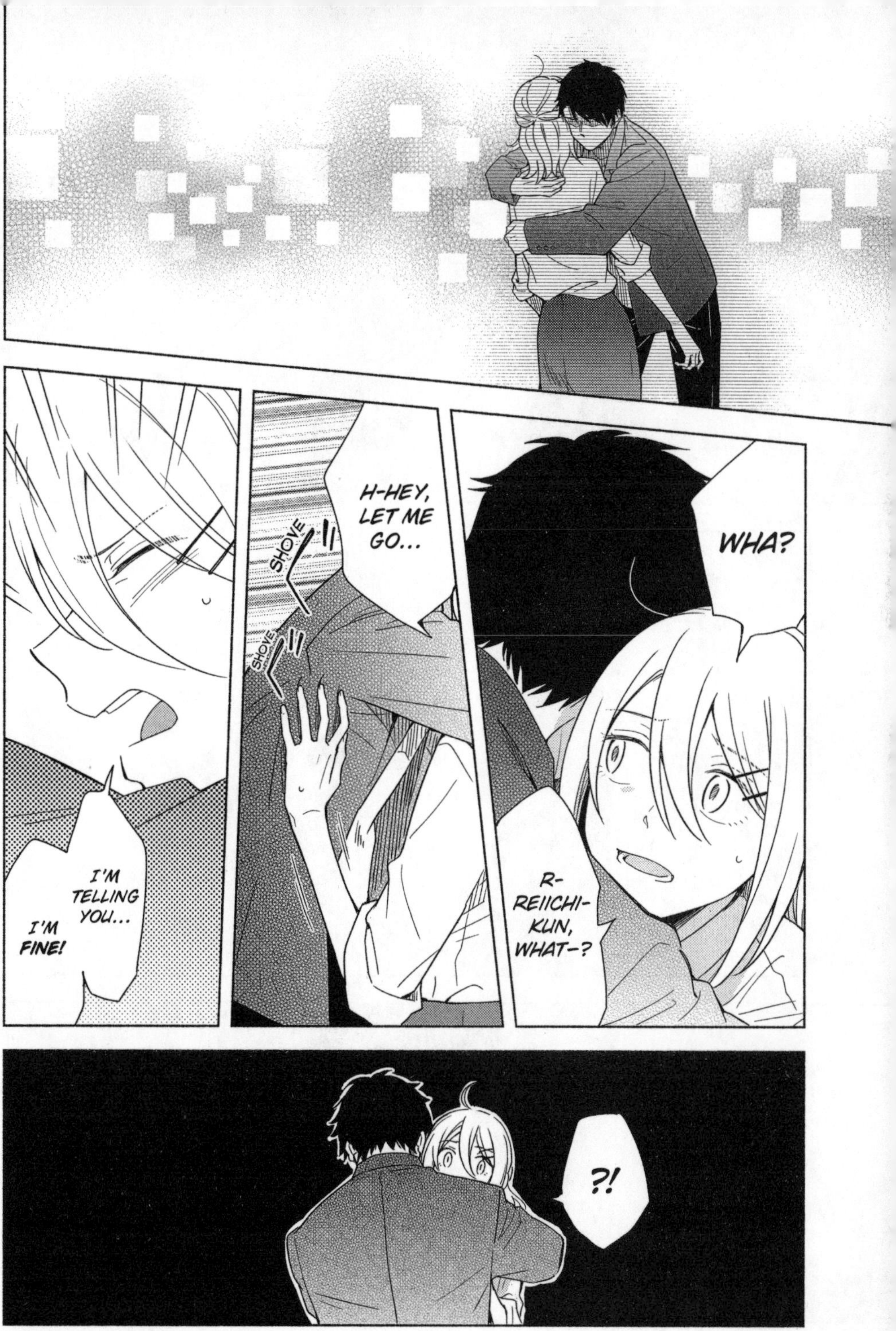
WHA?
R-REIICHI-KUN, WHAT-?
H-HEY, LET ME GO...
SHOVE
SHOVE
I'M TELLING YOU...
I'M FINE!
?!

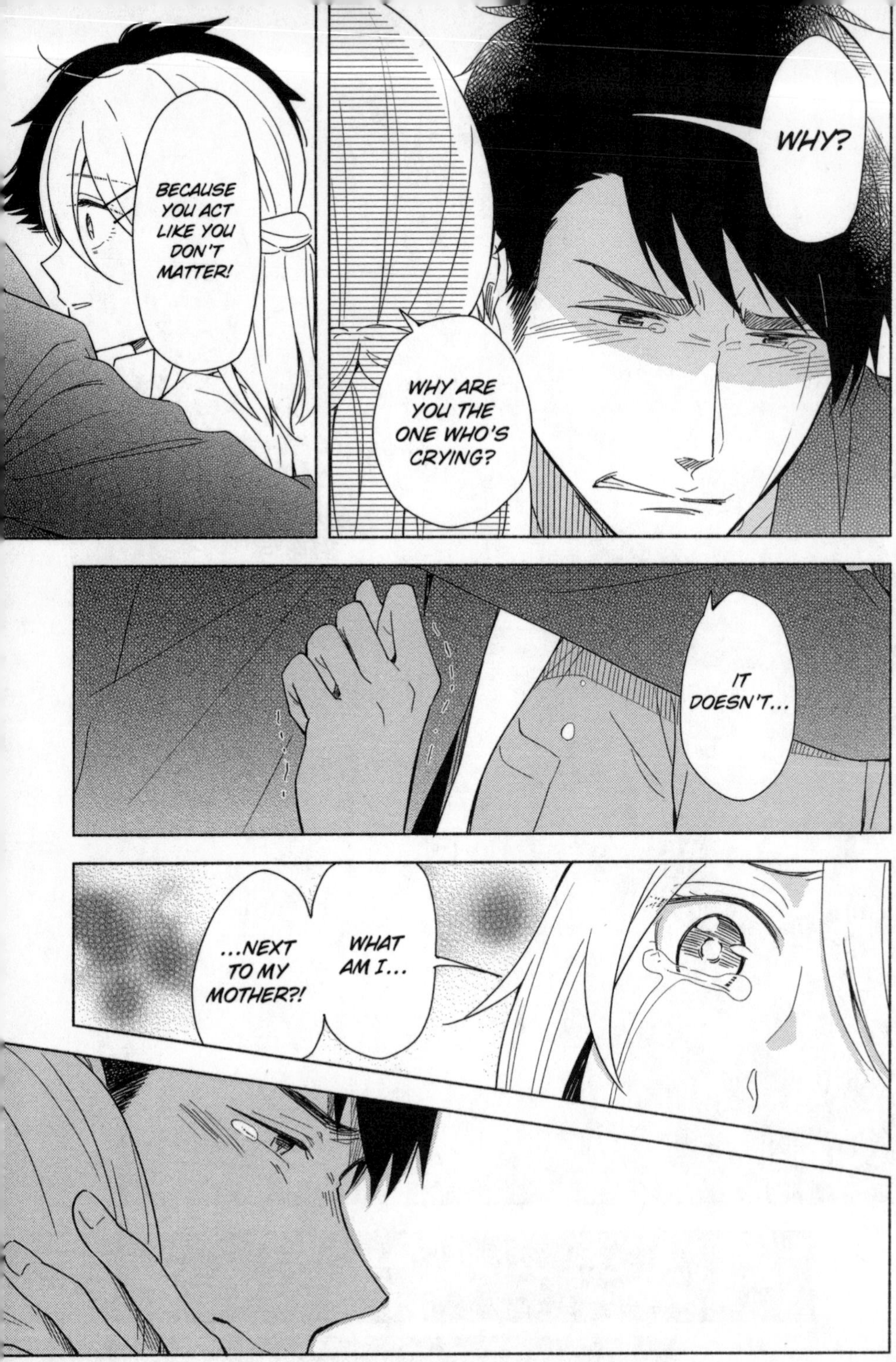
WHY?
WHY ARE YOU THE ONE WHO'S CRYING?
BECAUSE YOU ACT LIKE YOU DON'T MATTER!
IT DOESN'T...
WHAT AM I...
...NEXT TO MY MOTHER?!

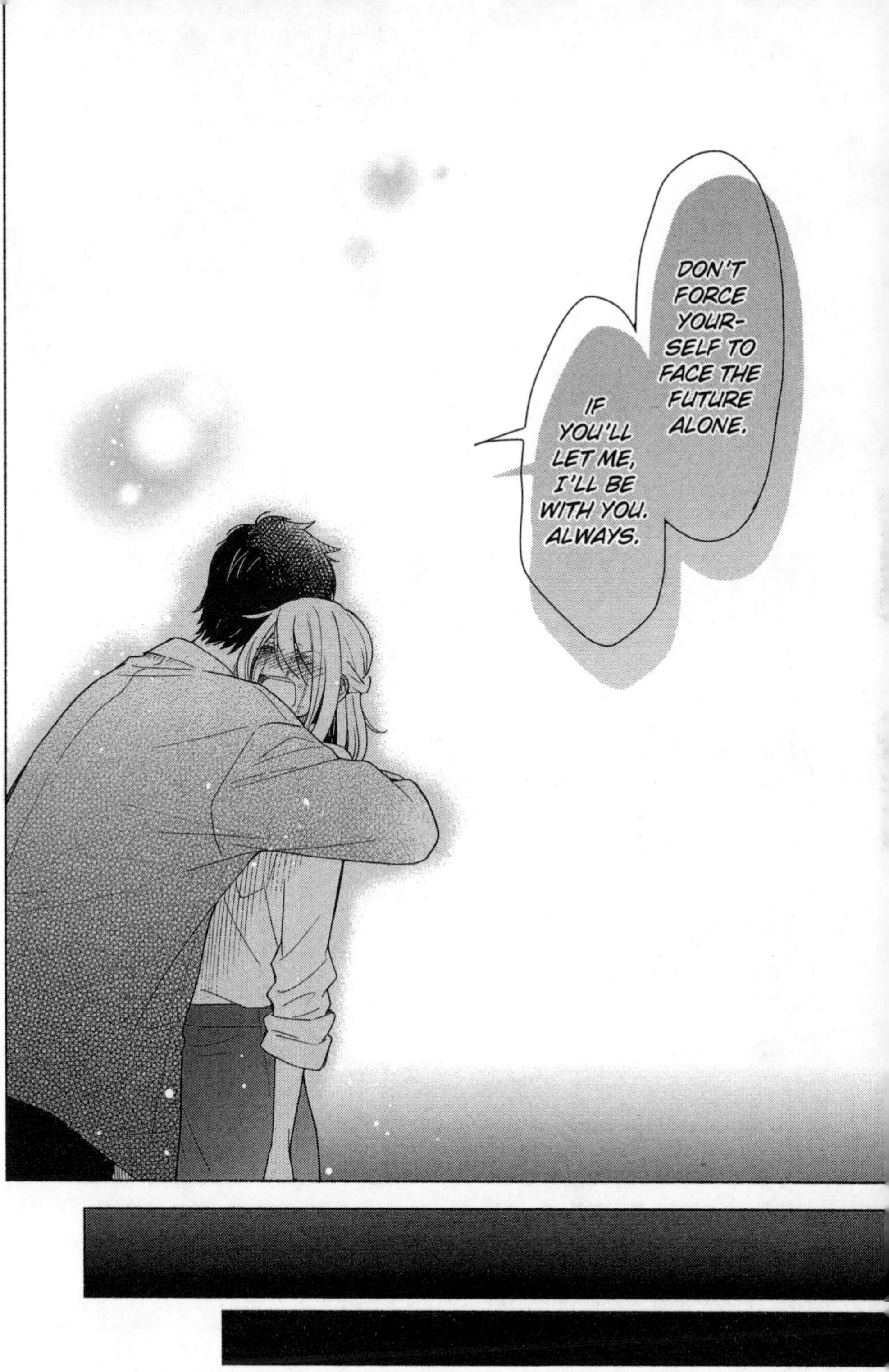
DON'T FORCE YOUR-SELF TO FACE THE FUTURE ALONE.
IF YOU'LL LET ME, I'LL BE WITH YOU. ALWAYS.

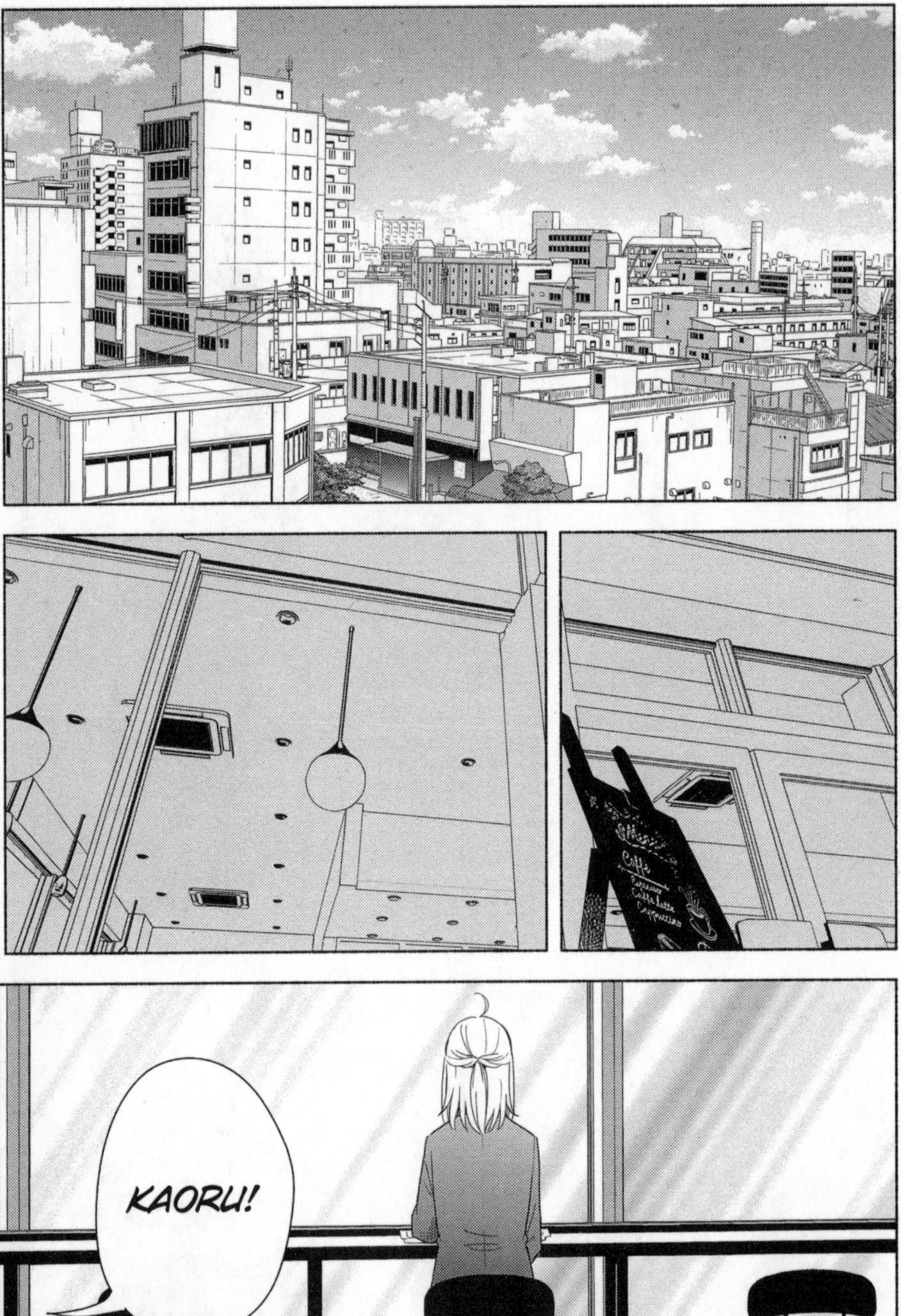
Caffe
Caffe latte
Cappuccino
KAORU!

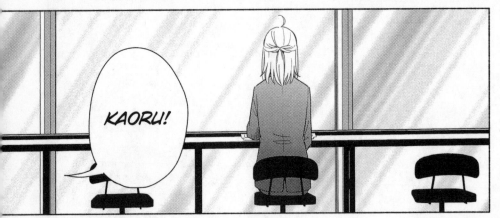

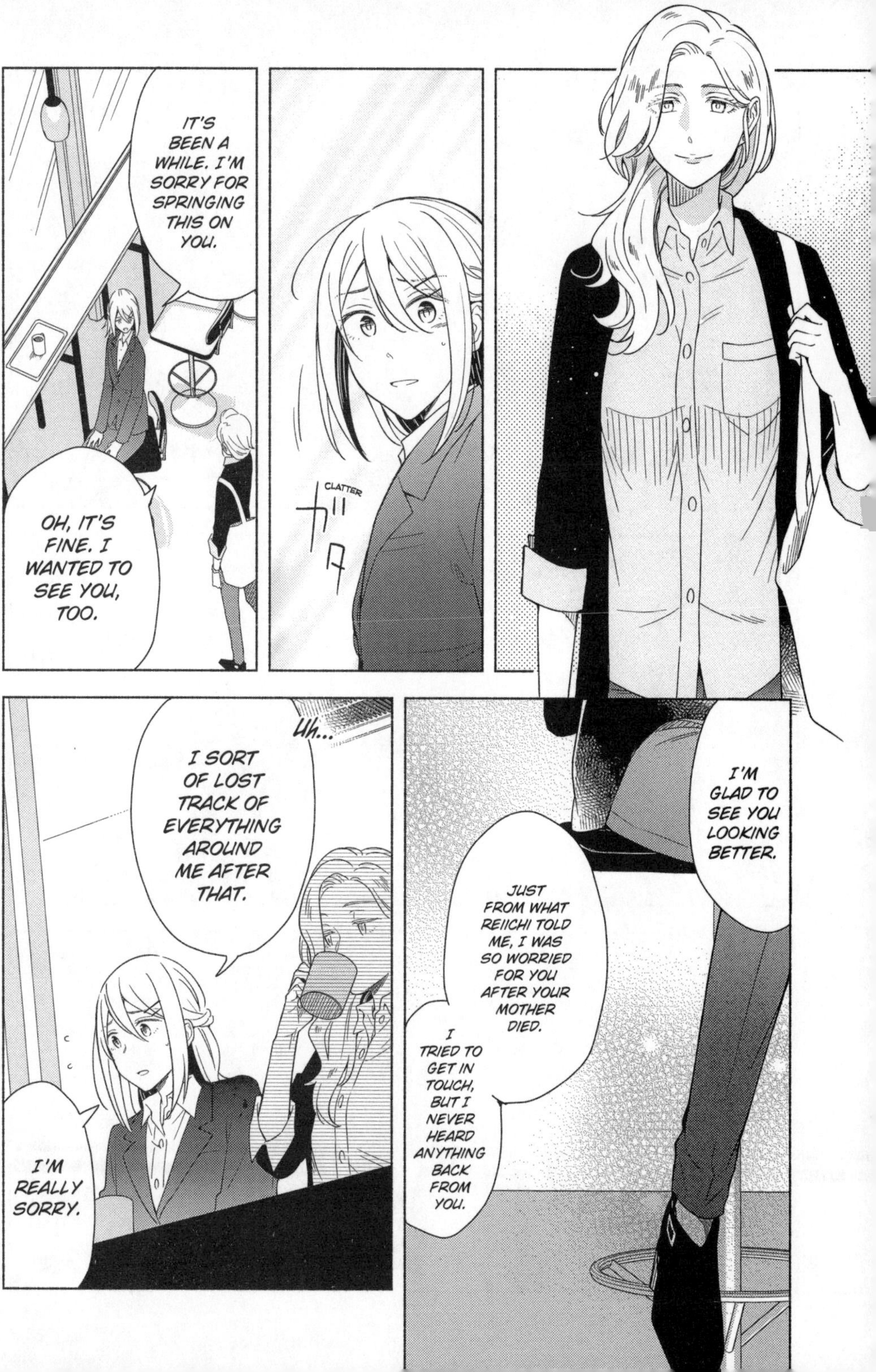
CLATTER
ガタ
IT'S BEEN A WHILE. I'M SORRY FOR SPRINGING THIS ON YOU.
OH, IT'S FINE. I WANTED TO SEE YOU, TOO.
I'M GLAD TO SEE YOU LOOKING BETTER.
JUST FROM WHAT REIICHI TOLD ME, I WAS SO WORRIED FOR YOU AFTER YOUR MOTHER DIED.
I TRIED TO GET IN TOUCH, BUT I NEVER HEARD ANYTHING BACK FROM YOU.
Uh...
I SORT OF LOST TRACK OF EVERYTHING AROUND ME AFTER THAT.
I'M REALLY SORRY.

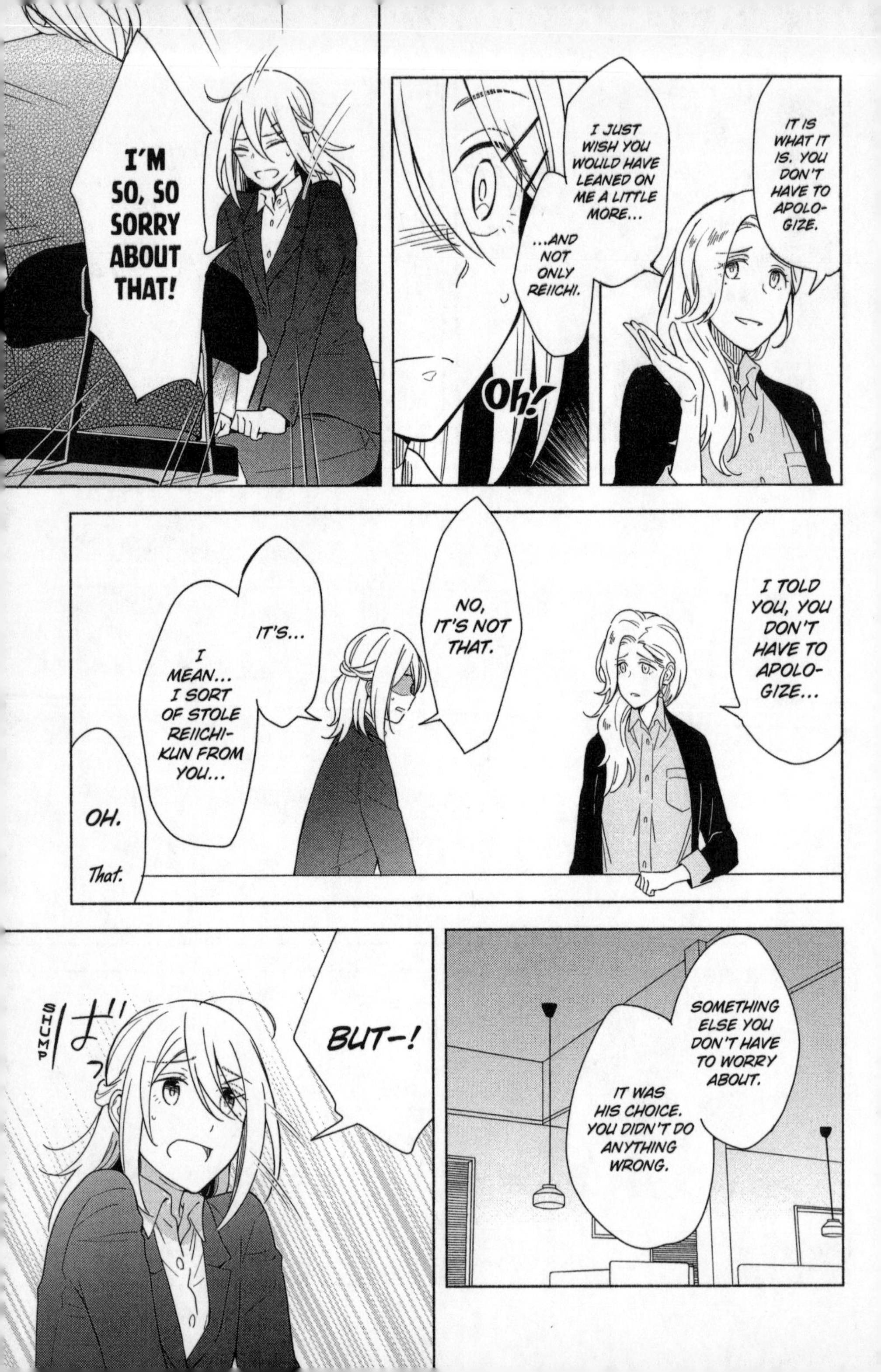
IT IS WHAT IT IS. YOU DON'T HAVE TO APOLOGIZE.
I JUST WISH YOU WOULD HAVE LEANED ON ME A LITTLE MORE...
...AND NOT ONLY REIICHI.
Oh!
I'M SO, SO SORRY ABOUT THAT!
I TOLD YOU, YOU DON'T HAVE TO APOLOGIZE...
NO, IT'S NOT THAT.
IT'S...
I MEAN... I SORT OF STOLE REIICHI-KUN FROM YOU...
OH.
That.
SOMETHING ELSE YOU DON'T HAVE TO WORRY ABOUT.
IT WAS HIS CHOICE. YOU DIDN'T DO ANYTHING WRONG.
BUT—!
SHUMP

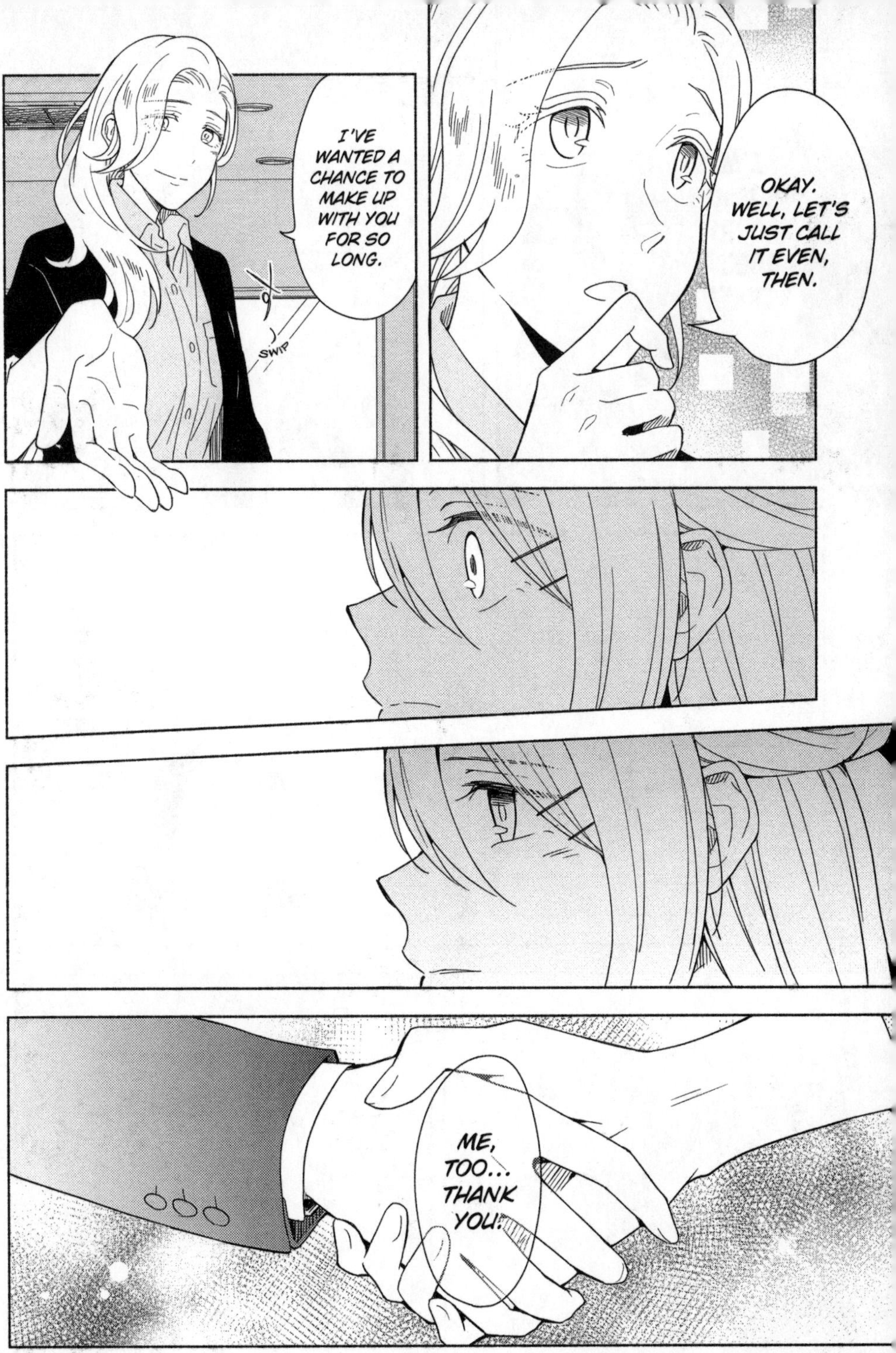
OKAY. WELL, LET'S JUST CALL IT EVEN, THEN.
I'VE WANTED A CHANCE TO MAKE UP WITH YOU FOR SO LONG.
SWIP
ME, TOO... THANK YOU!

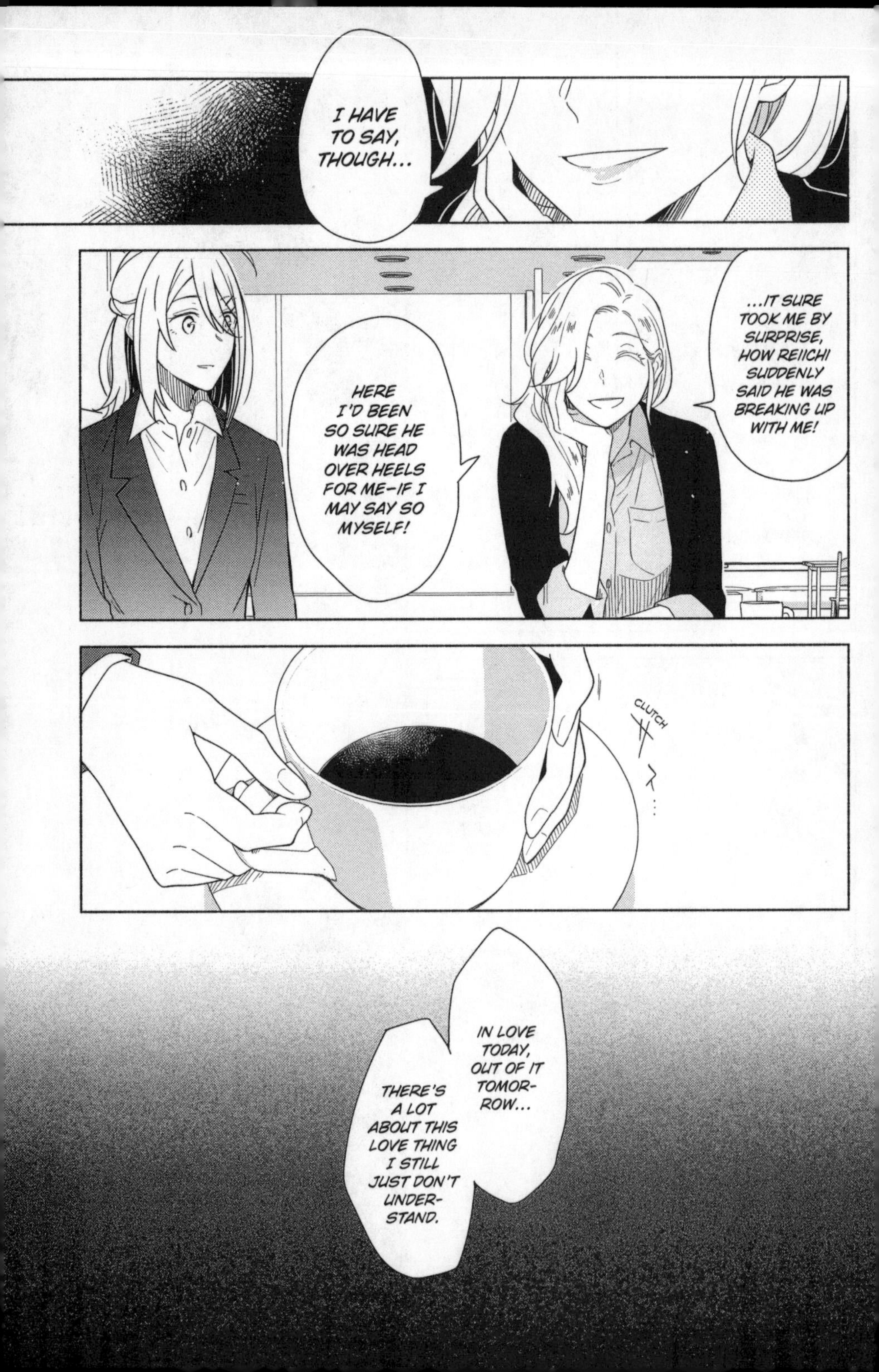
I HAVE TO SAY, THOUGH...
...IT SURE TOOK ME BY SURPRISE, HOW REIICHI SUDDENLY SAID HE WAS BREAKING UP WITH ME!
HERE I'D BEEN SO SURE HE WAS HEAD OVER HEELS FOR ME—IF I MAY SAY SO MYSELF!
CLUTCH
IN LOVE TODAY, OUT OF IT TOMORROW...
THERE'S A LOT ABOUT THIS LOVE THING I STILL JUST DON'T UNDERSTAND.

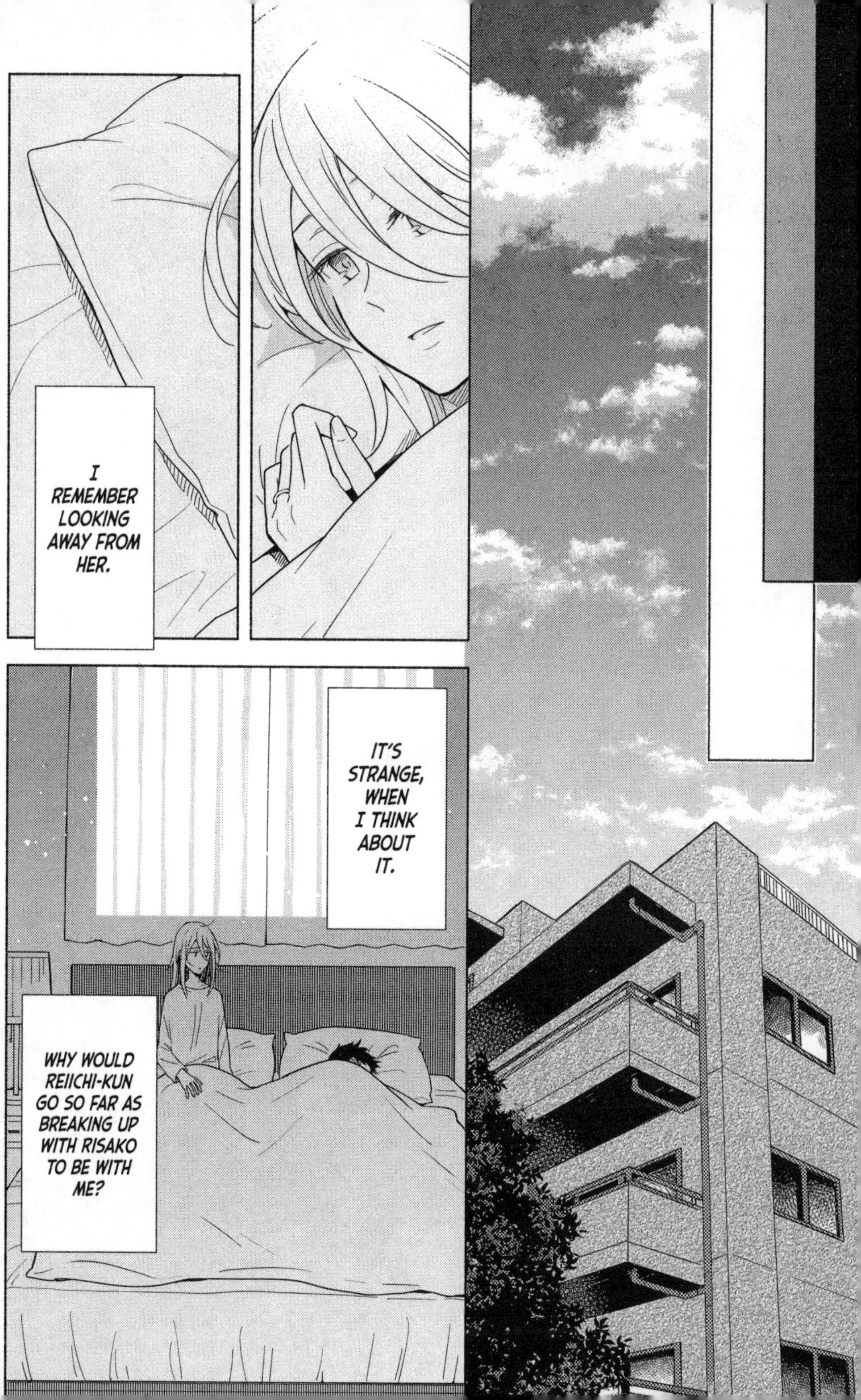
I REMEMBER LOOKING AWAY FROM HER.
IT'S STRANGE, WHEN I THINK ABOUT IT.
WHY WOULD REIICHI-KUN GO SO FAR AS BREAKING UP WITH RISAKO TO BE WITH ME?

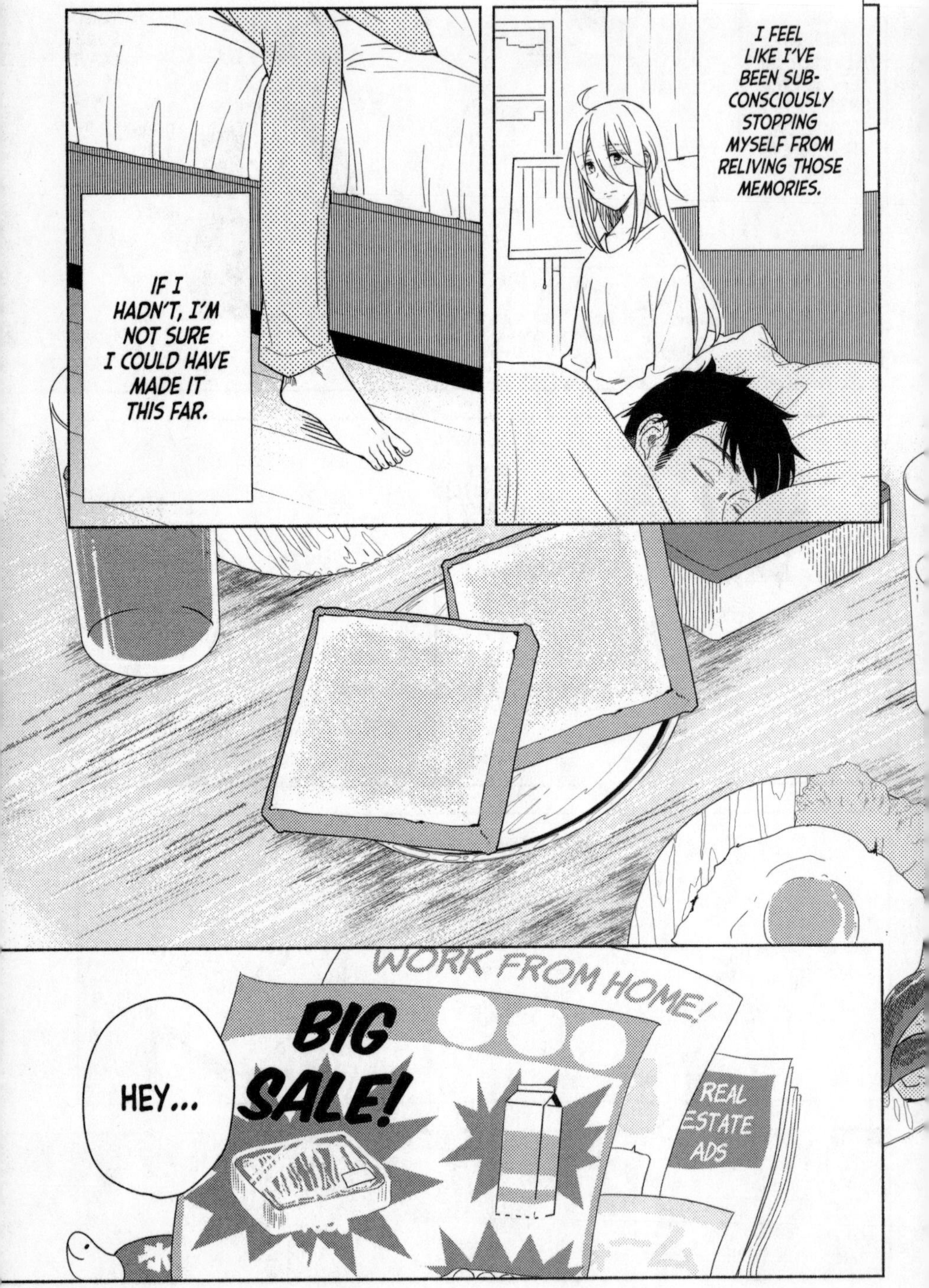
I FEEL LIKE I'VE BEEN SUB-CONSCIOUSLY STOPPING MYSELF FROM RELIVING THOSE MEMORIES.
IF I HADN'T, I'M NOT SURE I COULD HAVE MADE IT THIS FAR.
WORK FROM HOME!
REAL ESTATE ADS
BIG SALE!
HEY...

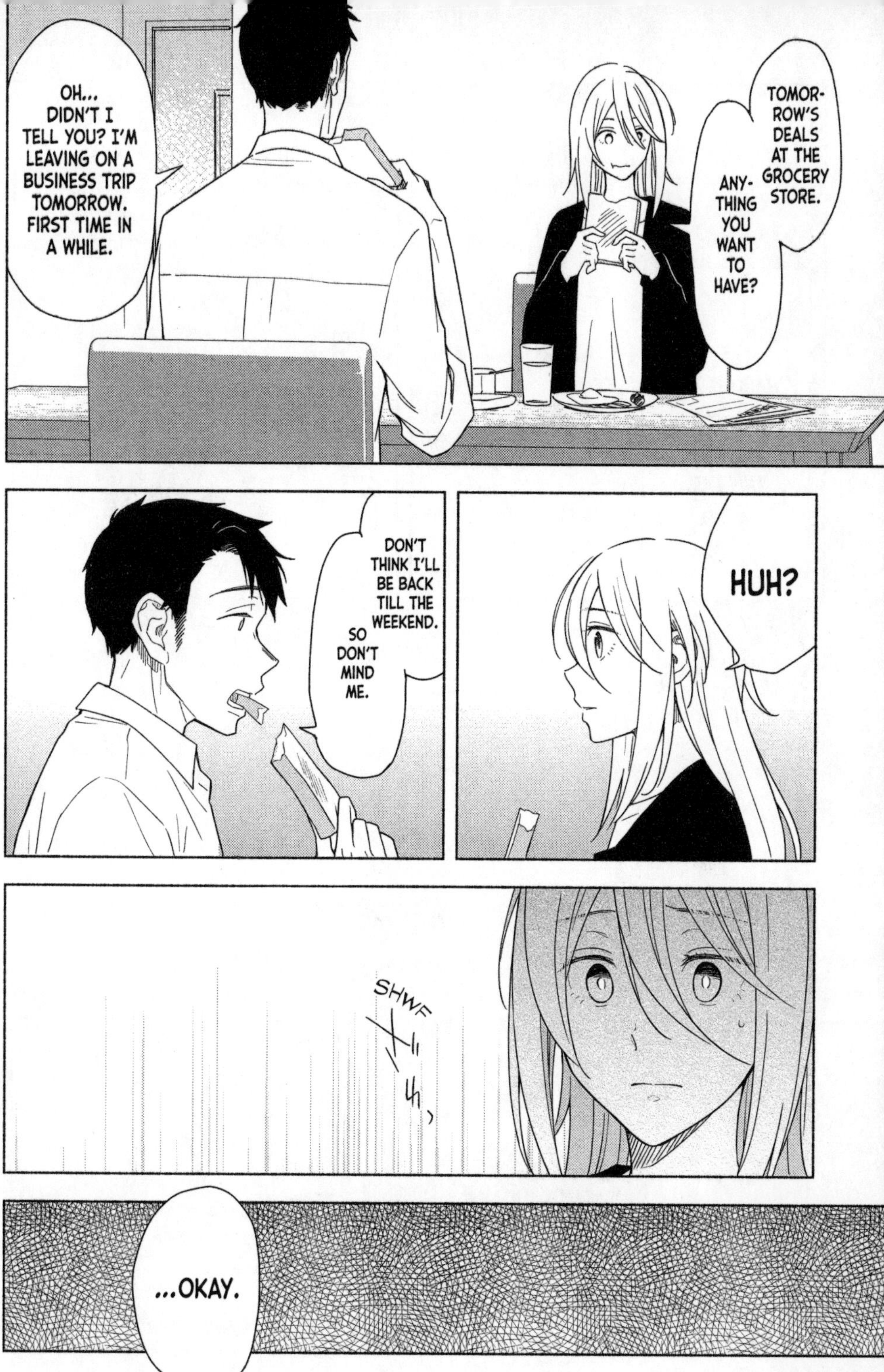
TOMORROW'S DEALS AT THE GROCERY STORE.
ANYTHING YOU WANT TO HAVE?
OH... DIDN'T I TELL YOU? I'M LEAVING ON A BUSINESS TRIP TOMORROW. FIRST TIME IN A WHILE.
HUH?
DON'T THINK I'LL BE BACK TILL THE WEEKEND.
SO DON'T MIND ME.
SHWF
...OKAY.

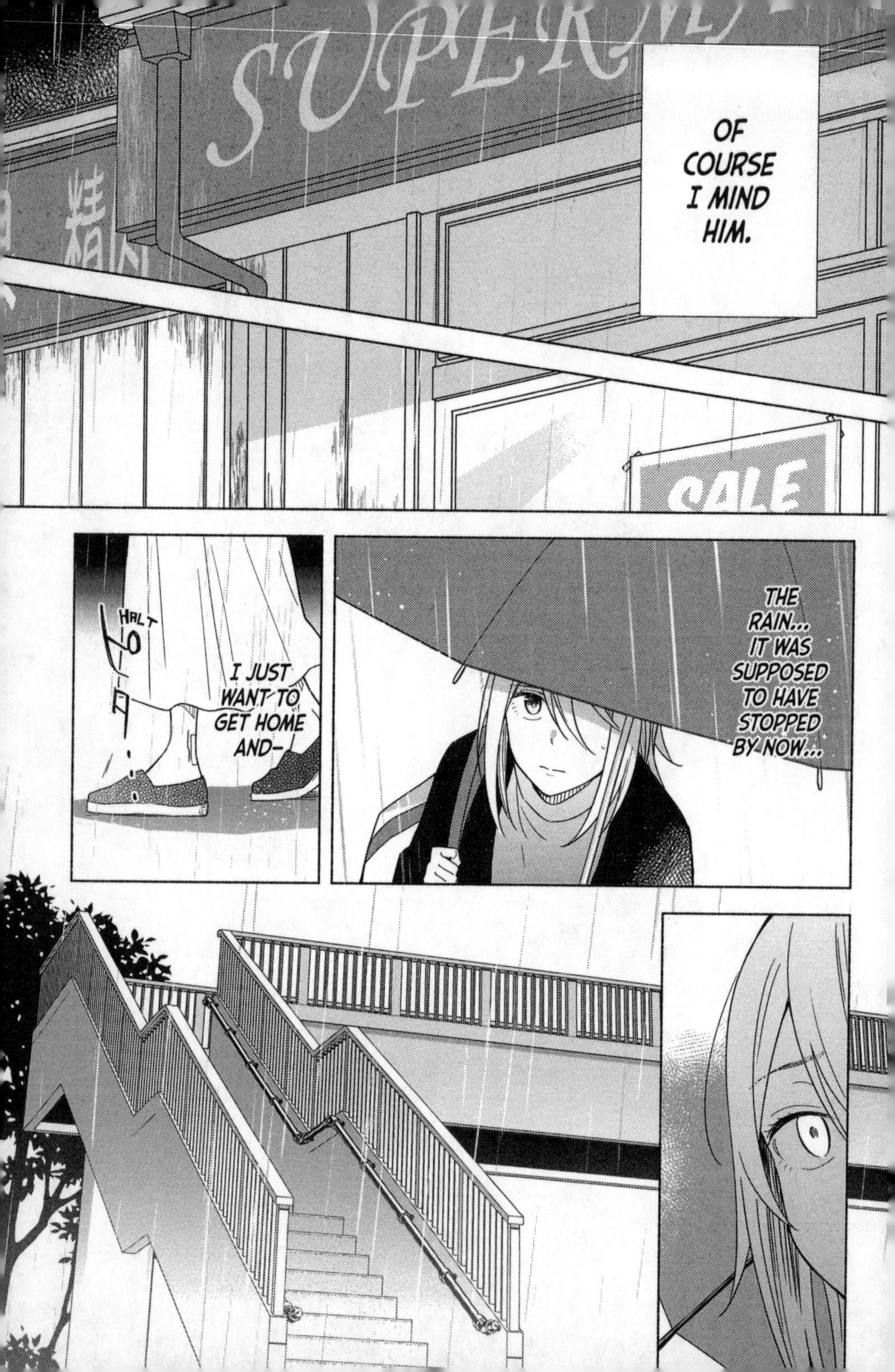
OF COURSE I MIND HIM.
SALE
THE RAIN... IT WAS SUPPOSED TO HAVE STOPPED BY NOW...
HALT
I JUST WANT TO GET HOME AND–

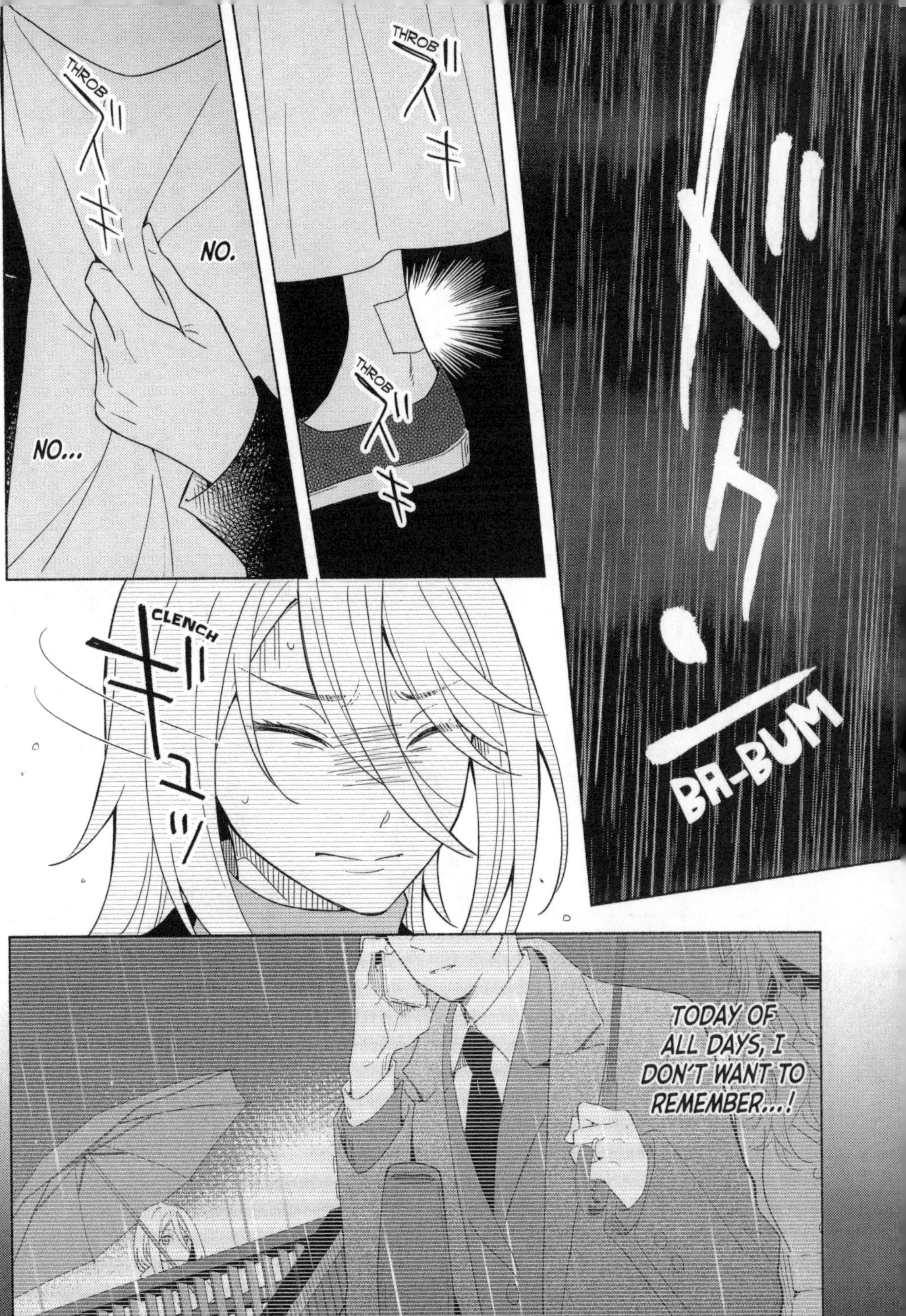
BA-BUM
THROB
THROB
THROB
NO.
NO...
CLENCH
TODAY OF ALL DAYS, I DON'T WANT TO REMEMBER...!

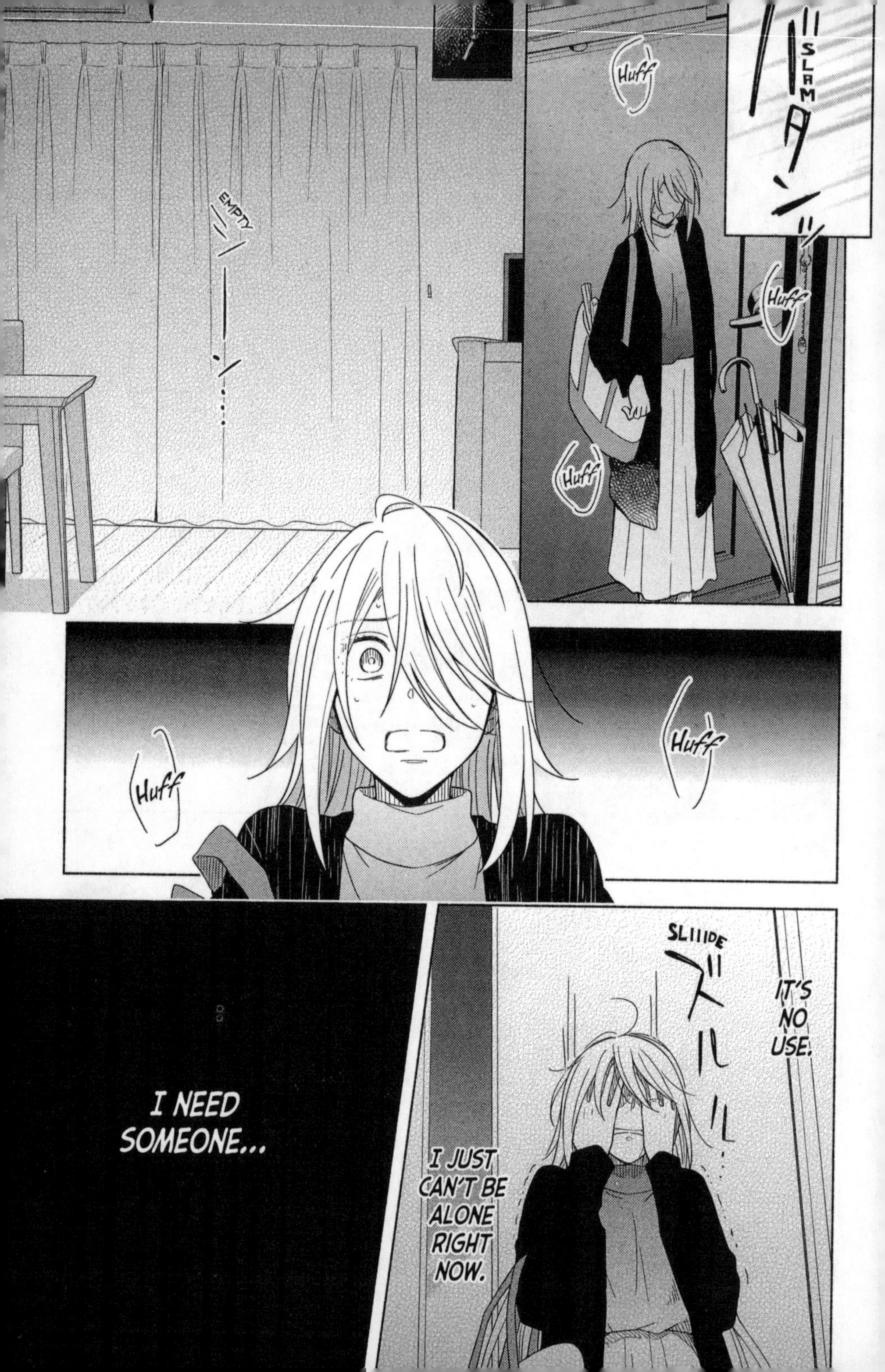
SLAM
Huff
Huff
Huff
EMPTY
Huff
Huff
SLIIIDE
IT'S NO USE.
I JUST CAN'T BE ALONE RIGHT NOW.
I NEED SOMEONE...

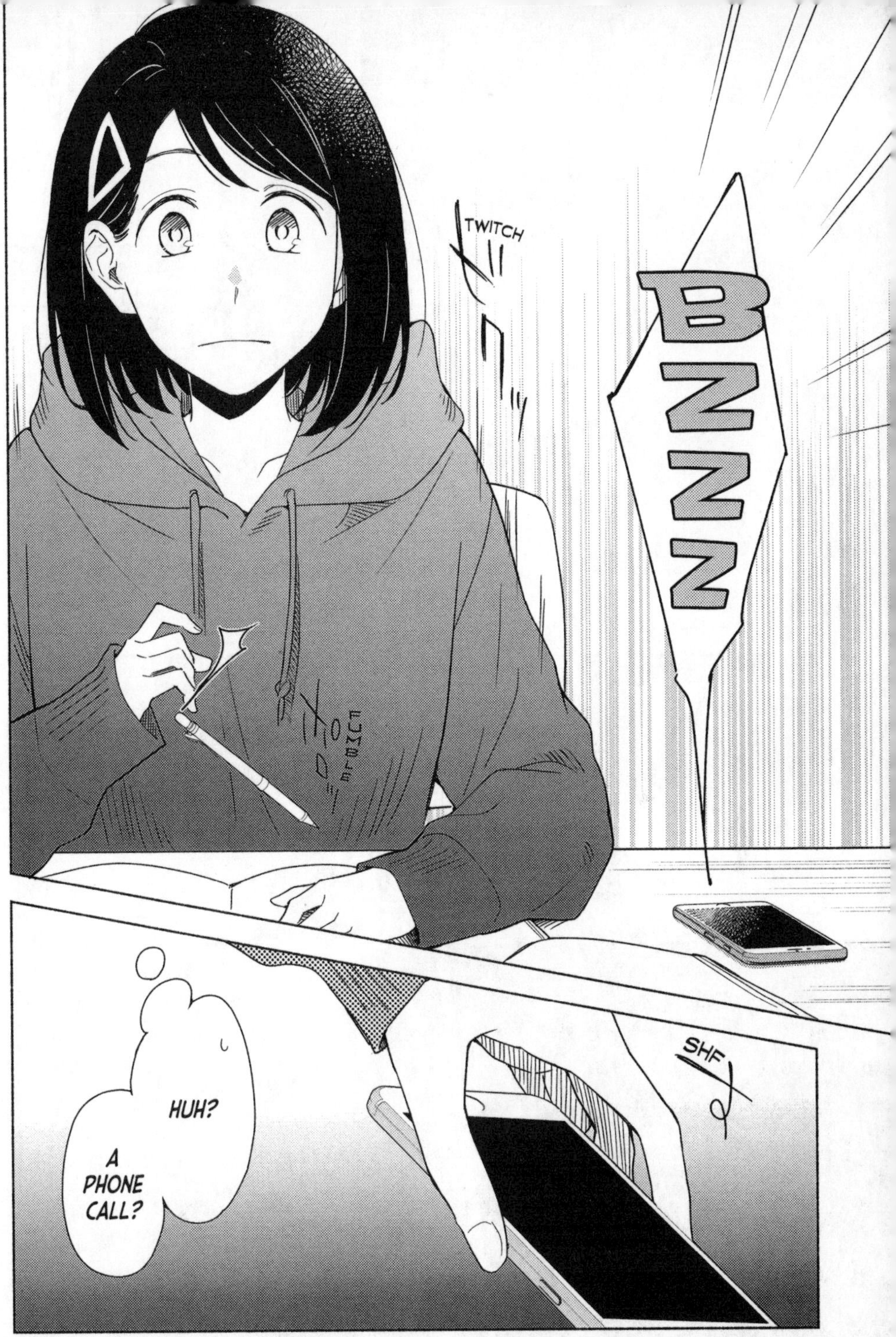
BZZZ
TWITCH
FUMBLE
SHF
HUH?
A PHONE CALL?

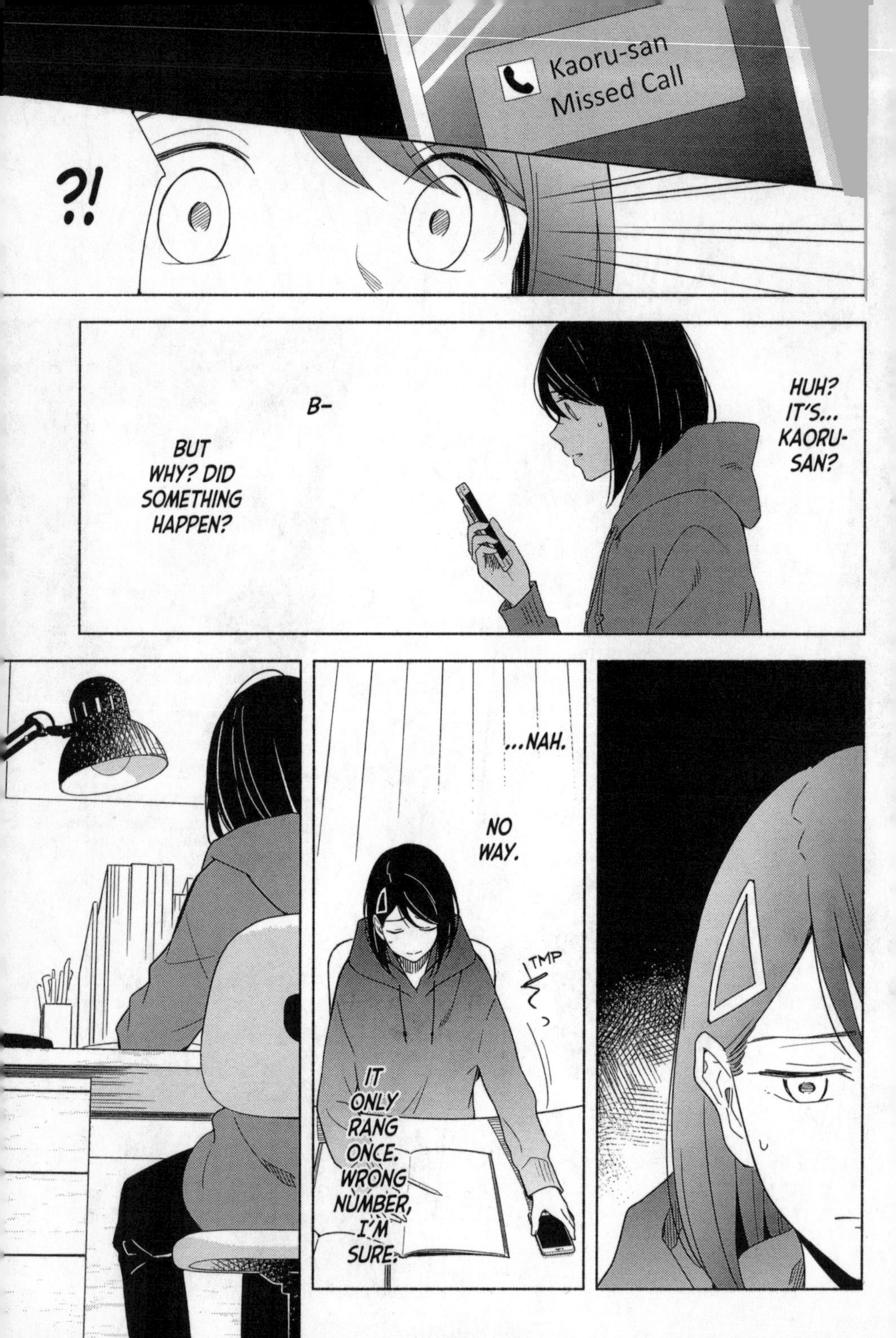
Kaoru-san
Missed Call
?!
HUH? IT'S... KAORU-SAN?
B-
BUT WHY? DID SOMETHING HAPPEN?
...NAH.
NO WAY.
TMP
IT ONLY RANG ONCE. WRONG NUMBER, I'M SURE.

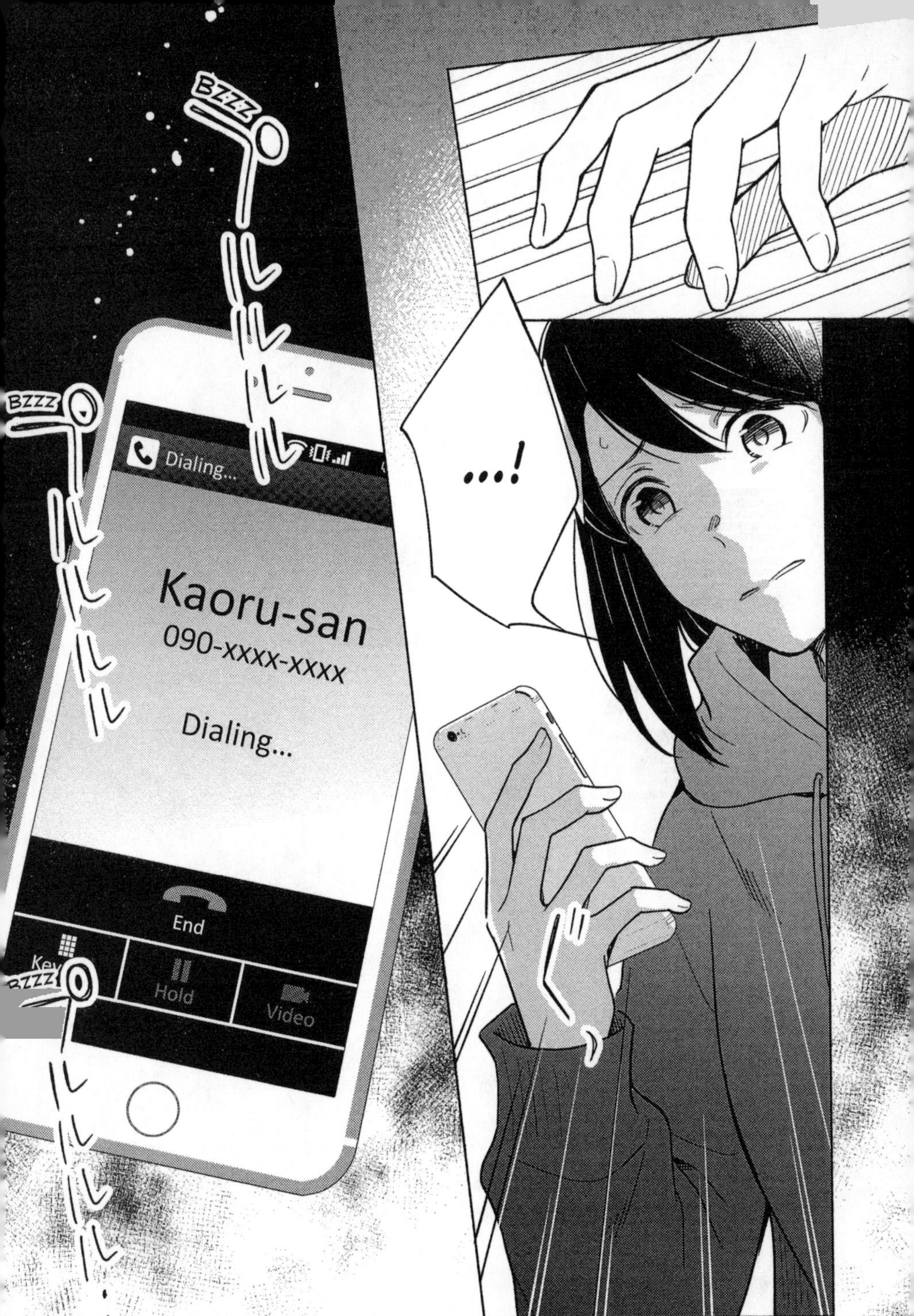

...!
BZZZ
Dialing...
Kaoru-san
090-xxxx-xxxx
Dialing...
End
Hold
Video
BZZZ
BZZZ

To be continued.

If I Could Reach You

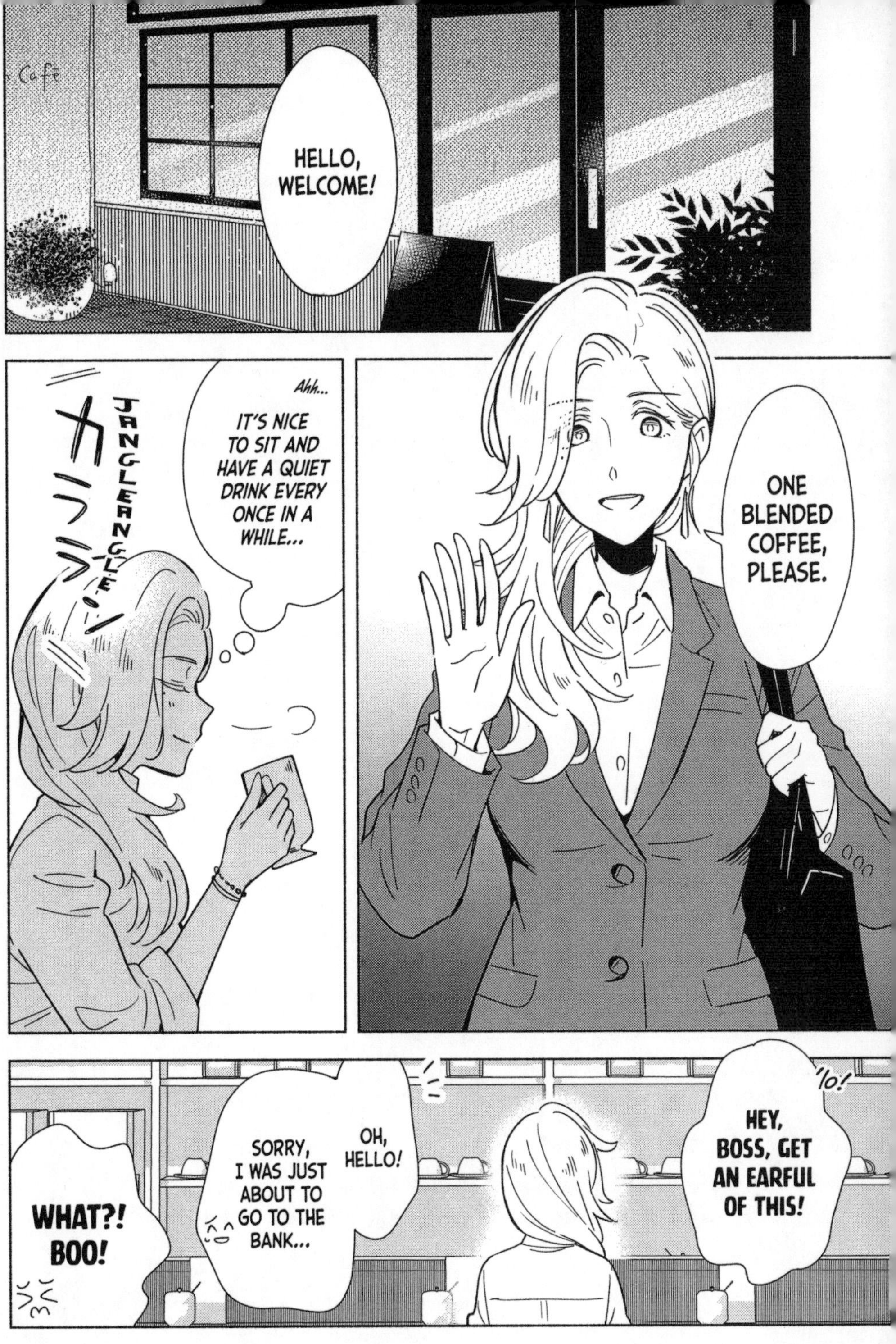
Café
HELLO, WELCOME!
ONE BLENDED COFFEE, PLEASE.
JANGLEANGLE
Ahh...
IT'S NICE TO SIT AND HAVE A QUIET DRINK EVERY ONCE IN A WHILE...
'llo!
HEY, BOSS, GET AN EARFUL OF THIS!
OH, HELLO!
SORRY, I WAS JUST ABOUT TO GO TO THE BANK...
WHAT?! BOO!

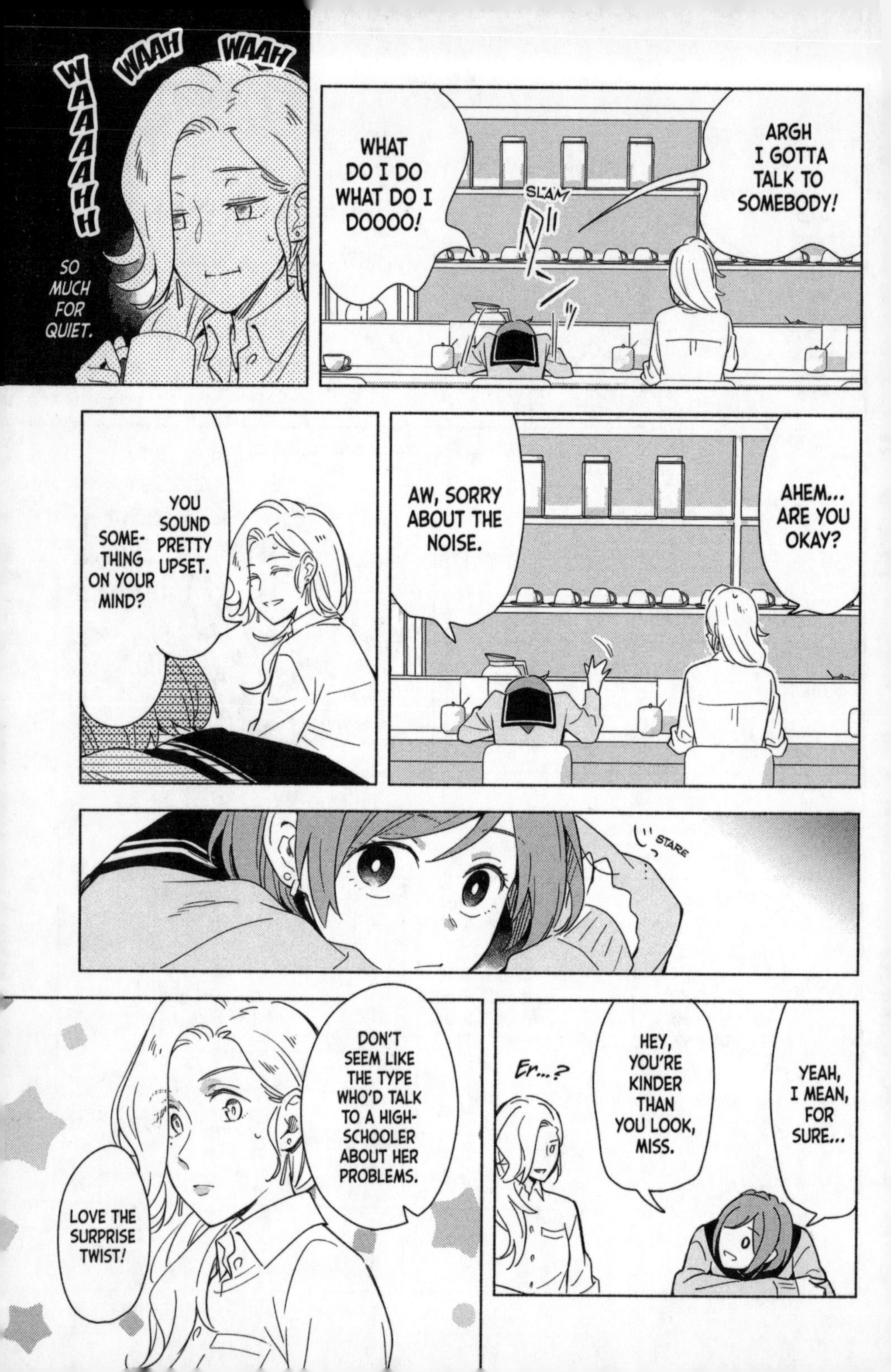
ARGH I GOTTA TALK TO SOMEBODY!
SLAM
WHAT DO I DO WHAT DO I DOOOO!
WAAAAAAHH
WAAH
WAAH
SO MUCH FOR QUIET.
AHEM... ARE YOU OKAY?
AW, SORRY ABOUT THE NOISE.
YOU SOUND PRETTY UPSET.
SOME-THING ON YOUR MIND?
STARE
YEAH, I MEAN, FOR SURE...
HEY, YOU'RE KINDER THAN YOU LOOK, MISS.
Er...?
DON'T SEEM LIKE THE TYPE WHO'D TALK TO A HIGH-SCHOOLER ABOUT HER PROBLEMS.
LOVE THE SURPRISE TWIST!

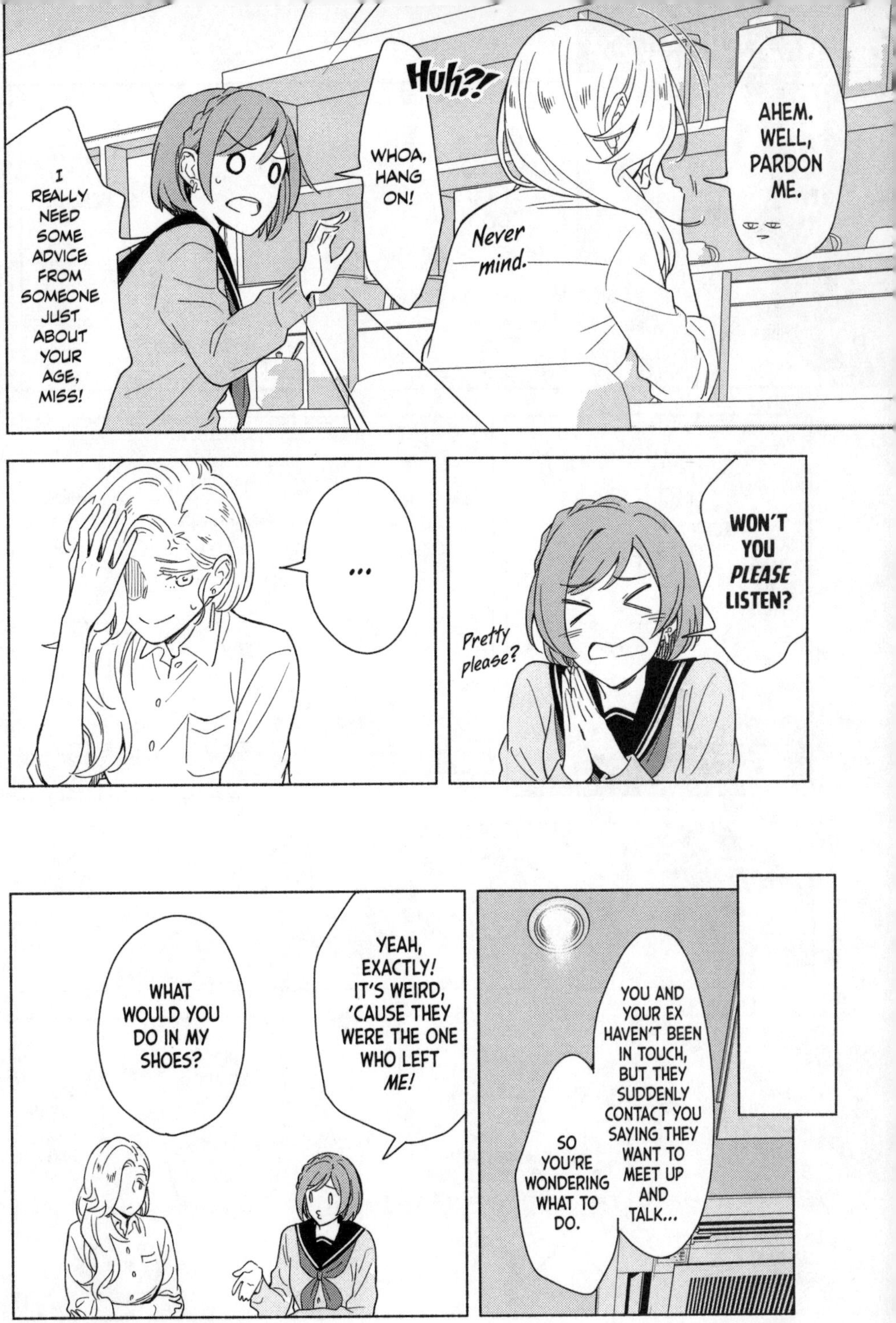
AHEM. WELL, PARDON ME.
Huh?!
Never mind.
WHOA, HANG ON!
I REALLY NEED SOME ADVICE FROM SOMEONE JUST ABOUT YOUR AGE, MISS!
WON'T YOU *PLEASE* LISTEN?
Pretty please?
...
YOU AND YOUR EX HAVEN'T BEEN IN TOUCH, BUT THEY SUDDENLY CONTACT YOU SAYING THEY WANT TO MEET UP AND TALK...
SO YOU'RE WONDERING WHAT TO DO.
YEAH, EXACTLY! IT'S WEIRD, 'CAUSE THEY WERE THE ONE WHO LEFT *ME*!
WHAT WOULD YOU DO IN MY SHOES?

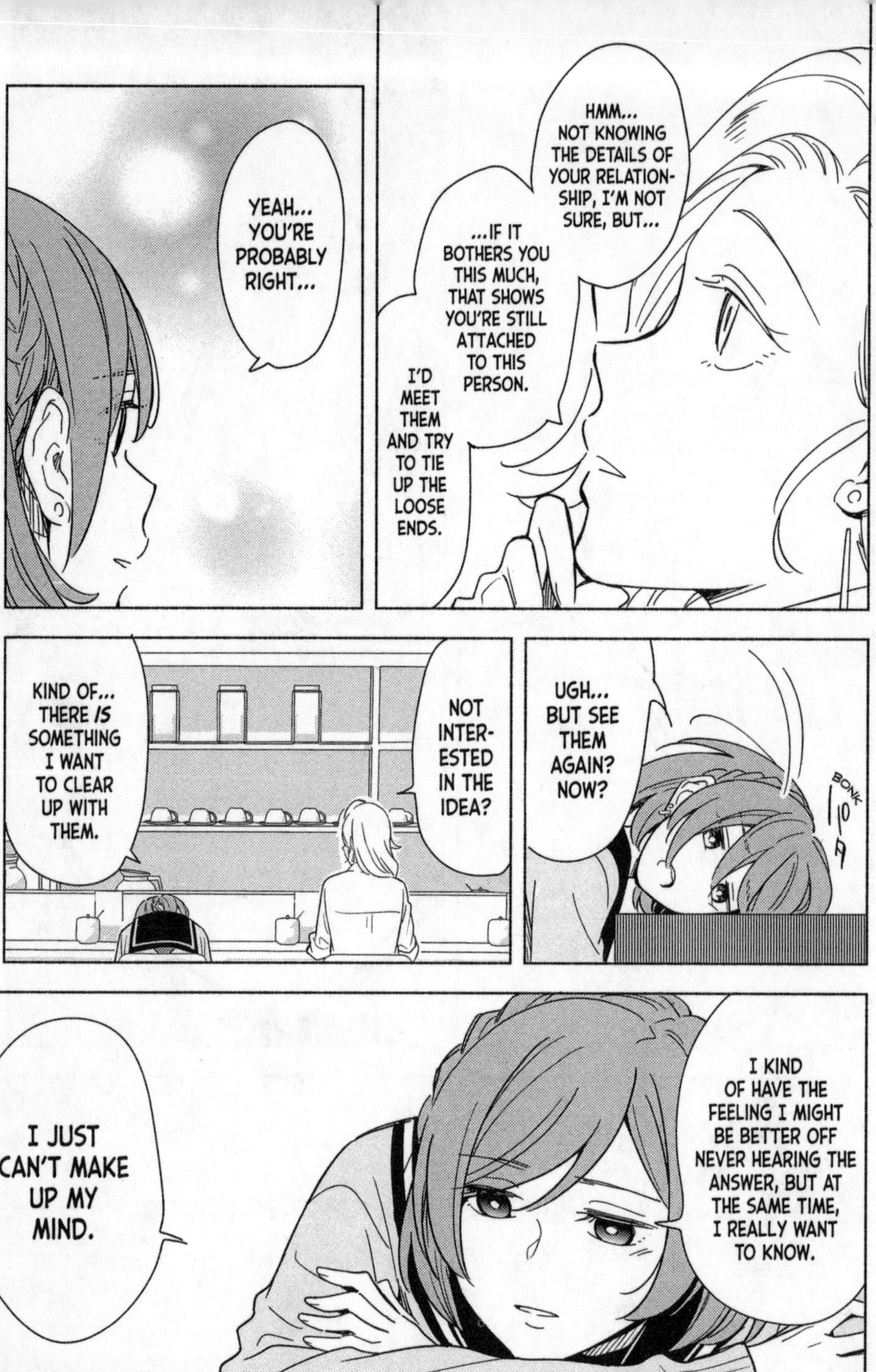
HMM... NOT KNOWING THE DETAILS OF YOUR RELATIONSHIP, I'M NOT SURE, BUT...
...IF IT BOTHERS YOU THIS MUCH, THAT SHOWS YOU'RE STILL ATTACHED TO THIS PERSON.
I'D MEET THEM AND TRY TO TIE UP THE LOOSE ENDS.
YEAH... YOU'RE PROBABLY RIGHT...
UGH... BUT SEE THEM AGAIN? NOW?
BONK
NOT INTERESTED IN THE IDEA?
KIND OF... THERE *IS* SOMETHING I WANT TO CLEAR UP WITH THEM.
I KIND OF HAVE THE FEELING I MIGHT BE BETTER OFF NEVER HEARING THE ANSWER, BUT AT THE SAME TIME, I REALLY WANT TO KNOW.
I JUST CAN'T MAKE UP MY MIND.

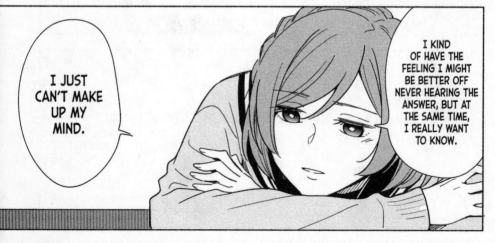

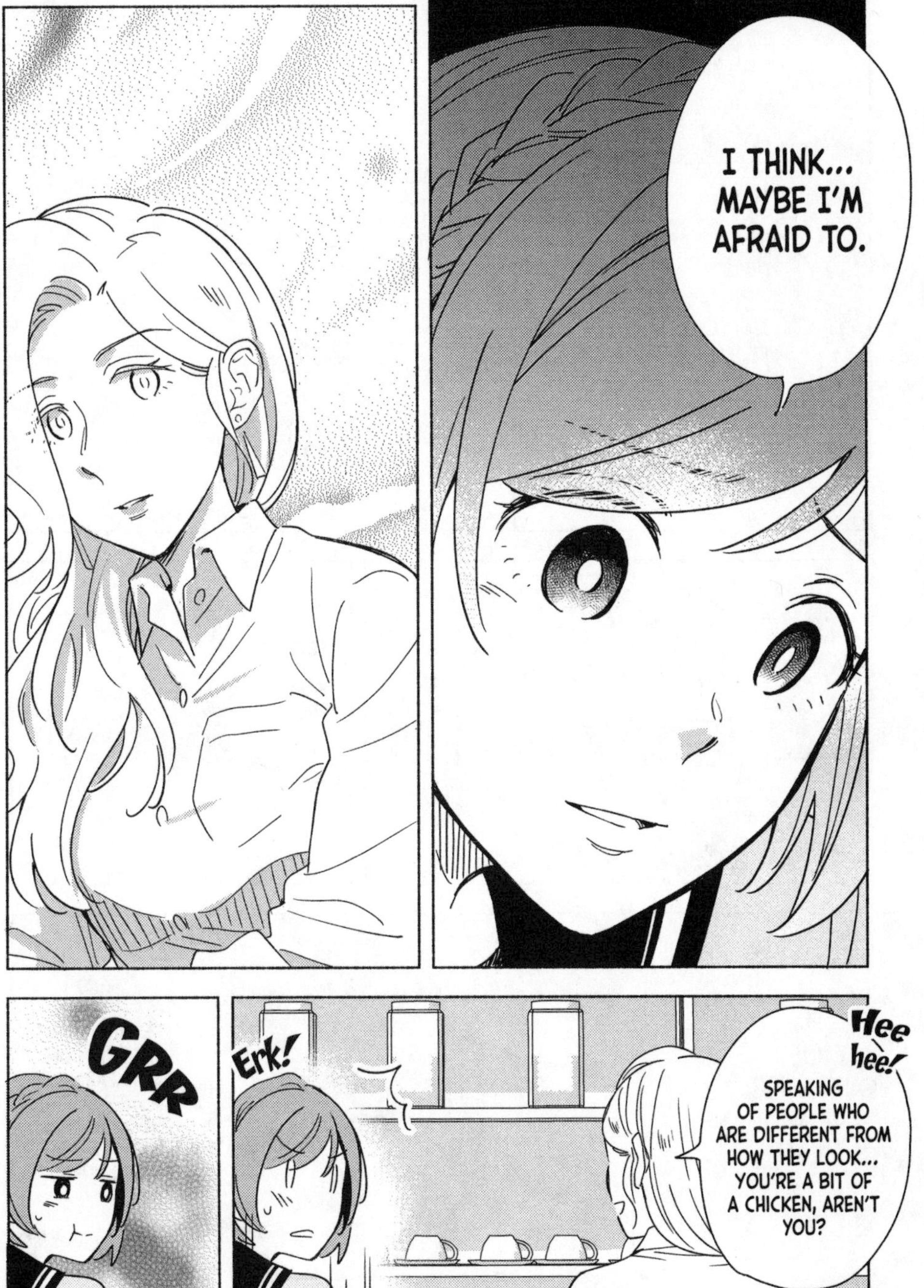
I THINK... MAYBE I'M AFRAID TO.
Hee hee!
SPEAKING OF PEOPLE WHO ARE DIFFERENT FROM HOW THEY LOOK... YOU'RE A BIT OF A CHICKEN, AREN'T YOU?
Erk!
GRR

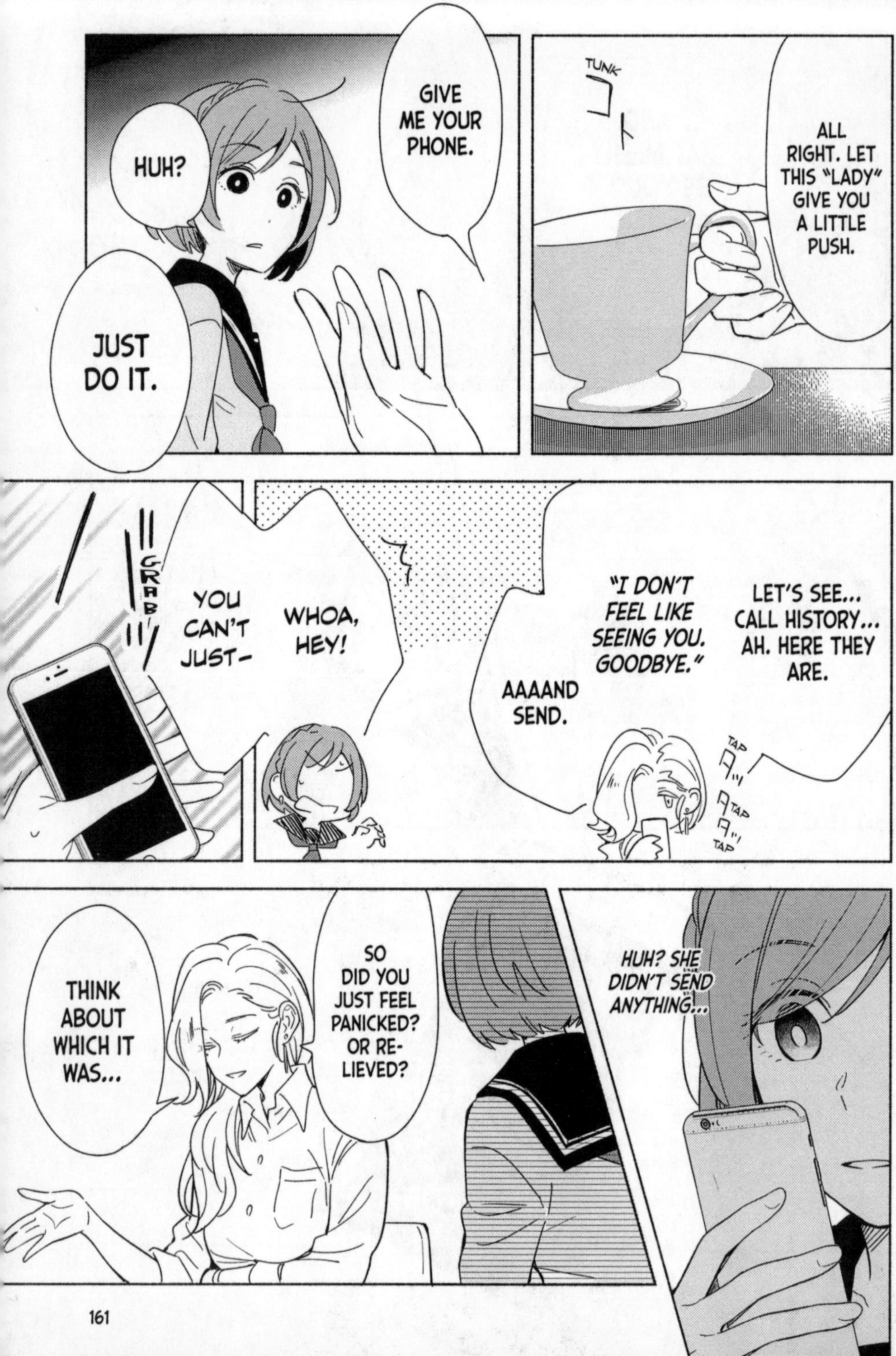
TUNK
ALL RIGHT. LET THIS "LADY" GIVE YOU A LITTLE PUSH.
GIVE ME YOUR PHONE.
HUH?
JUST DO IT.
LET'S SEE... CALL HISTORY... AH. HERE THEY ARE.
"I DON'T FEEL LIKE SEEING YOU. GOODBYE."
AAAAND SEND.
TAP
TAP
TAP
WHOA, HEY!
GRAB
YOU CAN'T JUST-
HUH? SHE DIDN'T SEND ANYTHING...
SO DID YOU JUST FEEL PANICKED? OR RE-LIEVED?
THINK ABOUT WHICH IT WAS...

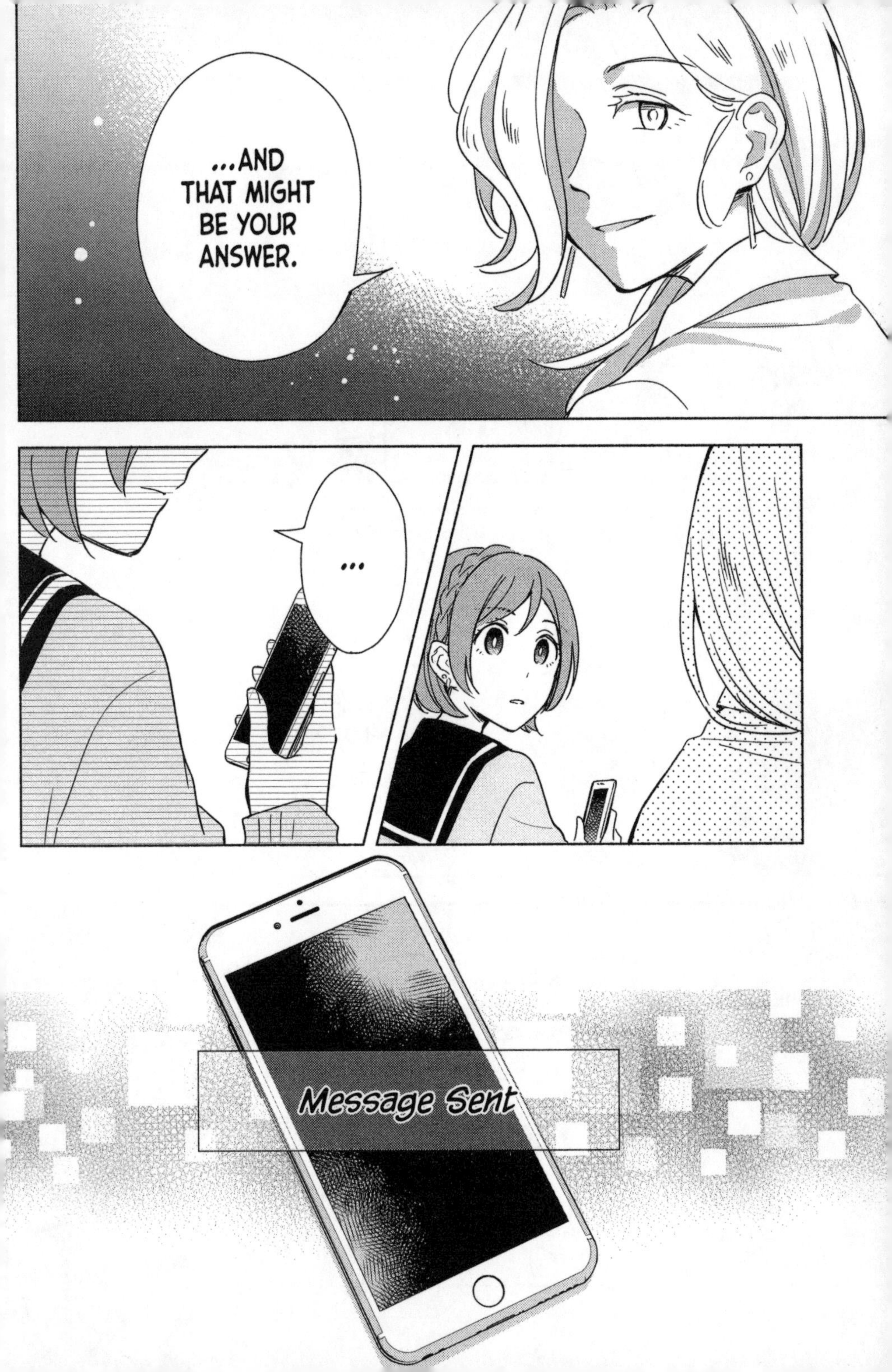
...AND THAT MIGHT BE YOUR ANSWER.
...
Message Sent

After-word

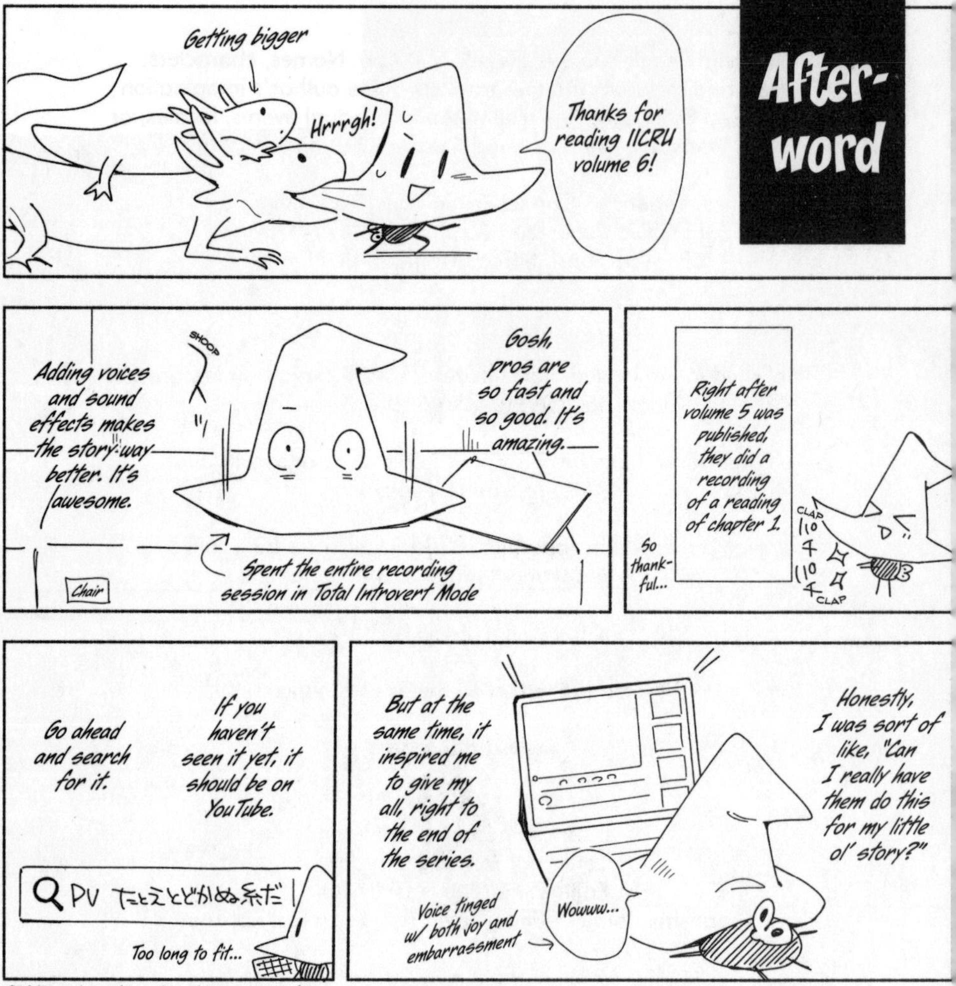
Thanks for reading IICRU volume 6!
Hrrrgh!
Getting bigger
Right after volume 5 was published, they did a recording of a reading of chapter 1.
CLAP
CLAP
So thankful...
Gosh, pros are so fast and so good. It's amazing.
SHOOP
Adding voices and sound effects makes the story way better. It's awesome.
Spent the entire recording session in Total Introvert Mode
Chair
Honestly, I was sort of like, "Can I really have them do this for my little ol' story?"
But at the same time, it inspired me to give my all, right to the end of the series.
Wowww...
Voice tinged w/ both joy and embarrassment
If you haven't seen it yet, it should be on YouTube.
Go ahead and search for it.
PV たとえとどかぬ糸だ
Too long to fit...

*PV (Promotional Video) Tatoe Todokanu Itodatoshitemo

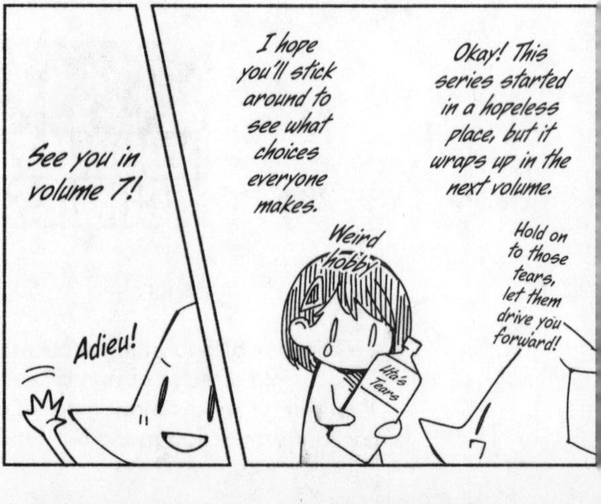
Okay! This series started in a hopeless place, but it wraps up in the next volume.
Hold on to those tears, let them drive you forward!
I hope you'll stick around to see what choices everyone makes.
Weird hobby
Uta's Tears
See you in volume 7!
Adieu!

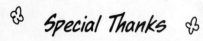

Special Thanks

Sato-san
Designer-san
Acha
And all my readers!

A Kodansha Comics Trade Paperback Original
If I Could Reach You 6 copyright © 2020 tMnR
English translation copyright © 2021 tMnR

Published in the United States by Kodansha Comics, an imprint of
Kodansha USA Publishing, LLC, New York.

Publication rights for this English edition arranged through
Kodansha Ltd, Tokyo.

First published in Japan in 2020 by Ichijinsha Inc., Tokyo
as *Tatoe Todokanu Itodatoshitemo*, volume 6.

ISBN 978-1-64651-155-6

Printed in the United States of America.

www.kodansha.us

9 8 7 6 5 4 3 2 1
Translation: Kevin Steinbach
Lettering: Jennifer Skarupa
Editing: Haruko Hashimoto
Kodansha Comics edition cover design by Phil Balsman

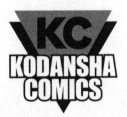

Publisher: Kiichiro Sugawara

Director of publishing services: Ben Applegate
Associate director of operations: Stephen Pakula
Publishing services managing editor: Noelle Webster
Assistant production manager: Emi Lotto, Angela Zurlo